Praise for *Following the Prophet*

For many, the hardest thing to understand about Muhammad is that his greatest legacy is the immense love for him in the hearts of Muslims worldwide. This book guides readers into the world of that love, why and how it has grown over the centuries, and how it has been expressed. What sets this book apart is that it starts this journey through a door of immense pain and fearful loss, which makes the light one encounters in its chapters all the more touching.
—Jonathan A. C. Brown, professor of Arabic and Islamic studies, Georgetown University

In this remarkable work, Sayilgan brings together the sacred past with an engaged present through his prophetically centered exploration of spirituality anchored in the Islamic tradition. The author provides us not only with an inviting and accessible narrative of the Prophet Muhammad's life, but also with an intimate look at his devotional repertoire and the community of faith that emerged around him and continues vibrantly down to the present.
—Martin T. Nguyen, professor of Islamic studies, Fairfield University

This accessible and thoughtful work offers a nuanced portrait of the Prophet Muhammad and other important figures, and a historical overview of early Islam, grounded in a wide range of Islamic sources. By presenting the Prophet's enduring legacy through the lens of Muslim devotional and historical memory, the book provides valuable insight for both Muslim readers seeking deeper spiritual understanding and non-Muslim readers interested in the foundations of early Islam.
—Syed Atif Rizwan, assistant professor of Islamic and interreligious studies, Catholic Theological Union

Following
the Prophet

Following the Prophet

The Life and Spiritual Legacy of Muhammad

Salih Sayilgan

FORTRESS PRESS
Minneapolis

FOLLOWING THE PROPHET
The Life and Spiritual Legacy of Muhammad

Copyright © 2025 Fortress Press. All rights reserved. Except for brief quotations in critical articles or reviews, no part of this book may be reproduced in any manner without prior written permission from the publisher. Email copyright@fortresspress.com or write to Permissions, Fortress Press, PO Box 1209, Minneapolis, MN 55440-1209.

Library of Congress Cataloging-in-Publication Data

Names: Sayilgan, Salih, author.
Title: Following the prophet : the life and spiritual legacy of Muhammad / Salih Sayilgan.
Description: Minneapolis : Fortress Press, [2025] | Includes bibliographical references and index.
Identifiers: LCCN 2025008359 (print) | LCCN 2025008360 (ebook) | ISBN 9798889833918 (paperback) | ISBN 9798889833925 (ebook)
Subjects: LCSH: Muḥammad, Prophet, -632—Biography. | LCGFT: Biographies.
Classification: LCC BP75 .S395 2025 (print) | LCC BP75 (ebook) | DDC 297.6/3092 [B]—dc23/eng/20250521
LC record available at https://lccn.loc.gov/2025008359
LC ebook record available at https://lccn.loc.gov/2025008360

Cover image: Detail of the name of the Prophet Muhammad written in Arabic language on the ceiling inside Ferhat Pasha Mosque, a 16th century Ottoman Islamic building. Sourced from Jasmin Merdan/Getty Images
Cover design: Emily Harris

Print ISBN: 979-8-8898-3391-8
eBook ISBN: 979-8-8898-3392-5

To Elif
May the light of the Prophet always shine upon you.

Say (O Prophet, to the people), "If you love God, follow me, and God will love you and forgive your sins. God is most forgiving and most merciful."

—Qur'an 3:31

CONTENTS

	Acknowledgments	xi
	Introduction	1
1.	Becoming the Prophet	11
2.	The Prophet's Spiritual Life and Character	67
3.	The Prophet's Spiritual Companions	137
4.	Following the Prophet	169
5.	Remembering the Prophet	197
6.	Conclusion	217
	Bibliography	223
	Index	227

ACKNOWLEDGMENTS

While this book is a monograph, in many ways, it also feels like a collective work, as it would not have been completed without the support of many people. Writing a book is a daily endeavor. It becomes a part of you. You do not just turn to the project when you are reading or drafting sentences; it requires constant thinking and attention. You sleep with it and wake up with it. Naturally, the content of the book weaves itself into your daily conversations and interactions. You begin making connections between your writing and everyday experiences. I have written a few other books, but writing this one felt particularly significant in this context, as it helped me become more attentive to the legacy of the Prophet among his followers and their love for him.

In this regard, I am especially thankful to Moutasem Atiya, Aamir Sheikh, Sami Zaharna, Kareem Monib, Yakup Kansizoglu, Hasan Awan, and Altijani Hussin. I not only learned many things about the Prophet from them, but I was also inspired by their love for him. I am also grateful to Mehmed Paksu, Fatih Kanca, Nurullah Celebi, Faris Kaya, and Mustafa Ulucay for supporting me in navigating resources about the Prophet in modern and Ottoman Turkish. Additionally, I have been moved by many families in my circles who embody the teachings of the Prophet in their daily lives. My special thanks go to the Munir, Siddique, Shikoh, Waheed, Puthawala, and Azizullah families, as well as to Basit Rauf, Hameeda Hameed, and Adina Ivanica.

The courses I have taught on Islam at Georgetown University almost always included sessions on the Prophet. My students' questions and critiques have deepened my understanding of various aspects of Muhammad's life. For several years, I have also been teaching as part of Georgetown University's Prison and Justice program. My inmate students' frank conversations about the Prophet have been particularly striking. I have observed that many of them follow Muhammad's example (Sunna) with love and dedication. Whenever the Prophet's name was mentioned in class or during their presentations, they would not hesitate to say, "Peace be upon him." They opened my eyes to another world where the legacy of the Prophet remains profoundly relevant. I am also grateful to my colleagues in the department for their collegiality and attentive ear, especially Paul L. Heck, Annalisa Butticci, Lauve H. Steenhuisen, Stephen M. Fields, Andrew Prevot, Leo D. Lefebure, Julia A. Lamm, and Alan C. Mitchell.

I would like to thank Ryan Hemmer for making Fortress Press the home for my book. Special thanks go to my editor, Adam Bursi, and his team at Fortress. Adam has shepherded this project from the very beginning, and his suggestions and critiques have significantly improved the manuscript. I am deeply grateful for his work and guidance throughout the process.

Finally, I could not have completed this project without the support of my family. My wife, Zeyneb, also a scholar of Islam, walked with me daily on this journey. Our conversations helped shape many of the ideas in this book. Our little daughter, Elif, has been a patient listener to these discussions—sometimes in silence, sometimes with active participation. To her, I dedicate this book.

INTRODUCTION

Imam Jalal al-Din al-Suyuti was one of the most prolific Muslim scholars of all time, making significant contributions to several Islamic sciences, particularly in the fields of hadith and Qur'anic commentary.[1] He memorized the entire Qur'an by the age of eight, studied under the leading scholars of his time, and memorized 200,000 hadiths. In his forties, he dedicated himself fully to worship and writing. His body of work, ranging from short treatises to multivolume books, exceeds 1,000 in number. Today, Suyuti's works remain widely read, and he is still regarded as one of the greatest Muslim scholars.

Suyuti's life was marked not only by scholarly achievements but also by serious personal tragedies. When Suyuti was just five years old, his father passed away; later in life, he experienced the devastating loss of his wife and both of his children. These painful experiences directly influenced Suyuti's writings: He authored several works addressing Islamic perspectives on coping with the death of children, emphasizing patience and steadfastness in the face of such trials. One of his notable books, *The Virtue of Remaining Steadfast When Losing a Child*, is a collection of hadith narrations from the Prophet Muhammad that provide guidance and comfort to those enduring the loss of a child.[2] The Prophet Muhammad himself had gone through similar tragedies, having lost his father before he was born and his mother when he was just six years old.

---

1. *Hadith* (pl. *ahadith*) literally means *speech* or *report* and, as a term, refers to a narrative record of what Muhammad said, did, and approved or disapproved of.

2. Imam Jalal al-Din al-Suyuti, *The Virtue of Remaining Steadfast When Losing a Child* (*Fadl al-Jalad 'Inda Faqd al-Walad*), trans. Abu Muhammad Zaid ibn Mahmud Haspatel (Inprint, 2016).

He had also endured the sorrow of burying six of his seven children, as well as losing his beloved wife Khadija at a critical time in his life. Faced with his own share of losses, Suyuti found solace in the Prophet's words and sought to share that comfort with others through his writings.

On the opening page of his book, Suyuti references the following verses from the Qur'an: "We shall certainly test you with fear and hunger, and loss of wealth, lives, and fruit. But [Prophet], give good news to those who endure patiently, those who say, when afflicted with a calamity, 'We belong to God and to Him we shall return.' They are the ones who will receive God's blessings and mercy, and it is they who are rightly guided."[3] Suyuti points out that some Qur'anic commentators interpret "the loss of fruit" in this passage as referring to the death of children, who are often described as the "fruit of the heart."[4] The same passage instructs the believers to say, "Indeed, we belong to God and to Him we shall return" (*inna lillahi wa inna ilayhi raji'un*) during times of trials and calamities. The significance of this expression, known as the *istirja'* (meaning *returning*), is further emphasized by Suyuti through a hadith of the Prophet: "Whoever recites *istirja'* at the time of calamity, God helps him back from his calamity, makes his end excellent, and makes for him a pious successor to please him."[5] In this narration, the Prophet highlights the significance of invoking the Qur'anic phrase of *istirja'* in response to tragedies. By doing so, God

---

3. Qur'an 2: 155–157. I have provided my own translation of the verses from the Qur'an. In addition, I consulted the following translations: Yusuf Ali, *The Meaning of the Holy Qur'an* (Amana, 2003); M. A. S. Abdel Haleem, *The Qur'an: English Translation and Parallel Arabic Text* (Oxford University Press, 2010); Majid Fakhry, *An Interpretation of the Qur'an: English Translation of the Meanings* (New York University Press, 2004); Seyyed Hossein Nasr et al., *The Study Quran: A New Translation and Commentary* (HarperOne, 2015); and Marmaduke Pickthall, *The Meaning of the Glorious Qur'an* (Everyman's Library, 1992).

4. Suyuti, *The Virtue of Remaining Steadfast When Losing a Child*, 33. Caner K. Dagli, "Commentary on Surat al Bakarah," in *The Study Quran: A New Translation and Commentary*, ed. Nasr et al. (HarperOne, 2015), 68.

5. Suyuti, *The Virtue of Remaining Steadfast When Losing a Child*, 34.

helps believers in enduring hardships, including the loss of a child, and ultimately grants them a great reward. Responding with *istirja'* is viewed as a demonstration of patience and reliance on God, essential aspects of Islamic spirituality modeled by the Prophet Muhammad.

For centuries, Muslim parents have sought out Suyuti's book on child loss, finding comfort and strength in the hadiths he compiled. In 2014, when Zaid Haspatel, a South African scholar of Islam, lost his son Muhammad, one of his friends gifted him an Arabic copy of Suyuti's book. Haspatel and his wife found great solace in the hadiths contained in the book, leading him to translate it into English to benefit other grieving parents. When my wife and I lost our daughter Meryem in a tragic accident in 2022, Suyuti's collection was one of the key resources that provided us with comfort during our time of grief. Many parents like us turn to the Prophet's words because he himself endured similar and even greater tragedies, including the loss of several children. As a messenger of God, his words carry profound significance and have a lasting impact on grieving parents.

In times of darkness and tragedy, the teachings of the Prophet offer light and healing in the lives of Muslims. Consider a world shrouded in darkness, where people endure suffering without understanding its purpose. They feel isolated, like strangers in a foreign land, lost and lonely. Uncertain of their origin and destination, they are plagued by anxieties about the future. Life seems devoid of meaning, and the world appears as a battlefield filled with violence, brutality, and injustice. Then imagine a light piercing through this darkness, illuminating the world. With this light, suffering gains meaning, and the world is no longer alien. The light reveals the purpose of life and clarifies what lies beyond, alleviating fears about the future. Life transforms from a struggle into an experience of solidarity. The world is no longer a brutal place but a divinely crafted space for human growth and progress.

For Muslims, this guiding light is the light of the Prophet Muhammad. His example is inseparable from the moral and spiritual life of a Muslim. As the Messenger of God and the channel for the Qur'an's revelation, he exemplifies how to live in accordance with

God's will. He serves as the ultimate model for leading a life of God consciousness (*taqwa*), providing hope and light during life's darkest moments—amid physical, emotional, and mental struggles and in times of grief and suffering.

Muhammad: A Living Spirit Transcending History

Within Islamic tradition, obedience to the Prophet Muhammad is regarded as obedience to God. The Qur'an emphasizes that if believers truly love God, they should follow the Prophet, and in doing so, they will be loved by God.[6] The connection between loving God and being loved by God is intricately tied to following the Prophet's example. Muhammad was often described as the "living Qur'an." When asked about the Prophet's character, his wife Aisha famously responded that his character (*akhlaq*) was the Qur'an itself.[7] Muhammad serves as the model for worshipping God and embodying patience, justice, simplicity, humility, resilience, and compassion. The prophetic example is at the core of Islamic ethics and spirituality.

However, this vital aspect of Muhammad's life is frequently overshadowed by controversies and historical details. Many biographies of the Prophet tend to be either apologetic, addressing polemical criticisms, or primarily focusing on the historical context in which he lived. These approaches have several limitations. First, they tend to overlook his character and spirituality. Second, and related to the first, they often fail to reveal the profound role the Prophet plays in the daily lives of Muslims and their deep love for him. Understanding the Prophet solely through the lens of his historical context does not fully capture the significance of a figure whose teachings have shaped the world and continue to guide nearly one-quarter of the global population today.

---

6. Qur'an 3:31.

7. Muslim ibn al-Hajjaj al-Naysaburi, *Sahih Muslim, kitab salat al-musafirin wa qasruha, bab jami'i salat al-layl wa man nama 'anhu aw marida*. The hadiths are cited according to the chapter-subchapter system.

Introduction

Muhammad's personality has evolved into a collective presence that has endured among his followers for centuries. His light remains vibrant and influential in the lives of Muslims today. His living spirit transcends the boundaries of seventh-century Arabia, a notion powerfully expressed by Bediuzzaman Said Nursi, a modern Ottoman scholar (d. 1960), through a compelling comparison:

> Imagine a peacock, a bird of stunning beauty, hatching from an egg, maturing, and then soaring into the skies. After it gains fame for its splendor, it would be foolish for someone to search for the bird's beauty, perfection, and achievements within the discarded eggshell left on the ground. In a similar way, anyone who examines the early life of our Prophet Muhammad (Peace and Blessings Be Upon Him) with a materialistic, superficial perspective cannot grasp the depth of his spiritual personality. Instead, one should view his early life, his human aspects, and the external conditions as a fragile shell, within which resides the radiant sun of both worlds—the tree of Muhammad (Peace and Blessings Be Upon Him). Like the Tuba tree,[8] this tree has emerged, nourished by Divine grace, and matured by the favor of the Lord. Thus, when encountering trivial details about the outward aspects of the Prophet's early life, one should not focus on them but instead lift their gaze to the light he has spread throughout the world.[9]

Nursi's point is that while the egg of a peacock contains certain qualities and elements, they are not as grand or significant as those found in the bird that emerged from the egg. Similarly, focusing only on the

---

8. The tuba tree holds symbolic significance in Islamic tradition, especially in depictions of paradise (*Jannah*). Described as a grand and awe-inspiring tree in the gardens of paradise, its roots are believed to reach into the highest heaven. According to tradition, the tuba tree is so vast that a rider could journey beneath its shade for a hundred years without reaching its edge.

9. Bediuzzaman Said Nursi, *Mesnev-i Nuriye* (Söz Basım, 2012), 113.

historical context and the events of Muhammad's life would not capture the complete picture of his person. He is much greater than this.

Our goal in this book, therefore, is to present a portrayal of Muhammad that surpasses the confines of seventh-century Arabia. We seek to unveil a portrait that has lived on in the hearts of Muslims across the centuries. Our focus will be not only on his character and spiritual legacy but also on how Muslims have remembered and reimagined his spirit over time as an expression of their love for God and God's messenger.

Elements of Islamic Spirituality

Since this work explores the Prophet's spiritual legacy, it may be helpful to offer a brief explanation of spirituality in Islam. First and foremost, Islamic spirituality is an expression of the love for God and God's creation. It begins with having faith in God and progresses to knowing God. The believer turns to the book of the universe, the Qur'an, and the teachings of the Prophet Muhammad to understand God's attributes: God is the Most Compassionate and the Most Merciful, the One who brings everything from nonexistence into existence. God is the Just, the All-Knowing, with nothing beyond God's knowledge. God is the Provider, the Most Gracious, the All-Forgiving, and the All-Loving. God is the One who inflicts death and gives life, the Most Holy—pure and without imperfection.

The Qur'an states that God created humans with the purpose of worshipping God: "I created jinn and humankind only to worship me."[10] As a result, perhaps no concept captures Islamic spirituality better than the term *'ibadah*, often translated as *submission, humility, obedience, servitude, devotion*, and especially *worship*. *'Ibadah* refers to the attitudes and actions a believer undertakes to express reverence, love, and obedience to God, with the intention of earning God's pleasure. In Islamic spirituality, worship is a comprehensive way of life that includes faith, rituals, and moral and ethical conduct (*akhlaq*). Going

---

10. Qur'an 51:56.

beyond simple belief and ritual, worship includes a believer's thoughts, feelings, and words. When they are directed toward God and bring the individual closer to God, they, too, are considered acts of worship.

Faith (*iman*) is defined in a number of hadiths as believing in God; God's angels, scriptures, and messengers; the resurrection and the hereafter; and predestination, both its good and its evil.[11] However, faith is understood to extend beyond these specific beliefs into embodied actions. On one occasion, the Prophet Muhammad stated that faith has over seventy branches: The highest branch is the declaration, "There is no god but God," while the lowest branch is the act of removing harm from people's paths.[12] Drawing from various hadiths, Muslim scholars have identified numerous branches of faith, which include reciting the Qur'an, maintaining cleanliness, adhering to the six articles of faith, practicing the five pillars of Islam, being thankful to God, avoiding waste, being truthful, refraining from hatred, practicing justice and piety, helping those in need, demonstrating humility, managing anger, caring for one's family, returning greetings, visiting those who are sick, attending funeral prayers, being generous, respecting those who are elderly, avoiding gossip, refraining from killing, and abstaining from impermissible food. These activities are all considered branches of faith and are integral to Islamic spirituality.

In discussions of Islamic rituals, the five pillars are often highlighted as fundamental aspects of worship. These include bearing witness that there is no god but God and that Muhammad is God's messenger, performing the five daily prayers, paying alms (*zakat*), fasting during the month of Ramadan, and making the pilgrimage (*hajj*) to the Kaaba.

However, there are many other practices that are also essential elements of Islamic worship and spirituality. Ethical, moral, and virtuous conduct are integral to Islamic spirituality, fostering the development of a beautiful character (*husn al-khulq*). Key traits include honesty,

---

11. The most prominent example is the hadith known as the Hadith of Gabriel, which is found in both *Sahih al-Bukhari* and *Sahih Muslim* collections.

12. *Sahih Muslim, kitab al-iman, bab bayani 'adadi shu'abi al-imani wa afdaliha wa 'adnaha wa al-fadilati al-haya'i wa kawnihi min al-iman.*

compassion, justice, fairness, fulfilling promises, humility, forgiveness, patience, generosity, gratitude, and good manners. Embodying these qualities is a fundamental aspect of one's spirituality. For Muslims, the Prophet Muhammad serves as the ultimate model for these attributes. Ethical conduct is closely connected to Islamic law (sharia) and is an essential part of one's spiritual life. In this way, law and spirituality in Islam are interconnected, not separate.

Worship as an Expression of Love for God

As stated above, fundamental to Islamic spirituality is the love for God and God's creation. Regarding God's mercy, the Qur'an mentions that it encompasses all things.[13] The Qur'an also describes the Prophet Muhammad as a mercy sent to the world: "And We have not sent you, [O Muhammad], except as a mercy to the worlds."[14] In this sense, the Prophet is the embodiment of God's mercy, sent to guide humanity in this life and lead it to salvation. The hadiths further emphasize God's mercy in creation. In one, the Prophet explains, "God has one hundred parts of mercy, of which He sent down one part to the jinn, mankind, animals, and insects, and through it, they love one another and show compassion to one another, and through it, wild animals care for their young. God has kept back ninety-nine parts of mercy with which to show mercy to His servants on the Day of Resurrection."[15] As believers grow in their knowledge of God and witness the manifestation of God's attributes in creation, they come to recognize the beauty, perfection, and generosity of God reflected in the world around them. This recognition naturally leads to a deep love for God. Worship becomes an expression of this love. The Prophet Muhammad is the ultimate example of how to express love for God through worship.

---

13. Qur'an 7:156.

14. Qur'an 21:107.

15. *Sahih Muslim, kitab al-tawba, bab fi al-haddi al-tawba wa al-farah biha.*

Introduction

Organization of Chapters and Sources

To present a holistic portrait of the Prophet's life and spiritual legacy, the first chapter begins with the story of Muhammad's journey to becoming the Messenger of God. It explores Muhammad's life before receiving revelation and delves into his childhood and young adulthood. The chapter also highlights significant events in his life during his prophethood and reactions to his message. The second chapter focuses on the spiritual life of the Prophet. It addresses his spiritual practices and offers insight into his daily life from a spiritual perspective. Given the connection between virtuous character and spirituality, this chapter also sheds light on the Prophet's virtues. The third chapter offers an overview of the Prophet's first companions, emphasizing their spirituality and love for him. The fourth chapter explores how the companions followed the Prophet's spiritual legacy and transmitted it to the next generations. The final chapter examines how Muhammad is remembered in Islamic culture and literature across centuries.

In exploring the Prophet's spiritual portrait, I have drawn on the Qur'an, hadith collections, biographical accounts (*sira*; plural *siyar*), and the extensive literature available about the Prophet in Arabic, Persian, Turkish, and English. This work is intended for any reader who wishes to understand the Prophet of Islam, Muhammad; his spiritual life; his role in Islamic piety; and how he is loved and revered by Muslims.

Whenever the Prophet's name is mentioned, it is customary in Islamic spiritual practice to invoke a prayer to express love and respect for him. With that in mind, I conclude this section with the traditional invocation: May God's peace and blessings be upon him (*salla allahu 'alayhi wa sallam*).

CHAPTER ONE

Becoming the Prophet

The year Muhammad was born, 570 CE, was known to Arabs in Mecca as the Year of the Elephant. According to tradition, Abraha, the ruler of Yemen, constructed a grand cathedral in Sanaa while the region was under the rule of the Christian kingdom of Abyssinia. Abraha's aim was to establish this cathedral as the primary pilgrimage site in the region, diverting attention away from the Kaaba in Mecca. Aware of Abraha's intentions, a man associated with the Quraysh tribe, the custodians of the Kaaba, traveled to Sanaa and deliberately defiled the new temple. In retaliation, Abraha launched an attack on the Kaaba with his army, aiming to take revenge. His forces included war elephants, which he intended to use to destroy the Kaaba.

Along their journey, Abraha's forces seized everything in their path, including two hundred camels belonging to Abd al-Muttalib, Muhammad's grandfather. Abd al-Muttalib, the leader of the Banu Hashim clan of the Quraysh tribe, also served as the custodian of the Kaaba. While camped a few miles outside of Mecca, Abraha sent a messenger to the city to speak with their representative. He wanted to communicate that his intention was not to engage in battle or shed blood but only to destroy the Kaaba. Abd al-Muttalib and his sons accompanied the messenger to meet with him. Abraha welcomed Abd al-Muttalib with respect. However, instead of discussing the Kaaba, Abd al-Muttalib brought up the issue of his camels that had been seized by Abraha's army. Surprised by Abd al-Muttalib's words, Abraha remarked, "I'm astonished that you are more concerned about your camels than the Kaaba." Abd al-Muttalib replied, "I am the owner of the camels; the owner of the Kaaba is God, and He will protect it." This response angered Abraha, who asserted that nothing could stop him from destroying the Kaaba. He returned Abd al-Muttalib's camels and ordered his army to prepare for the attack.

However, when the elephants were directed toward the Kaaba, they knelt down and refused to move. But when turned toward Yemen, they marched willingly. Soon after, a swarm of birds appeared, pelting Abraha's army with stones. The Qur'an relates this incident: "Do you [Prophet] not see how your Lord dealt with the army of the elephant? Did He not make their plans into misguidance? He sent flocks of birds against them, pelting them with stones of hard-baked clay, leaving them like chewed-up straw."[1] Thus, God safeguarded the Kaaba from Abraha's attack in the same year the Prophet Muhammad was born.

Muhammad's Father: Abdullah

Abdullah, the Prophet's father, was a highly respected figure among his people. It is said that his father, Abd al-Muttalib, rediscovered the well of Zamzam through a series of visions.[2] Abd al-Muttalib, along with his only son at the time, Harith, claimed the guardianship of the well. However, other prominent leaders of the tribe also maintained their right to oversee the well, arguing that it belonged to their ancestor Ishmael and that they had a share in it. They also pointed out to Abd al-Muttalib that, with only one son, he lacked the support needed to take on the responsibility alone. In a patriarchal society, these remarks deeply hurt Abd al-Muttalib.

Abd al-Muttalib prayed that if God blessed him with ten sons, he would sacrifice one of them at the Kaaba's sanctuary. Eventually, God

---

1. Qur'an 105:1–5.

2. The well of Zamzam is a sacred well located within the Grand Mosque (*Masjid al-Haram*) in Mecca, approximately 20 meters (66 feet) east of the Kaaba. Its history traces back to the time of Prophet Abraham (*Ibrahim*) and his family. According to Islamic tradition, when Hagar (*Hajar*) and her son Ishmael (*Ismail*) were left in the barren desert by Abraham, they desperately searched for water. In response to Hagar's struggle, God miraculously caused water to gush forth from the ground, creating the well of Zamzam. Over time, the Zamzam well became buried under silt and was forgotten until it was rediscovered by the Prophet Muhammad's grandfather.

accepted his prayer, and he was blessed with ten sons, one of whom was Abdullah, the Prophet's father. When the time came, Abd al-Muttalib gathered his children and informed them of his prayer and promise to God. They all agreed to honor their father's vow. Abd al-Muttalib distributed ten arrows, each with one of his sons' names written on it. He then collected the arrows to cast them in the Kaaba's sanctuary, in front of the people. The plan was to sacrifice the son whose name appeared. When the arrow was drawn, it bore Abdullah's name—Abd al-Muttalib's most beloved son.

However, the people of the city strongly opposed the idea of sacrificing Abdullah, arguing that such an act would set a dangerous precedent and that there was no justification for sacrificing someone like Abdullah. On the community's advice, Abd al-Muttalib agreed to consult a wise woman in Yathrib (Medina) to see if there was an alternative. She asked about the customary blood compensation for a man in their tribe, and he replied that it was ten camels. The woman suggested placing ten camels alongside Abdullah and casting lots. If the lot fell on Abdullah, ten more camels should be added each time until the lot fell on the camels. Once it did, the camels would be sacrificed, signaling that God had accepted the offering. After ten rounds, the lot finally fell on the camels. To be certain, they cast lots a few more times, and each time, the result was the same. In the end, one hundred camels were sacrificed, and their meat was distributed among the people of Mecca. Reflecting on the prophet Abraham's attempt to sacrifice his son Ishmael, as well as his father Abdullah's story, Muhammad once remarked, "I am the son of two sacrifices."[3]

Abdullah's Marriage to Amina

Abdullah had reached an age when he was ready for marriage. After careful consideration, Abd al-Muttalib decided that Amina, the daughter of Wahb, would be the best match for his son. He approached Amina's father, who agreed to the marriage. Amina and Abdullah

---

3. Mustafa Fayda, "Muhammed," in *İslam Ansiklopedisi* (Türkiye Diyanet Vakfı, 2020), 30:407.

were soon married. It is said that the light of prophecy was visible on Abdullah's face. After marrying Amina, that light transferred to her, signifying that she was pregnant with a child.

Like many of his family members, Abdullah was involved in trade. A few months after his marriage, he joined a caravan headed for Syria. On his return journey to Mecca, Abdullah fell ill and never made it home. He passed away in Medina, where he was buried. Amina was left a young widow, and her child would grow up without ever knowing his father.

The Birth of Muhammad

A few months after Abdullah's death, Amina gave birth to a baby boy, whom they named Muhammad (meaning *the one who is praised*). Although Abdullah did not leave much behind in terms of wealth or property, he left a son who would go on to transform not only the region but also the entire world. Tradition recounts numerous miracles and extraordinary events surrounding Muhammad's birth. He was born circumcised, with his umbilical cord already severed. Additionally, between his shoulders was the mark of prophecy (*khatm al-nubuwwah*). The night was illuminated by his light. Süleyman Çelebi (d. 1422), who composed one of the most prominent poems about Muhammad in Ottoman literature, relates to the Prophet's mother's experience concerning his birth:

> The beloved mother said: "At the beginning,
> Saw I a strange light as if the sun was spinning
>
> Lightning flashed suddenly from my house on that night,
> It reached the skies and with it the world became bright
>
> From the heavens descended angels row on row,
> Like the Ka'ba, round and round my house they did go."[4]

---

4. Süleyman Çelebi, *Vesiletün Necat*. For the translation, see, Syed Tanvir Wasti, "The Mevlid or Nativity Poem by Süleyman Çelebi," in *Tehseel*, vol. 1:3 (Islamic Research

Foster Care in the Desert

It was traditional to send children to live with Bedouins in the desert, where they would be cared for by wet nurses. The desert environment was healthier for their growth and offered them the chance to learn pure Arabic. Families in the city, who were typically more affluent, would support the Bedouin families who took in their children. For the Bedouins, this tradition of fostering was an opportunity to establish a lasting connection with one of the prominent families. The foster mother would gain a new son, who would regard her as a second mother and feel a lifelong sense of filial duty toward her. He would also consider himself a brother to her biological children. This bond was more than just symbolic; among the Arabs, it was believed that the qualities of the nurse were transmitted to the child through breastfeeding.[5]

One of the Bedouin tribes that had a reputation for nursing and caring for children was the Banu Sa'd. Their women would periodically come to Mecca and take the newborn children with them to the desert. During one of the visits, all the children were taken except baby Muhammad. He was an orphan, and the foster families were aware that they would not receive much in return, as Muhammad's family was poor and had little to offer. One of the Bedouin women, Halima, had not found a child to foster. Instead of returning to the desert without any child, she and her husband, Harith, agreed to take Muhammad with them. The tradition reports that once they had Muhammad as their foster child, the family experienced so many blessings. Halima described some of them as follows: "We arrived at our tents in the land of Bani Sa'd, a place I knew to be the most barren on God's earth. However, after we brought Muhammad to live with us, my flock would return each evening well-fed and full of milk. We milked them and drank, even when others had none. Our neighbors would tell their shepherds, 'Go graze your flocks where his flock grazes,' referring to my shepherd.

Academy, 2018), 22.

5. Martin Lings, *Muhammad: His Life Based on the Earliest Sources* (Inner Traditions, 2006), 24.

Yet, their flocks returned hungry and without milk, while mine came back well-nourished and abundant in milk. We continued to enjoy this prosperity and blessing from God until the child turned two, and I weaned him."[6]

Opening the Heart of Muhammad

After two years, it was time for Muhammad to return to his mother. When they arrived, Amina requested Halima to keep Muhammad a bit longer due to a plague in Mecca. Muhammad stayed with them for a few additional months. During this period, another remarkable event occurred. One day, while Muhammad was with his foster brother Abdullah outside the tent, Abdullah rushed to his parents, saying, "Two men in white garments came, laid Muhammad down, opened his chest, and began to stir it with their hands." When Halima and her husband came outside, they found Muhammad looking pale and asked him what had happened. Muhammad explained, "Two men in white came to me, laid me down, opened my chest, and searched it, though I do not know for what purpose."[7]

Years later, the Prophet himself recounted this childhood event. When his companions asked him to share something about himself, he responded, "I am the prayer of my father Abraham, the good news of my brother Jesus, and the dream of my mother. When she was pregnant with me, there was a light in her that illuminated the places in Damascus." He then described the event in the desert: "Two men clothed in white came to me with a gold basin full of snow. They took hold of me, split open my chest, and brought forth my heart. They also split it open, removed a black clot which they cast away, and then washed my heart and chest with the snow."[8] The heart is not only central to the

---

6. Ibn Ishaq, *The Life of Muhammad*, trans. A. Guillaume (Oxford University Press, 1967), 71.

7. Ibn Ishaq, *Life of Muhammad*, 72.

8. Ibn Ishaq, *Life of Muhammad*, 72.

physical body but also central to spirituality. It is possible that during this washing process, the Prophet's heart was spiritually expanded and filled with knowledge, wisdom, divine light, and inspiration.[9]

This incident worried Halima and her husband, prompting them to return Muhammad to his mother, Amina, to ensure his safety. When they told what had happened, Amina remained unconcerned, knowing that great things awaited her son. Muhammad then stayed with his mother in Mecca. He continued to show respect to Halima and supported her family throughout his life. He would occasionally share his experiences with his companions, saying, "I am the true Arab among you because I am a Qurayshi. I stayed with Banu Sa'd in the desert, suckled milk there, and my language is their language."[10]

The Death of Muhammad's Mother

When Muhammad was six years old, his mother took him to see their relatives in Yathrib (Medina) and visit his father Abdullah's grave. Amina's servant, Umm Ayman, also accompanied them. On their way back to Mecca, Amina fell ill and passed away. She was buried in Abwa, a village between Mecca and Medina. Amid the sorrow of losing his mother, it was Umm Ayman who comforted Muhammad. He would often refer to her as "my mother after my mother." Growing up without parents was a challenge for Muhammad, but God assured his protection. During difficult times in the early years of his prophethood, God reminded him of this promise: "Did He [God] not find you an orphan and shelter you?"[11] Years later, the Prophet visited his mother's grave with his companions and became emotional, shedding tears. When his companions asked what caused his tears, the Prophet replied,

---

9. Salih Suruç, *Kainatın Efendisi: Peygamberimizin Hayatı* (Nesil, 2016), 82.

10. Ibn Ishaq, *Life of Muhammad*, 72.

11. Qur'an 93:6.

"I remembered my mother's love and compassion for me during my childhood."[12]

The Orphan and the Shepherd

After Aminah's death, Abd al-Muttalib took full responsibility for his orphaned grandson, Muhammad. He provided special care for him, considering him a precious trust from his beloved son Abdullah. Abd al-Muttalib would take Muhammad with him wherever he went. Being advanced in age, Abd al-Muttalib cared for Muhammad for only a few years. Before his death, he entrusted Muhammad to his son Abu Talib, Muhammad's uncle.

Abu Talib and his wife, Fatima, were compassionate and caring toward Muhammad and were well respected among their people. Despite having a large family and limited resources, they took care of him. Muhammad also contributed to the family's support by tending sheep and goats. He spent many days alone in the hills above Mecca or on the slopes of the surrounding valleys, herding the animals.[13]

Muhammad often spoke about this period of his life. One time, he and his companions were picking wild fruits from a tree. Muhammad provided tips on finding the best fruits, knowledge only a shepherd would possess. When his companions asked if he had been a shepherd, Muhammad replied that every prophet had been a shepherd. He himself had tended the sheep of the people of Mecca. Drawing from his experience, Muhammad used this metaphor in his teachings: "All of you are shepherds, and each of you is responsible for his flock. The leader of a people is a shepherd and is responsible for his flock. A man is the shepherd of his household and is responsible for his family. A servant is the shepherd of his master's property and is responsible for it. Each of you is a shepherd and responsible for your flock."[14]

---

12. Ibn Sa'd, *Kitab al-Tabakat al-Kubra*, ed. 'Ali Muhammad 'Amr (Maktabah al-Khanji, 2001), 1:95.

13. Ibn Sa'ad, *Kitab al-Tabakat al-Kubra*, 1:103.

14. Al-Bukhari, *al-Adab al-Mufrad*, kitab al-malika, bab al-'abdu ra'in.

Travel to Syria and the Monk Bahira

Like the other family members, Muhammad's uncle Abu Talib was involved in trade and often traveled to Syria with his tribe's trade caravan. When Muhammad was in his early teens, Abu Talib took him along on one of these journeys. During a stop in Bosra, a desert town known for being the retreat of a monk named Bahira, the monk noticed a cloud shading the young Muhammad among the group. Bahira approached and closely observed Muhammad, discovering the seal of prophethood between his shoulders. Recognizing all the signs of prophecy he had read about in his Christian scriptures, Bahira identified Muhammad as the Paraclete, the "Comforter and Most Praised," foretold by the true teachings of Jesus. Bahira advised Abu Talib to return Muhammad to Mecca, cautioning him to be wary of the Jews of Arabia, who might try to harm a prophet not from their community. The monk assured Abu Talib that a "great future" lies before the young boy.[15]

Later, the Qur'an would refer to people like Bahira among the Christians: "When they listen to what has been revealed to the Messenger, you see their eyes overflowing with tears for recognizing the truth. They say, 'Our Lord! We believe, so count us among the witnesses.'"[16] The Qur'an would also mention the words of Jesus predicting the coming of the Prophet Muhammad: "Jesus, son of Mary, said, 'Children of Israel, I am sent to you by God, confirming the Torah that came before me and bringing good news of a messenger after me whose name will be Ahmad.' Yet when he came to them with clear signs, they said, 'This is pure magic.'"[17] The name Ahmad in this verse is understood in Islamic tradition as another name for the Prophet Muhammad and means *the one who is highly praised*. In light of this verse, many Muslim scholars have interpreted the Greek word *paraclete* (meaning *advocate* or *comforter*) in the New Testament (John 14:15–16) as a reference to the Prophet Muhammad: "If you love me, you will keep my

---

15. Ibn Ishaq, *Life of Muhammad*, 81.

16. Qur'an 5:83.

17. Qur'an 61:6.

commandments. And I will ask the Father, and He will give you another advocate (*paraclete*), to be with you forever."[18]

A Righteous and Trustworthy Person

Muhammad was known among his people as a righteous and trustworthy person (*al-amin*). When the Byzantine emperor Heraclius inquired about Muhammad's character to one of his former fiercest enemies, Abu Sufyan, he responded, "Muhammad never breaks his promises, he never lies, and he always speaks the truth."[19]

Muhammad participated in what we might today call social justice efforts. Notably, he joined the Alliance of the Virtuous (*hilf al-fudul*), a coalition formed to protect people from injustices within Meccan society, where tribal conflicts occasionally arose, and vulnerable individuals visiting the city for pilgrimage and trade often faced oppression and unfair treatment. The alliance's founders and members pledged to defend the rights of those who were weak, poor, and vulnerable. Years later, Muhammad would reflect on this action: "I was present in the house of Abdullah ibn Jud'an for such an excellent pact that I would not trade my part in it for a herd of red camels; even now, in Islam, if I were called to it, I would gladly respond."[20]

This prophetic approach would serve as a source of inspiration for future generations of Muslims. Emulating the Prophet's example, Muslims would support efforts that advance peace and justice in societies. A contemporary instance of such an initiative is the Alliance of Virtue, founded in 2018 by religious leaders from Jewish, Christian, and Muslim communities. This program aims to bring together leaders from different faiths to work toward the common good, fostering peaceful

---

18. Joseph E. B. Lumbard, *Commentary on Surat al-Saff*, in *The Study Quran: A New Translation and Commentary*, ed. Nasr et al. (HarperOne, 2015), 1366.

19. *Sahih Muslim, kitab al-jihad wa al-siyar, bab kitab al-nabi salla allahu alayhi wa sallam ila hiraql yad'uhu ila al-Islam.*

20. Ibn Ishaq, *Life of Muhammad*, 57.

coexistence. Instead of emphasizing theological differences, the initiative focuses on collaboration based on the inherent dignity of all people and the pursuit of shared goals.[21]

Marriage to Khadija

By his mid-twenties, Muhammad had gained a strong reputation in Meccan society for his admirable character. Impressed by his integrity and achievements, Khadija, a widowed businesswoman, hired him. Over time, she grew fond of him and eventually proposed marriage. When they wed, Muhammad was twenty-five, and Khadija was fifteen years his senior.[22] After their marriage, Muhammad left his uncle's home to live with Khadija. With his improved financial situation, he also brought his young cousin Ali ibn Abi Talib to live with them. This arrangement helped support his uncle Abu Talib, who was struggling financially with a large family to care for, as having Ali in Muhammad's household eased some of his uncle's responsibilities.

Muhammad and Khadija had six children together: two sons, Qasim and Abdullah, and four daughters, Zainab, Ruqayya, Umm Kulthum, and Fatima. Of these, only Fatima survived him. His marriage to Khadija was monogamous and lasted twenty-five years, until her passing. Muhammad deeply loved Khadija and always cherished her support and generosity during difficult times. After Khadija's death, one of the Prophet's wives, Aisha, would later admit that she was not jealous of any of the Prophet's other wives except for Khadija. Muhammad often spoke fondly of Khadija, and whenever he sacrificed an animal, he would share it with her friends. When Aisha expressed her displeasure, Muhammad reminded her that Khadija was the mother of his children

---

21. For more information on the initiative, see "History of Alliance of Virtues," Alliance of Virtues, September 9, 2024, https://www.allianceofvirtues.com/english/history.asp.

22. Given the number of children Khadija had with Muhammad, some Islamic sources suggest she was likely younger than forty when she first married the Prophet.

and had many admirable qualities.[23] In a hadith, Muhammad stated that Mary, the daughter of Imran, was the best woman of her time, and the best woman of his community (*umma*) was Khadija.[24]

After Khadija's death, Muhammad entered into many other marriages, primarily with widows who had children from previous marriages and were in need of assistance and protection. For instance, Sawda bint Zam'a was the first woman he married after Khadija's passing. An early follower of the Prophet, Sawda was a widow with five children. Marriage to Muhammad provided her with safety and support to raise her children. Additionally, Muhammad engaged in political marriages to establish peace among the tribes of Arabia. Polygamous marriages and unions for political reasons were quite common in the Near East. At one point, he had nine wives. Muhammad did not have any children with these women, except with his wife Maria al-Qibtiyya, who bore him a son named Ibrahim, who died in infancy.

Conflict over the Renovation of the Kaaba

Muhammad was highly respected and admired by his people, often playing a key role in mediating conflicts. For example, the Meccans occasionally needed to renovate the Kaaba due to damage from natural disasters, sometimes requiring a complete rebuild. Each tribe was responsible for a part of the construction. On one occasion, a major conflict arose over who would place the sacred Black Stone (*al-Hajar al-Aswad*).[25] The leaders agreed that the first person to enter through the main gate of the Kaaba would mediate the dispute. Muhammad

---

23. *Sahih al-Bukhari, kitab manakib al-ansar, bab tazwij al-nabiyyi salla allahu 'alayhi wa sallam khadija wa fadliha radiya allahu 'anha.*

24. *Sahih al-Bukhari, kitab manakib al-ansar, bab tazwij al-nabiyyi salla allahu 'alayhi wa sallam khadija wa fadliha radiya allahu 'anha.*

25. *Al-Hajar al-Aswad* is a sacred Black Stone located at the eastern corner of the Kaaba. According to Islamic tradition, the stone was placed in the Kaaba by the prophet Abraham and his son Ishmael. It marks the starting point for the circumambulation (*tawaf*) performed by pilgrims during Hajj and Umrah.

was the first to arrive, and his appearance was met with celebration, as he was considered trustworthy. When the situation was explained to him, he requested a cloak to be laid on the ground and had the stone placed on it. Representatives from each clan held the cloak and lifted it together to the height of the wall, and Muhammad then placed the stone with his own hands, thus preventing a major violent conflict among the tribes of Quraysh.[26]

The First Revelations and Converts

Unlike many in Meccan society, Muhammad was one of the few who did not follow the prevalent polytheistic beliefs and practices, instead adhering to the monotheistic *hanif* tradition. On the rare occasions when he tried to engage in such practices, God miraculously intervened to protect him. For example, he once attempted to attend a dance at a wedding, but as he approached the location, he fell asleep and did not wake up until sunrise.[27]

In his mid-thirties, Muhammad began regularly withdrawing from society to meditate. This time spent in solitude, removed from daily life, had a deep effect on his spirituality. He frequently visited the Cave of Hira on Nur Mountain (the Mountain of Light) near Mecca to engage in reflection, prayer, and worship, especially in the month of Ramadan.

During one of these retreats in 610 CE, at the age of forty, Muhammad had an experience that would profoundly change the course of history. The archangel Gabriel appeared to him in a striking and intense visitation, commanding him to "read" (*iqra*). Muhammad responded, "I do not know how to read!" He then narrated the rest of his experience as follows:

> The angel seized me forcefully and pressed me so hard that I could no longer endure it. He then released me and again

---

26. Ibn Ishaq, *Life of Muhammad*, 57.

27. Al-Tabari, *Tarikh al-Tabari: Tarikh al-Rusul wa al-Muluk*, vol. 2, ed. Muhammad Abu al-Fadl Ibrahim (Dar al-Maarif, 1967), 279.

asked me to read. I replied, "I do not know how to read." He caught me once more, pressing me a second time until I could not bear it. After releasing me, he asked me once more to read, but I responded again, "I do not know how to read!" For the third time, he seized me, pressed me, then released me and said, "Read! In the name of your Lord who created: He created man from a clinging form. Read! Your Lord is the Most Bountiful One who taught by the pen, who taught man what he did not know."[28]

This exchange between Muhammad and Archangel Gabriel is marked as the first revealed verses of the Qur'an. It was also during this occasion that Gabriel taught Muhammad how to do ablution (*wudu*) and prayer (*salat*).[29] As this was the first revelation Muhammad had ever received, he did not initially understand what was happening. Some sources indicate he was concerned, even terrified, by the experience. His tentative response to the angelic call was "I do not know how to read." When Gabriel repeated his command, Muhammad again answered, "I do not know how to read" because he was "unlettered" (*ummi*) and could neither read nor write.[30]

Following the incident, Muhammad rushed to Khadija and shared what had occurred. She reassured him with these words: "Don't worry, and don't be sad. God will not put a beloved servant of his to shame. I know that you always speak the truth. You take care of what is entrusted to you. You are good to your relatives and neighbors. You treat them with compassion. You help the poor and needy. You open your door to them. Be patient! You will be the prophet of the community."[31] Khadija's full confidence in her husband led her to become the first follower of Islam.

---

28. *Sahih al-Bukhari, kitab bad' al-wahy, bab kayfa kana bad' al-wahy 'ila rasul allah salla allahu 'alayhi wa sallam.*

29. Ibn Ishaq, *Life of Muhammad*, 112.

30. Qur'an 29:48; 7:157.

31. Muslim bin al-Hajjaj, *Sahih Muslim, kitab al-iman, bab bad' al-wahy ila rasul allahi salla allahu 'alayhi wa sallam.*

In order to better understand the situation, Khadija brought Muhammad to her Christian cousin Waraqa ibn Nawfal, an elderly scholar well-versed in both the Gospel and the Torah. On hearing Muhammad's story, Waraqa confirmed that Muhammad had indeed received a revelation from God. He warned that people would resist Muhammad's message, predicting that he and his followers would face persecution and expulsion from Mecca. While Waraqa's words were encouraging, Muhammad and Khadija struggled to understand why they would be persecuted and expelled. Waraqa explained, "Yes, they will drive you from your homeland. No prophet who has received revelation like you has avoided persecution for their teachings. If I live to see the days when you publicly deliver the message of revelation, I will support you with all the resources I have."[32]

After the initial experience, Muhammad did not receive any further revelation for some time. During this distressing period of silence, his opponents took the opportunity to criticize him, with some even claiming that Muhammad's Lord had abandoned him. The Prophet started to fear that he had somehow displeased God, although his wife, Khadija, assured him this was not the case. Eventually, the revelations resumed, bringing him further reassurance:

> By the morning brightness and by the night when it is still, your Lord has not forsaken you [Prophet], nor does He hate you, and the next life will be better for you than this one; your Lord is sure to give you so much that you will be well satisfied. Did He not find you an orphan and shelter you? Did He not find you lost and guide you? Did He not find you needy then satisfied your needs? So do not oppress the orphan, and do not chide the one who asks for help; talk about the blessings of your Lord.[33]

---

32. Ibn Ishaq, *Life of Muhammad*, 107, and *Sahih al-Bukhari, kitab bad' al-wahy, bab kayfa kana bad' al-wahy 'ila rasul allah salla allahu 'alayhi wa sallam*.

33. Qur'an 93:1–11.

In another revelation, God instructed the Prophet to rise and proclaim the new message to the community, urging him to "be patient" in God's cause.[34] The Qur'an was gradually revealed and would continue until Muhammad's death, often addressing the questions and challenges faced by the emerging Muslim community, first in Mecca and later in Medina. The Meccan verses laid the foundation of faith (*iman*), focusing on themes such as belief in one God, life after death, resurrection, accountability in the hereafter, worship, and justice.

The First Converts

The next person to embrace the new message after Khadija was Ali ibn Abi Talib, the Prophet's cousin who lived with them. Shortly after the first revelation, Ali saw Muhammad and Khadija praying together. When they finished, Ali asked what they were doing. The Prophet replied, "This is a faith ordained by God. I invite you to believe in one God and abandon idol worship." Ali said he needed to consult with his father, Abu Talib. The Prophet responded, "If you choose to accept this message, do so now. If not, please keep what you have seen and our conversation confidential." Ali assured him he would keep it to himself. However, he returned the next day and told the Prophet he wanted to convert. He reasoned that God did not seek his father's approval to create him, so he did not need his father's permission to worship the God who created him.[35]

Ali would later become one of the Prophet's most influential followers. He married the Prophet's daughter, Fatima, and became the fourth successor of the Muslim community after the Prophet's death. Fatima was Muhammad's only child to outlive him, and the Prophet's lineage continued through her children, Hasan and Husayn. Ali's father, Abu Talib, did not accept the new message, choosing instead

---

34. Qur'an 74:1–7.

35. Ibn Ishaq, *Life of Muhammad*, 115, and Suruç, *Kainatın Efendisi*, 166.

to adhere to the religion of his forefathers. However, he continued to protect Muhammad until his death.

The Opposition to the Revelation

After Ali's conversion, Zayd ibn Haritha, the Prophet's adopted son, and Abu Bakr, the Prophet's close friend and a merchant, also converted, as did several slaves, including Bilal ibn Rabah, Sumayya bint Khabbat, and her husband, Yasir ibn Amir. The increasing number of converts alarmed the elites in Mecca. Many individuals, including some close members of the Prophet's extended family, opposed his message, fearing that the new religion threatened their tribal customs, economy, and social order. Among the dissenters was Muhammad's uncle Abu Lahab, one of the Prophet's staunchest enemies, who, along with his wife, became symbols of resistance to the new faith.[36]

In a new piece of revelation, God instructed the Prophet to start spreading the message of the Qur'an, beginning with his relatives.[37] One day, Muhammad climbed a hill just outside Mecca and called together the elders of Quraysh, including Abu Lahab. He asked them, "If I told you an army was coming over that hill, would you believe me?" They replied, "Yes, for we have never known you to tell anything but the truth." The Prophet then said, "In that case, I am a warner sent to you against a tremendous punishment." Abu Lahab responded, "May your hands perish this day. Is this why you have summoned all of us here?"[38] On this occasion, Muhammad received a revelation condemning Abu Lahab and his wife to hell: "May the hands of Abu Lahab perish! May he perish! Neither his wealth nor his gains will help him: he will burn

---

36. Qur'an 111:1–5.

37. Qur'an 26:214.

38. *Sahih al-Bukhari, kitab al-tafsir, bab wa tabb ma aghna 'anhu maluhu wa ma kasab.*

in the Flaming Fire— and so will his wife, the firewood-carrier, with a palm-fibre rope around her neck."[39]

Abu Lahab was a prominent figure in the Prophet's clan and the wealthiest of Muhammad's uncles. After the death of the Prophet's other uncle, Abu Talib, Abu Lahab assumed the leadership of the clan. He violently opposed Muhammad's message and persecuted many of his followers, collaborating with the Prophet's enemies to undermine his efforts. Abu Lahab and his wife became notorious for their insults and assaults against Muhammad. Living nearby, they often stoned his house and threw excrement at his door.[40] Abu Lahab's wife would carry bundles of thorns and scatter them in the Prophet's path.

Muhammad's adversaries even used the death of his sons to discredit him. In Arabian culture, it was believed that noble lineage could only be maintained through male descendants. Therefore, with all of Muhammad's sons dying in infancy, they considered him a man "without posterity," believing he would have no heirs to continue his legacy and that he would be forgotten after his death.[41] In this difficult time, support and comfort for the Prophet came from God through revelation: "We have truly bestowed abundant good upon you [Prophet], so pray and sacrifice your Lord alone. It is your enemy who is without posterity."[42] As we will explore in the following chapters, although Muhammad's sons did not survive to carry on his legacy, he had many devoted followers who loved him, adhered to his teachings, and passed on his message to future generations.

Efforts to Make a Deal with Muhammad

Muhammad's opponents believed he had wronged them in a way that no one would dare to do against their own tribe. They responded to

---

39. Qur'an 111:1–5.

40. Ibn Ishaq, *Life of Muhammad*, 191.

41. Ibn Ishaq, *Life of Muhammad*, 180.

42. Qur'an 108:1–3.

the Prophet and his message by saying, "You criticize our ancestors, disgrace our religious practices, belittle our beliefs, insult our gods, and divide our people. You have done the worst thing possible to us."[43] The Meccans sought various ways to stop Muhammad from preaching in Mecca, even offering him wealth and leadership in exchange for abandoning his mission. When his uncle Abu Talib attempted to persuade him on behalf of the tribe, Muhammad replied, "Even if they placed the sun in my right hand and the moon in my left, I will not give up my mission."[44] On another occasion, some Meccan leaders proposed a compromise: The Prophet would worship their gods for a year, and they would worship his God for a year. The guiding response came from God through revelation, and the answer was a firm no: "Say [Prophet], 'Disbelievers: I do not worship what you worship, you do not worship what I worship, I will never worship what you worship, you will never worship: you have your religion and I have mine."[45]

Attempts to Undermine the Revelation

Unable to dissuade Muhammad from his mission, the Meccan leaders sought other ways to undermine the revelation, making several accusations against him. The Qur'an directly addresses these claims. One accusation was that Muhammad derived his teachings from a local Christian rather than from the archangel Gabriel: "Indeed, We know very well that they say, 'No one is teaching him except a human,' but the language of the person they refer to is foreign, while this revelation is in clear Arabic."[46] Here, the Qur'an counters derisive claims by highlighting that the individual they claim as the source does not know Arabic, whereas the Qur'an is revealed in pure Arabic.

---

43. Ibn Ishaq, *Life of Muhammad*, 119, 133.

44. Ibn Ishaq, *Life of Muhammad*, 119.

45. Qur'an 109:1–6.

46. Qur'an 16:103.

Another charge from the Meccans was that Muhammad was either a soothsayer or possessed. They also alleged that he fabricated the revelations from confused dreams or poetry. The Qur'an brings up their claims: "Yet they say, 'This [revelation] is a set of confused dreams! No, he made it up! No, he must be a poet!'"[47] Some Meccans went further, dismissing Qur'anic passages as ancient fables or the product of sorcery.[48] Through these varied and inconsistent accusations, the Meccans aimed to discredit Muhammad's teachings as human fabrications rather than divine revelation.

Additionally, Meccans demanded that Muhammad show them extraordinary signs to prove his prophethood. The Qur'an addresses their demands as follows: "They say, 'We will not believe in you [Muhammad] until you make a spring gush out of the ground for us; or until you have a garden of date palms and grapevines, and make rivers flow through them; or make the sky fall upon us in pieces, as you have claimed; or bring God and the angels before us face to face; or have a house made of gold; or ascend to Heaven—even then, we will not believe in your ascension until you bring down unto us a book we can read.'"[49] God then instructed the Prophet on how to respond to their unrealistic expectations: "Glory be to my Lord! Am I not only a human messenger?"[50] The Qur'an frequently recounts the insincere demands made by previous generations to their prophets. Now the Meccans were making similar requests. In his response, the Prophet emphasized not only his humanity but also his reliance on God to bring about any extraordinary event or miracle.

In dealing with Muhammad, the Meccan opponents also sought the help of Jewish rabbis in Medina and sent a delegation to consult them. Since the Jews were part of a revelation-based tradition and had the Torah as their scripture, the Meccans believed that Jewish scholars

---

47. Qur'an 21:5.

48. Qur'an 25:5 and 6:7.

49. Qur'an 17:90–93.

50. Qur'an 17:93.

could provide them with some solutions. They gave the Meccan delegation three questions: If Muhammad could answer them, he would be considered God's prophet; if he could not, he would be deemed a false prophet. One question was about the seven sleepers (*ashab al-kahf*), another was about the traveler (*dhu'l-qarnayn*) who reached the ends of the earth in the East and West, and the third was about the nature of the Spirit (*al-ruh*). When the delegation presented these questions to the Prophet, he replied, "I will tell you the answers tomorrow," expecting to receive a revelation. However, when they returned the next day, Muhammad still could not provide the answers. It took fifteen days for the Prophet to receive the revelation addressing these questions, a waiting period that was stressful for him. The Qur'an clarified the situation with this verse: "Do not say of anything, 'I will do that tomorrow,' without adding, 'God willing.'" The Qur'an then gave detailed accounts of the first two questions and responded to the third with "[Prophet], they ask you about the Spirit. Say, 'The Spirit is part of my Lord's domain. You have only been given a little knowledge.'"[51] This story affirmed that the Prophet's knowledge depended on revelation and that he could access it only with God's permission.

Although they witnessed numerous signs of Muhammad's prophecy, many of the Meccan elites persisted in their disbelief. They continuously sought to challenge the Prophet whenever possible. On one occasion, a few Meccan leaders approached the Prophet and said, "If you are truly a Prophet of God, then split the moon into two parts." The Prophet asked, "Would you then believe in me?" They replied yes. The Prophet made a sign with his finger, and the moon was miraculously divided into two. Yet they dismissed this extraordinary event as sorcery. The Qur'an addresses their persistent disbelief: "The Hour draws near; the moon is split in two. Whenever the disbelievers see a sign, they turn away and say, 'Same old sorcery!' They reject the truth and follow their own desires."[52]

---

51. Qur'an 17:85.

52. Qur'an 54:1–3.

Despite his critics, Muhammad continued his mission. Many new converts joined his community of believers. The Qur'an challenged Muhammad's opponents to produce something comparable to the new divine revelations but affirmed that they could not and would never be able to do so: "If you have doubts about what we have revealed to Our servant, then produce a single sura like it and call your helpers other than God, if what you say is true."[53]

Persecutions and Tortures

Failing to stop the spread of Muhammad's message with dialogue, the Meccan elites resorted to insults, boycotts, persecution, and the torture of Muhammad's followers. For example, Sumayya and Yasir, an enslaved couple, were tortured to death by their master, Abu Jahl, a prominent opponent of the Prophet, because of their faith in the new revelation. Known as Abu Hakam (the father of wisdom) in Mecca, he was renamed Abu Jahl (the father of ignorance) by the Prophet due to his blind rejection of the revelation and hostility toward Islam. Both Sumayya and Yasir are remembered as the first martyrs of Islam. Another follower of the Prophet who faced severe torture was Bilal ibn Rabah, a slave of Umayya ibn Khalaf. Umayya was well-known for his aggression toward the Prophet and his followers. After secretly converting to Islam upon learning about the Qur'an's message, Bilal faced brutal persecution when Umayya discovered his conversion. Umayya would starve Bilal and torture him under the scorching sun as a public display to intimidate other Muslims. Abu Bakr eventually purchased Bilal from Umayya and set him free. Bilal then became the Prophet's special *muezzin* (the one who calls to prayer).

First Immigrants and Refugees in Abyssinia

As the situation in Mecca became unbearable for the new converts, the Prophet instructed his followers to emigrate to Abyssinia, explaining

---

53. Qur'an 2:23–24.

that its ruling king did not tolerate injustice and that the land was welcoming. He advised them to stay there until God relieved them of their hardship.[54] Around eighty of his followers, including his son-in-law, Uthman ibn Affan, and his wife, Ruqayya (the Prophet's daughter), along with his cousin Ja'far ibn Abi Talib and his wife, sought refuge there. They departed Mecca discreetly and in small groups. Abyssinia was chosen for several reasons. First, the Meccans had a trade relationship with the region, making it a familiar territory. Second, Abyssinia was ruled by a Christian king known for his sense of justice, under whom they hoped to freely practice their faith. The Qur'an had distinguished Jews and Christians from the polytheists of Mecca by calling them "People of the Book" (*ahl al-kitab*), indicating that, like the new Muslim community, they had divinely revealed scriptures.

When the Meccans learned that some of the Prophet's companions had fled to Abyssinia, they sent a delegation bearing gifts to persuade the king to return them to Mecca. The king, however, decided to hear both sides before making any decision. The Meccans argued that the Muslims had abandoned the customs of their ancestors and introduced an unfamiliar religion.[55] The king then turned to the Muslims, asking them to explain their beliefs and the message of Prophet Muhammad. Ja'far ibn Abi Talib spoke on their behalf:

> O King, we were a people lost in ignorance, worshiping idols, consuming dead animals, committing immoral acts, breaking family ties, mistreating visitors, and allowing the strong to oppress the weak. This was our way of life until God sent us a messenger, whose noble lineage, truthfulness, trustworthiness, and compassion we knew well. He called us to recognize the oneness of God and to worship Him, abandoning the stones and images that we and our ancestors had worshiped. He instructed us to speak the truth, fulfill our commitments,

---

54. Ibn Ishaq, *Life of Muhammad*, 146.

55. Lings, *Muhammad*, 83.

honor family ties, and practice hospitality. He urged us to refrain from crimes and bloodshed. He forbade us from committing immoral acts, telling lies, exploiting the property of orphans, and defaming chaste women. He commanded us to worship God alone, without associating anything with Him, and he taught us about prayer, charity, and fasting. So we accepted his message, believed in him, and followed what he brought to us from God. We worshipped God alone, without associating anything with Him, and we regarded as forbidden what he forbade and as lawful what he declared lawful.[56]

The king then asked if they could share an example of the revelation brought by their Prophet. In response, Ja'far recited a passage from the Qur'anic chapter about Mary:

> Mention in the Qur'an the story of Mary. She withdrew from her family to a place to the east and secluded herself away; We sent Our Spirit to appear before her in the form of a perfected man. She said, "I seek the Lord of Mercy's protection against you: if you have any fear of Him [do not approach]!" but he said, "I am but a Messenger from your Lord, [come] to announce to you the gift of a pure son." She said, "How can I have a son when no man has touched me? I have not been unchaste," and he said, "This is what your Lord said: 'It is easy for Me—We shall make him a sign to all people, a blessing from Us.'"[57]

It is reported that the king was deeply moved by the Qur'anic recitation of the story of Mary and Jesus. However, the Meccan delegation continued their efforts to persuade the king, claiming that Muslims deny the divinity of Jesus. The king turned to Ja'far again, asking about

---

56. Ibn Ishaq, *Life of Muhammad*, 151–152.

57. Qur'an 19:16–21.

the new revelation's view of Jesus. Ja'far responded with the Qur'anic description: "We say of him only what has been revealed to us—that he is the servant of God, His messenger, His Spirit, and His Word, which He cast unto Mary, the blessed virgin."[58] The king then picked up a stick, drew a line, and remarked, "The difference between us and you is no thicker than this line." He assured the Muslims that they could live peacefully in Abyssinia for as long as they wished. The king rejected the Meccans' request and returned their gifts.

The Conversion of Hamza and Umar

Meanwhile, the conversion of two prominent figures in Mecca added a new dimension to the sixth year of the Prophet's mission. One of them was Hamza ibn Abd al-Muttalib, the Prophet's uncle. On returning from a hunting trip, Hamza learned that Abu Jahl and his companions had insulted and verbally abused the Prophet. Furious, Hamza forcefully confronted Abu Jahl and declared that from then on, he was a Muslim and would stand with the Prophet and his followers. Hamza then went to the Prophet, offering comfort and informing him of his decision. This courageous stand against the Prophet's opponents earned Hamza a place as one of the most celebrated heroes in Islamic history. In the years that followed, Hamza fought alongside the Prophet and ultimately gave his life in a battle against the Meccans. He remains an iconic figure in Arabic, Persian, and Turkish literature, especially for his heroism. A literary genre called *Hamzaname* in Turkish culture is dedicated to Hamza's legacy, where he is honored as the "master of martyrs" in Islamic tradition.

The other figure was Umar ibn al-Khattab, a key figure among the Meccan elite who would later become one of Muhammad's main companions and the second caliph after the Prophet's death. Umar had a profound impact on the early Muslim community. Initially, Umar had been a fierce opponent of Muhammad and his followers, known for persecuting and torturing those who converted to Islam within his

---

58. Lings, *Muhammad*, 86.

tribe. According to tradition, Muhammad prayed for God to strengthen Islam through the conversion of one of the two major Meccan leaders: Umar ibn al-Khattab or ʿAmr ibn Hisham (Abu Jahl).[59]

Disturbed by the growing number of converts and perceiving Muhammad as a source of division within his tribe and families, Umar decided the only solution was to kill him. On his way to carry out this plan, Umar encountered a follower of Muhammad who warned him that Muhammad's clan would not tolerate his death. The man also informed Umar that Umar's own sister and brother-in-law had both converted to Islam. This news angered Umar, and he headed to his sister's house, where he found them reciting verses from the Qur'an (Surah Ta Ha).

Demanding to see the text, Umar was initially refused, prompting him to violently confront them. Eventually, they relented, allowing him to read the passages himself. This direct encounter with the Qur'an's words softened Umar's heart, and he was deeply moved by its beauty and message. Umar then sought out Muhammad, not to confront him but to embrace the message of Islam. Following Umar's conversion, Muhammad began to openly spread his message, inviting not only his relatives but also the wider Meccan community to hear the revelations he had received.

The Boycott and Embargo

The Meccan leadership continued to devise new obstacles to halt the Prophet and the spread of his message. Their latest strategy was a complete boycott of the Prophet's entire clan, aimed at pressuring its leaders, particularly Abu Talib, to abandon Muhammad. An embargo was imposed on the Prophet's family and his followers, with its terms written and placed in the Kaaba for public awareness.[60] These terms

---

59. *Jami' al-Tirmidhi, kitab al-manaqib ʿan rasul allahu salla ʿalayhi wa sallam, bab fi manaqib Umar ibn al-Khattab radi Allahu ʿanhu.*

60. Ibn Ishaq, *Life of Muhammad*, 159.

included prohibiting marriage with members of the Prophet's clan and banning all trade with them. This boycott lasted nearly three years, leaving many in a state of starvation and famine. The Prophet, his wife Khadija, his uncle Abu Talib, and Abu Bakr spent all their resources to support their people during this period. Finally, with the encouragement of several influential figures who had familial ties with the Prophet's followers, the embargo was lifted.

The Year of Sadness

With the end of the boycott came relief, but the Prophet and his community were soon shaken by the loss of two pivotal figures in his life. The first was his uncle Abu Talib. Although he did not accept Muhammad's message, Abu Talib had consistently protected him from harm at the hands of the Meccan leaders. The second loss was his wife and closest companion, Khadija, who passed away just a few months after Abu Talib. Khadija was the first Muslim and had offered unwavering support to the Prophet and his mission from the very beginning. Their deaths left a profound void in his life, and the Prophet named the year of their passing the "Year of Sadness" (*'am al-huzn*) due to the depth of his grief.

Following Abu Talib's death, Abu Lahab—a fierce opponent of the Prophet—took over the leadership of Muhammad's clan. This shift meant the Prophet would no longer have the clan's protection, leaving him vulnerable to his adversaries. The Meccans, sensing this vulnerability, intensified their persecution of the Prophet and his followers. One day, an enemy threw dirt on him, and as he returned home covered in dust, one of his daughters wept at the sight. The Prophet consoled her, saying, "Don't cry, my daughter! Surely, God will protect your father."[61] On another occasion, while the Prophet was praying near the Kaaba, a polytheist threw the placenta of a newborn camel—still filled with blood and filth—onto him. In yet another incident, one of his opponents went even further, attempting to strangle the Prophet while he was in prostration during prayer. Witnessing this, Abu Bakr

---

61. Ibn Ishaq, *Life of Muhammad*, 191.

intervened, exclaiming, "Will you kill a man just because he says, 'My Lord is Allah'?"[62]

Continuing his mission in Mecca was becoming more challenging than ever, and the Prophet's safety was at serious risk. Muhammad urgently began to explore options outside of Mecca. The most promising choice seemed to be the city of Taif, located southeast of Mecca, where he could potentially seek the protection of the Thaqif tribe and continue his mission. So Muhammad set out for Taif with his adopted son, Zayd.

However, the response from the people of Taif was disheartening. Not only did they reject Muhammad's request, but they also chased him and his companion out of the city. Both left Taif wounded; Muhammad's feet bled from the stones thrown at him, and Zayd suffered a head injury.[63] When they finally reached a safe place on their return to Mecca, the Prophet turned to God in supplication, seeking solace and refuge:

> To You, my Lord, I complain of my weakness, my helplessness, and the humiliation inflicted upon me by the people. Most Compassionate and Merciful, You are the Lord of the weak, and You are my Lord. To whom do You leave me? To a stranger who treats me with hostility? Or to an enemy, You have empowered against me? As long as You are not displeased with me, I can endure whatever I face. Yet, I would be much happier with Your mercy. I seek refuge in the light of Your face, which dispels all darkness and rightly guides all matters in this world and the Hereafter. May I never incur Your wrath or be subject to Your anger. I submit to You until I earn Your pleasure. Everything is powerless without Your support.[64]

---

62. *Sahih al-Bukhari, kitab fadail ashab al-nabiyy salla allahu 'alayhi wa sallam, bab qawl al-nabiyy salla allahu 'alayhi wa sallam, "law kuntu muttakhizan khalila."*

63. Ibn Ishaq, *Life of Muhammad*, 192–193.

64. Ibn Ishaq, *Life of Muhammad*, 193.

On Muhammad's way back to Mecca, Gabriel appeared to him and conveyed that he was aware of the hurtful words and treatment Muhammad had received from his people. The angel told the Prophet that if he wished, God could destroy them. However, out of compassion, Muhammad replied that he did not want them to be destroyed. He expressed his only wish: that God would bring forth descendants from their lineage who would worship God alone and not associate any partners with God.[65]

The Prophet needed to return to Mecca but knew it would not be safe without the protection of a prominent figure. As he approached Mecca, he sought the protection of Mutʿim ibn ʿAdi, a chief of one of the Quraysh clans. Mutʿim accepted Muhammad's request, allowing him to reenter Mecca under the protection of Mutʿim and his family. The Prophet remembered Mutʿim's support years later, even after the latter's death. Later, after fleeing to Medina, the Muslim community would face the Meccans in several battles. During one of them, the Battle of Badr, Mutʿim was killed while fighting for the Meccans, many of whom were taken captive. After the battle, a Meccan delegation came to Medina requesting the release of the captives, and Mutʿim's son, Jubayr, was among them. When the Prophet saw Jubayr, he said, "If Mutʿim were alive and spoke to me about these captives, I would release them all."[66] With these words, the Prophet expressed his gratitude to Mutʿim for his support during a difficult time.[67]

The Night Journey and Ascension to Heaven

During this challenging time in the Prophet Muhammad's life, one of the most significant events occurred: his night journey (*isra*) and

---

65. *Sahih Muslim*, kitab al-jihad wa al-siyar, bab ma laqiya al-nabiyy salla allahu ʿalayhi wa sallam min adha al-mushrikina wa al-munafiqina.

66. *Sahih al-Bukhari*, kitab al-khumus, bab ma manna al-nabiyy salla Allahu ʿalayhi wa sallam ʿala al-usara min ghayri an yukhammas.

67. Suruç, *Kainatın Efendisi*, 261.

ascension to heaven (*mi'raj*). One night, while near the Kaaba, the archangel Gabriel took Muhammad from there to Jerusalem. From Jerusalem, he ascended through the seven heavens, ultimately encountering God directly.[68] Along this journey, he met major prophets, including Abraham, Moses, and Jesus, and led them in prayer—a gesture understood as affirming his prophethood and his role as the "seal of all prophets," as stated in the Qur'an.[69]

A chapter in the Qur'an, Surat al-Isra, is named after this event. Its opening verse describes the journey: "Glory be to the One Who took His servant by night from the sacred place of worship to the furthest place of worship, whose surroundings We have blessed, to show him some of Our signs: Indeed, He alone is the All Hearing, the All Seeing."[70] From this verse, we know that God wanted to reveal signs (*ayat*) to the Prophet through this experience. During the journey, the Prophet witnessed divine manifestations throughout the universe, observing the beauty and perfection of God's creation. The truths of faith became even clearer to him.[71]

On this sacred journey, God gifted the Prophet and his followers with the duty to perform the five daily prayers. Initially, God prescribed fifty prayers daily, but on Moses's advice, the Prophet requested a reduction from God until the number was set to five times.[72] Additionally, the Prophet received a revelation that became the foundation of the Islamic creed: "The Messenger believes in what has been sent down to him from his Lord, as do the faithful. They all believe in God, His angels, His scriptures, and His messengers. 'We make no distinction

---

68. Qur'an 53:9.

69. Lings, *Muhammad*, 104.

70. Qur'an 17:1.

71. While the vast majority of Muslim scholars believe the journey was both physical and spiritual, some hold that it was only a spiritual experience.

72. Ibn Ishaq, *Life of Muhammad*, 186–187.

between any of His messengers,' they say, 'We hear and obey. Grant us Your forgiveness, our Lord. To You we all return!'"[73]

When reports of Muhammad's ascension spread, some questioned the story's authenticity. However, Abu Bakr, a close companion, firmly declared, "If Muhammad said so, I believe it happened." In recognition of his firm faith, the Prophet honored him with the title *al-Siddiq*, meaning "the truthful one."[74]

Due to its importance in the Qur'an and hadith, the Prophet's night journey and ascension became a central theme in Islamic literature. A genre in Turkish and Persian literature known as *miʻrajname* is dedicated to descriptions of this event. Jerusalem, as the site of the Prophet's journey, became Islam's third holiest city, after Mecca and Medina. Later, Muslims constructed the Al-Aqsa Mosque on the spot from which the Prophet is believed to have ascended to heaven.[75]

The night journey affirmed God's mercy and glory, the existence of heaven, and the eternal world. Muhammad not only experienced the joy of being in God's presence but also brought believers the hopeful news that they, too, could attain closeness to God. This experience provided Muhammad great comfort, motivating and reenergizing him to persevere in his mission despite the challenges he and his followers faced.

The Aqaba Pledges: Paving the Way for Migration

Muhammad continued his efforts to spread the Qur'anic message, particularly during the pilgrimage season in Mecca, when he would meet visitors and invite them to embrace his teachings. During one of these seasons, he encountered a group from Yathrib (later known as Medina). After speaking with the Prophet, six individuals accepted his message.

---

73. Qur'an 2:285.

74. Ibn Ishaq, *Life of Muhammad*, 181.

75. The spot in Jerusalem where Muhammad is believed to have ascended to heaven is thought to be the ancient site of the Jewish temple, which was destroyed by the Romans centuries earlier.

These new followers came from the two major polytheistic tribes in Yathrib: the Aws and the Khazraj. Significantly, the people of Yathrib were already somewhat familiar with the concept of divine revelation due to the substantial Jewish presence in their city, and they had heard of the Jewish expectation of a Prophet. Additionally, the Aws and Khazraj tribes had been embroiled in conflicts for decades, and Muhammad's message offered the prospect of peace. These factors made members of the Aws and Khazraj tribes more receptive to Muhammad's message.

On returning to Yathrib, these new converts began spreading Muhammad's message within their circles, leading to additional conversions. The following year, twelve Muslims from Yathrib visited Mecca. The Prophet personally met them at a place called Aqaba, near Mecca, where they pledged their allegiance to him. As part of this first Aqaba pledge, they agreed to abandon polytheism, worship only one God, refrain from theft, avoid fornication, abstain from infanticide, refrain from slander, and uphold righteousness.

After the pledge, the Prophet sent Mus'ab ibn Umayr, a young companion, to Yathrib to teach the new followers the Qur'an and how to pray (*salat*). Mus'ab's efforts, combined with those of the new converts, sparked a wave of conversions, including several prominent figures from both tribes.

In the following years, over seventy people from Yathrib came to Mecca during the pilgrimage season in order to pledge their allegiance to Muhammad. In this second pledge at Aqaba, the Prophet expressed his intention to migrate to Yathrib. In response, the people of Yathrib vowed to protect him as they would their own families, marking a significant step toward the eventual migration of the Muslim community.[76] All these factors indicated that Yathrib could serve as a safe alternative to Mecca for Muhammad and his followers. Ultimately, the people of Yathrib proved to be highly receptive to the Prophet's teachings.

Following the second pledge of allegiance, Muhammad encouraged his followers to emigrate to Medina. Many heeded his advice and discreetly left Mecca, except for Umar, who made his departure public.

---

76. Ibn Ishaq, *Life of Muhamamd*, 203.

The Prophet, along with his companion Abu Bakr and his family, as well as Ali ibn Abi Talib and his mother, remained behind. However, some followers were prevented from emigrating due to their families' opposition.

The growing Muslim presence in Medina alarmed the Meccans, as they feared this shift would threaten their trade routes. So they sought a decisive solution: to kill Muhammad before he could leave for Medina. One night, they surrounded the house where Muhammad was staying, intending to carry out their plan. The Prophet became aware of their plan through divine revelation. Acting swiftly, he miraculously escaped their scheme. The Qur'an references this plot: "Remember [Prophet] when the disbelievers plotted to capture, kill, or expel you. They schemed, and so did God: He is the best of schemers."[77] When their plot failed, the Quraysh offered a reward of one hundred camels to anyone who could find the Prophet. Muhammad and his companion Abu Bakr sought refuge in a cave (*ghar thawr*) for three nights.

The Prophet's opponents tracked them to the entrance of the cave. When Abu Bakr became anxious about their situation, Muhammad reassured him, saying, "Do not worry, God is with us." At the entrance, the trackers noticed that the cave's mouth was completely covered by a spider's web; just before it was a dove's nest. They concluded that Muhammad and his companion could not be inside since the undisturbed, intricate spider's web indicated no one had entered. Consequently, they left without searching the cave. This miraculous protection of the Prophet and his companion is recounted in the Qur'an: "Even if you do not help the Prophet, God helped him when the disbelievers drove him out: when the two of them were in the cave, he [Muhammad] said to his companion, 'Do not worry, God is with us,' and God sent His calm down to him, aided him with forces invisible to you, and thwarted the disbelievers' plan. God's plan is superior: God is almighty and wise."[78]

---

77. Qur'an 8:30.

78. Qur'an 9:40.

After facing various obstacles and making several stops along the way, the Prophet and his companion Abu Bakr finally arrived in Medina, a journey that took approximately two weeks. Muhammad's followers, who had been eagerly anticipating his arrival, were overjoyed to welcome him to their city. They greeted him with heartfelt songs of celebration:

> The full moon rose over us
> From the valley of Peace
> And it is incumbent upon us to show gratitude
> For as long as anyone in existence calls out to God
> O our Messenger amongst us
> Who comes with the exhortations to be heeded
> You have brought to this city nobility.
> Welcome you who call us to a good way.[79]

This song became a symbol of the Prophet's migration among Muslims. In 2015, Ottawa's Children's Choir in Canada performed this song as the country welcomed Syrian refugees. The video of the performance went viral on social media, bringing many Muslims to tears.[80] The implication was that the Prophet and his companions were refugees warmly received in Medina with this song. The Canadian choir mirrored the warmth of the people of Medina in welcoming the Muslim refugees.

Leaving his hometown of Mecca was not easy for the Prophet. According to tradition, as he departed, he looked back and lamented, "Of all God's earth, you are the dearest place to me and the most beloved to God. Had my people not driven me out, I would never have left

---

79. It is widely believed within the Muslim community that the people of Medina welcomed the Prophet with these words.

80. Gloria Henriquez, "Internet in Tears over Video of Kids Choir Performing Arabic Welcome Song," *Global News*, December 12, 2015, https://globalnews.ca/news/2397785/this-video-of-kids-singing-in-arabic-to-welcome-syrian-refugees-has-the-internet-in-tears/.

you."[81] However, for the Muslim residents of Yathrib, Muhammad's presence brought immense value and honor to their city. With the Messenger of God residing there, the city became known as Medina al-Nabi, meaning City of the Prophet. Muhammad's emigration (*hijra*) from Mecca to Medina in 622 CE marks the beginning of the Islamic calendar, which is thus known as the *Hijri* calendar. Despite his deep love for Mecca, Muhammad chose to remain in Medina even after the conquest of Mecca and would eventually die there.

The Prophet as a Guest in Medina

With the Prophet's arrival, the question was: Who would have the honor of hosting him? Muhammad did not have a place to stay, and many eagerly wished to host the Prophet and his companion. To avoid disappointing anyone, he said he would stay at the house closest to where his camel knelt down. This turned out to be the home of Abu Ayyub al-Ansari. The Prophet stayed with Abu Ayyub's family as a guest for seven months.

During this time, the Prophet and his companions constructed a mosque in Medina, known as al-Masjid al-Nabawi (the Prophet's Mosque), along with attached rooms for the Prophet and his family, who joined him later. The mosque was built from dried mud bricks, supported by palm trunks, and covered with palm branches. It served as the heart of the Muslim community, functioning as a place for communal prayer and education. The Prophet also received guests and dignitaries there. Over the course of Islamic history, the mosque has undergone numerous expansions, restorations, and renovations. Today, the site of the Prophet's Mosque is a major pilgrimage destination for Muslims, where the Prophet is buried along with some of his companions, including Abu Bakr and Umar ibn al-Khattab. For Muslims, it is regarded as the most sacred place after the Kaaba.

---

81. Lings, *Muhammad*, 121.

The Bonds Between the Refugees and Their Hosts

One of the first actions the Prophet took on arriving in Medina was to foster peace and unity among its people. Many of his companions from Mecca had left behind all they owned and were now settling in Medina as refugees. To support this transition, the Prophet paired his Meccan companions (*muhajirun* or *immigrants*) with the residents of Medina (*ansar* or *helpers*). The Medinan Muslims warmly welcomed their Meccan brethren, and this pairing ensured that each Medinan family would intentionally host and support a Meccan family. This arrangement provided not only financial assistance but also emotional support, ensuring no one was left behind. Moreover, this initiative established a bond of brotherhood rooted in the new revelation, transcending tribal affiliations. The *ansar* willingly shared their resources with the *muhajirun*, demonstrating selflessness and solidarity. In fact, before specific instructions regarding inheritance were revealed, a *muhajir* could even inherit from an *ansar*.

A striking example of this brotherly bond is the story of Abdurrahman ibn 'Awf and Sa'd ibn al-Rabi', whom the Prophet paired together. Abdurrahman was an immigrant from Mecca, while Sa'd was one of the wealthiest Muslims in Medina. On being united in this bond of brotherhood, Sa'd approached Abdurrahman and said, "I am one of the wealthiest among the Ansar, and I want to share my wealth with you. I also have two wives—look at them and let me know which one you prefer. I will divorce her, and after her waiting period ['iddah] is over, you can marry her."[82]

Abdurrahman, however, graciously declined this offer and simply asked Sa'd to show him the market. This story highlights the extraordinary level of generosity and support the *ansar* were willing to extend to the immigrants. At the same time, it also demonstrates the independence and self-respect of the *muhajirun*, who were eager to work and establish their own livelihoods rather than solely relying on the

---

82. *Sahih al-Bukhari, kitab manaqib al-ansar, bab 'ikha'u al-nabiyy salla allahu 'alayhi wa sallam bayn al-muhajirina wa al-ansar.*

generosity of the *ansar*. The immigrants were determined not to become a burden on their welcoming community, embodying the spirit of mutual respect and cooperation.

The remarkable relationship between the immigrants (*muhajirun*) and helpers (*ansar*) in Medina established a lasting model of brotherhood based on faith, which has inspired Muslims for generations. The Qur'an honors their sacrifice and dedication in several verses, such as "The first to lead the way, the Emigrants and the Helpers, and those who followed them in goodness—God is well pleased with them, and they are well pleased with Him. He has prepared for them gardens beneath which rivers flow, wherein they will abide forever. That is the supreme triumph."[83] Another verse highlights the virtues of the helpers and their selflessness toward their immigrant brothers and sisters: "As for those who had already settled in Medina and embraced the faith before the arrival of the immigrants, they show love for those who migrated to them seeking refuge, harboring no envy in their hearts for what has been given to the newcomers. They prioritize the needs of the migrants over their own, even when they themselves are in need. Truly successful are those who are saved from the selfishness of their own souls."[84] These verses not only celebrate the profound relationship between the immigrants and helpers but also recognize their support for the Prophet during challenging times. Their unity and mutual care remain a powerful example of faith-driven solidarity and generosity.

Revelations and Transformations in Medina

In Medina, the Prophet Muhammad would continue to receive Qur'anic revelations until his death. The revelations in Mecca emphasized the foundations of faith, including belief in one God, recognition of God's signs (*ayat*) in creation, and sacred history through the stories of the prophets. They also reaffirmed belief in Muhammad's prophethood and

---

83. Qur'an 9:100.

84. Qur'an 59:9.

resurrection, the hereafter, and the day of judgment. The Qur'anic verses revealed in Medina, however, placed a greater focus on practical matters. These included the institution of rituals such as praying, fasting, almsgiving, and pilgrimage, as well as guidance on relationships with other religious communities, personal manners, governance, marriage, business transactions, justice, and ethics. In many instances, the Qur'an addressed specific challenges faced by the Muslim community, offering solutions and directives for their immediate and long-term needs.

The Qur'anic approach to change and transformation in Medina was gradual and considerate of human nature. For instance, when the Prophet emigrated to Medina, drinking and gambling were common practices in the community. Recognizing the challenges of addiction, the Qur'an addressed these issues incrementally. In the first stage, the Qur'an introduced the principle that while intoxicants and gambling might offer some benefit, their harm outweighed it: "They ask you [Prophet] about intoxicants and gambling: say, 'There is great sin in both, and some benefit for people, but the sin is greater than the benefit.'"[85] This verse encouraged many Muslims to avoid these practices due to their harmful effects, though some continued. In fact, a number of individuals still came to communal prayers while intoxicated.

In the next stage, the Qur'an more directly addressed this issue, cautioning believers against attending prayer while under the influence of alcohol: "You who believe, do not approach prayer when you are drunk, until you understand what you are saying."[86] Given that Muslims prayed five times a day, this restriction made it increasingly difficult for them to drink without affecting their worship, prompting further caution.

Finally, the Qur'an delivered a complete prohibition of intoxicants, gambling, and other practices: "You who believe, intoxicants, gambling, idolatrous practices, and [divining with] arrows are repugnant acts—Satan's doing. Shun them so that you may prosper. With intoxicants

---

85. Qur'an 2:219.

86. Qur'an 4:43.

and gambling, Satan seeks only to incite enmity and hatred among you and to stop you from remembering God and prayer. Will you not give them up?"[87] This verse not only banned alcohol and gambling outright but also condemned idolatry and the pagan practice of using divining arrows for decision-making or distribution of goods, describing them as evil acts inspired by Satan. With this decisive prohibition, the consumption of alcohol and other banned practices disappeared from Muslim life in Medina.

Witnessing the Prophet's Miracles

In the company of the Prophet, the companions often witnessed extraordinary miracles that strengthened their faith. On one occasion, the Prophet noticed that Abu Hurayra was suffering from extreme hunger and invited him to his home. Inside, there was only a single bowl of milk. The Prophet instructed Abu Hurayra to invite the Ahl al-Suffa—the "People of the Bench," a group of poor and homeless people who resided on a shaded bench (*suffa*) in the Prophet's Mosque—to join them. Though initially disheartened, as the milk seemed insufficient even for one person, Abu Hurayra obeyed and called his fellow residents. To his astonishment, each member of the Ahl al-Suffa drank from the bowl and was fully satisfied. When it was Abu Hurayra's turn, he, too, drank until he was full. Finally, the Prophet himself drank the remaining milk, saying, "In the name of God" (*bismillah*).[88]

On another occasion, Anas ibn Malik, a close companion of the Prophet, recounted a remarkable event. Around three hundred companions, including members of the Ahl al-Suffa, were gathered outside the mosque in Medina for the late afternoon (*'asr*) prayer. However, there was not enough water for ablution (*wudu*). The Prophet requested

---

87. Qur'an 5:90–91.

88. *Sahih al-Bukhari, kitab al-riqaq, bab kayfa kana 'ayshu al-nabiyy salla allahu 'alayhi wa sallam wa ashabihi wa takhallihim min al-dunya.*

a small cup of water, placed his hands into it, and miraculously, water began to flow from his fingers. The companions were able to perform their ablutions and even drink from the blessed water.[89] These events not only highlight the Prophet's ability to perform miracles through divine aid but also reflect his deep concern and care for the well-being of his companions, fostering a strong sense of community and reinforcing faith in divine provision.

The Prophet's miracles were not limited to multiplying food and water. When the Prophet's Mosque was first built, it did not have a pulpit. The Prophet Muhammad would deliver sermons while leaning on a dried palm trunk. This arrangement continued for a long time. Later, at the request of his companions, a three-step pulpit was constructed. The palm trunk was set aside, and the Prophet began using the pulpit to address the people. When the Prophet ascended the newly built pulpit and delivered his first sermon, painful cries resembling the sound of a grieving female camel were heard. The people looked around but saw neither a pregnant camel nor a calf. The source of the cries was the dried palm trunk! Its weeping, like a camel in distress, was heard by the Prophet and everyone present in the mosque. The weeping did not stop until the Prophet descended from the pulpit and approached the trunk. He placed his hand on it and comforted it, after which it fell silent. Turning to his companions, he said, "If I had not embraced and comforted it, it would have continued to cry like this until the Day of Judgment because of being separated from the Messenger of God." At the Prophet's request, the trunk was buried in a hole dug beneath the pulpit.

This extraordinary event was a clear miracle, demonstrating that the Prophet was recognized not only by humans, jinn, angels, and animals but even by inanimate objects like a dried palm trunk. Mawlana Jalaluddin Rumi, a prominent thirteenth-century Muslim scholar and Sufi poet, alludes to this story in his *Masnavi*, urging the heedless to

---

89. *Sahih al-Bukhari, kitab al-manaqib, bab 'alamat al-nubuwwa fi al-'islam.*

pay attention to the Prophet's message and admonishing them not to remain less responsive than a piece of wood.[90]

Multireligious Unity and Disharmony

In Medina, the Prophet Muhammad not only focused on establishing the Muslim community but also sought to foster peaceful coexistence with other communities in the city. To achieve harmony and stability, he initiated a multireligious pact among the city's major groups: the polytheistic Arabs, the three Jewish tribes, and the nascent Muslim community. This agreement, commonly referred to as the Constitution of Medina or the Charter of Medina, outlined the framework for intercommunity relations.

According to the charter, all parties were granted freedom in their internal affairs, including the practice of their religions. At the same time, they agreed to unite and stand in solidarity against external threats, particularly from Muhammad's opponents in Mecca. The agreement also ensured the protection of lives and property for everyone in the city. A key aspect of the charter was its prohibition against alliances among the Jewish tribes, the Medinan polytheists, and the Meccans that could jeopardize the Muslim community in Medina. Additionally, the Prophet Muhammad was recognized as the ultimate authority, entrusted with mediating disputes and upholding the principles outlined in the agreement. This initiative not only established Medina as a peaceful and cohesive society but also solidified Muhammad's leadership in the city.

Despite the establishment of the Constitution of Medina, tensions between the Muslim and Jewish communities remained unresolved. While a few members of the Jewish community, such as Abdullah ibn Salaam and his family, accepted the Prophet's message, the vast majority chose not to follow Muhammad. Although the Prophet's teachings closely aligned with the Jewish tradition, the Jewish tribes were

---

90. Jalaluddin Rumi, *The Masnavi of Rumi*, trans. Alan Williams (I. B. Tauris, 2022), 1:141.

anticipating a prophet to arise from among their own people. Over time, these tensions escalated as some Jewish tribes violated the principles outlined in the Constitution of Medina. They also collaborated with the Quraysh of Mecca, the Prophet's opponents, against the Muslim community. This breach of trust led to accusations of treason against the Jewish tribes, ultimately resulting in their expulsion from Medina.

The Hypocrites

Another group frequently mentioned in the Qur'anic verses that were revealed in Medina is the hypocrites (*munafiqun*). In fact, the sixty-third chapter of the Qur'an is named after them. These individuals outwardly declared themselves to be Muslims but did not sincerely embrace the faith. For political and material benefits, they found it advantageous to appear to be Muslim while secretly undermining the Prophet Muhammad and his mission. Although the hypocrites publicly acknowledged Muhammad as a prophet, they continued to align themselves with his enemies in private.

The Qur'an highlights the hypocrites' behavior and attributes, stating, "When the hypocrites come to you [Prophet], they say, 'We bear witness that you are the Messenger of God.' God knows that you truly are His Messenger, and He bears witness that the hypocrites are liars. They use their oaths as a cover, hindering others from the way of God: Evil indeed is what they do. This is because they professed faith and then rejected it, so their hearts have been sealed, and they do not understand."[91] This passage illustrates the duplicity of the hypocrites, emphasizing their insincerity and role in obstructing the path of God.

The hypocrites sought not only to create divisions within the Muslim community but also to make life in Medina more challenging for the believers. For instance, while they outwardly participated in the Muslim community's activities, such as joining military expeditions, they would often withdraw midway under flimsy excuses. This behavior left the Muslim forces vulnerable and weakened their position. The

---

91. Qur'an 63:1–3.

Qur'an warns that the hypocrites' duplicity will ultimately be exposed, and they will face dire consequences in the hereafter. Numerous hadiths of the Prophet Muhammad also describe the traits of the hypocrites. In one narration, he said, "The signs of a hypocrite are four. Whoever possesses even one of them exhibits a characteristic of hypocrisy until they abandon it: when entrusted with something, they betray the trust; when they speak, they lie; when they make a covenant, they break it; and when they argue, they behave in a reckless, offensive, and insulting manner."[92] This description underscores the moral and ethical flaws of hypocrisy and serves as a reminder for self-reflection and integrity in both words and actions.

Wars with the Quraysh of Mecca

Meanwhile, the number of people embracing Islam continued to grow, with many Arab tribes from across the Arabian Peninsula joining the new faith. However, the growing strength and influence of the Muslim community seriously concerned the Meccan elite. They sought to undermine the Muslims by communicating with other groups in Medina, warning that supporting the Muslims could lead to war.

Anticipating potential threats from the Meccans, the Prophet Muhammad and his followers took proactive measures to defend themselves. This marked a shift in their approach compared to their time in Mecca, where they had responded to persecution and torture with patience and forbearance. In Medina, the Muslims adopted a more active stance in self-defense. To keep the Meccan Quraysh in check, the Prophet arranged a number of military expeditions to the routes of the Quraysh trade caravans. While the Muslim community did not directly attack any caravan, this intimidation alarmed the Meccans, which would lead to many battles until a treaty was eventually reached between the two parties in 628 CE.

This shift in strategy was reinforced by a new revelation granting the Muslim community permission to fight back when attacked. The

---

92. *Sahih al-Bukhari, kitab al-'iman, bab 'alamat al-munafiq.*

Qur'an states, "Permission is given to those who are fought because they have been wronged—and truly God has the power to help them."[93] The following verse explains the reasoning behind this permission: "Those who have been expelled unjustly from their homes only for saying, 'Our Lord is God.' If God did not repel some people by means of others, many monasteries, churches, synagogues, and mosques, where God's name is mentioned, would have been destroyed. And God will surely help those who help Him—truly God is strong and mighty."[94] These verses highlight several justifications for self-defense and retaliation. First, the Prophet's followers were unjustly expelled from their homeland simply for their faith in one God, with their properties confiscated by the Meccan aggressors. Second, oppressors and those who commit injustices must be checked by people who seek justice; otherwise, they would destroy places of worship—whether Jewish, Christian, or Muslim—where God's name is honored. In essence, the Qur'an sanctions war as a last resort to protect the freedom of religion and prevent the destruction of sacred spaces, underscoring the principle of justice and the defense of faith.

The Battle of Badr

The first major fight between the Meccans and the Muslims—known as the Battle of Badr— ensued in 624, the second year after the *hijra*. The conflict began when the Prophet sent an expedition to intercept a Quraysh caravan returning from Syria. The goal was to seize the caravan's goods, which were considered rightful compensation for the wealth and property the Quraysh had confiscated from the Muslims in Mecca. The caravan, led by Abu Sufyan, became aware of the Muslims' plan. In response, Abu Sufyan changed the caravan's route to ensure a safe return to Mecca and sent an urgent message to the Quraysh for reinforcements, warning that the caravan was at risk of attack. The Quraysh,

---

93. Qur'an 22:39.

94. Qur'an 22:40.

already seeking an opportunity to confront the Muslims, used this as a pretext to mobilize their army, intending to crush the growing Muslim presence in Medina.

By the time the Muslim forces reached Badr, a strategic stop on the caravan route, the Quraysh caravan had safely made its way to Mecca. However, the Quraysh army continued with their plan to confront the Muslims. Meanwhile, the Prophet and his companions, camping near Badr, were initially unaware of the advancing Meccan army. When they received news of the Meccans' approach, the Muslims faced a critical decision: either retreat to Medina or prepare for battle. It is reported that the Prophet sent Umar ibn al-Khattab as an envoy to persuade the Quraysh to avoid war and return to Mecca. Despite these efforts, the Meccans were determined to fight. After consulting his companions, the Prophet decided to confront the Quraysh forces at Badr.

Although the Quraysh army outnumbered the Muslims by more than three to one, the Muslims achieved a decisive victory. The Quraysh suffered significant losses, with seventy men killed, including key leaders such as Abu Jahl and Umayya ibn Khalaf, while only fourteen Muslims were martyred. The Qur'an references the Battle of Badr in several verses, emphasizing that the Muslim victory was achieved with divine assistance. It highlights how angels were sent by God to support the Muslims during the battle, strengthening their resolve and securing their triumph.[95] This miraculous victory not only boosted the morale of the Muslim community but also enhanced the Prophet's reputation and solidified the standing of Islam in Arabia. The triumph at Badr attracted new followers to the faith and marked a significant turning point in the establishment of the Muslim state.

The Battle of Uhud

The defeat of the Quraysh at Badr fueled their desire for revenge, intensifying their aggression against the Muslim community. Losing many of their leaders left the Meccans determined to retaliate. In the following

---

95. Qur'an 3:123–125; 8:9, 12, 17.

year (625 CE), they organized a larger and more prepared force to launch an attack on the Muslims in Medina. This time, their army numbered three thousand soldiers.

When Muhammad learned of their plans, he consulted with his companions and decided to confront the Quraysh army at Uhud, a location a few miles north of Medina. Initially, the Muslim forces consisted of one thousand fighters, but on the way to Uhud, Abdullah ibn Ubayy, the leader of the hypocrites, withdrew along with three hundred of his followers, leaving the Muslim army with only seven hundred soldiers.

Muslims initially gained the upper hand in the battle, advancing against the Quraysh forces. However, a critical mistake turned the tide. A group of Muslim archers stationed at a strategic position disobeyed the Prophet's instructions to remain in their posts. Believing the battle was already won, they left their positions to collect the spoils of war. Taking advantage of this lapse, the Quraysh regrouped and launched a sudden counterattack, turning the battle in their favor. The Muslim forces suffered heavy losses, and the Prophet himself was wounded. A rumor even spread that he had been killed, further shaking the morale of the Muslims. More than seventy Muslims were killed in the battle, including some of the Prophet's closest companions. Among them were Hamza ibn Abd al-Muttalib, the Prophet's beloved uncle, and Musʿab ibn Umayr, who had played a key role in spreading Islam in Medina before the immigration.

Despite the losses, the Muslims managed to regroup by the end of the battle and pursued the retreating Quraysh. While the Battle of Uhud inflicted significant casualties on the Muslim side, the Meccans failed to achieve their ultimate goal of annihilating the Muslim community or taking control of Medina.

The Battle of Trench

The Meccans sought more decisive ways to weaken or eliminate the Muslim community, as the Prophet Muhammad and his followers continued to challenge their authority. The Muslim community in Medina was steadily growing, and its influence posed a threat to the Meccans' caravan routes.

To neutralize this threat, the Meccans sought to form alliances with various Arab and Jewish tribes. In 627 CE, they assembled an army of ten thousand men and marched toward Medina. Learning of their plans, the Prophet decided to defend the city rather than meet the Meccan forces in open combat, as their numbers greatly outmatched the Muslims.

Seeking counsel from his companions, the Prophet adopted a suggestion from Salman al-Farsi, a companion of Persian origin, who proposed digging a trench around the vulnerable parts of the city. This defensive measure was unfamiliar to Arabian warfare but proved highly effective. The trench was completed just in time before the Meccans arrived. It caught the Meccan army off guard, halting their advance and forcing them into a prolonged siege. For nearly a month, the Meccans encamped outside Medina, unable to breach the trench. Harsh weather conditions, food shortages, and the resilience of the Muslim defenders demoralized the Meccan forces, ultimately forcing them to retreat without achieving their objectives.

The thirty-third chapter of the Qur'an, the Confederates (*Surat al-Ahzab*), takes its name from this event. The Qur'an vividly describes the siege and the emotional strain it placed on the Muslim community: "You who believe, remember the blessing of God upon you when mighty armies massed against you: We sent a violent wind and invisible forces against them. God sees all that you do. They massed against you from above and below; your eyes rolled [with fear], your hearts rose into your throats, and you thought many things about God."[96] As in the Battle of Badr, the Qur'an emphasizes divine assistance in this moment of vulnerability, describing how God sent a fierce wind and unseen forces, including angels, to aid the Muslims.

The Siege of Medina, also known as the Battle of the Trench, marked the final major offensive by the Meccans against the Muslim community in Medina. This event not only demonstrated the effectiveness of the Prophet's leadership and strategy but also brought to light the faith and perseverance of the Muslim community in the face of overwhelming aggression.

---

96. Qur'an 33:9–10.

The Treaty: Victory in Disguise

The following year, the Prophet had a vision in which he saw himself visiting the Kaaba with his companions. Acting on this vision, he resolved to perform the lesser pilgrimage (*'umrah*) to Mecca. Around 1,400 Muslims donned the pilgrimage attire (*ihram*) and set out on the journey. They departed Medina unarmed, signaling their peaceful intentions, as their sole purpose was to perform the pilgrimage, not to engage in conflict. However, given the tense relations with the Quraysh, it was uncertain whether they would be granted entry.

On reaching Hudaybiyyah, a location just outside Mecca, the Prophet sent an envoy to negotiate with the Quraysh. The Quraysh, however, firmly refused to allow Muhammad and his followers into the city. After extensive discussions, representatives from both sides agreed on a treaty, which included the following terms:

1. The Muslims would return to Medina without performing their pilgrimage that year. However, they would be allowed to visit the Kaaba the following year and remain in Mecca for three days.
2. Any man who fled Mecca, embraced Islam, and joined the Prophet's community in Medina would be returned to Mecca. Conversely, any member of the Prophet's community who fled to Mecca would not be returned to Medina.
3. Other Arab tribes were free to ally with either the Muslims or the Quraysh, but all parties were bound to honor the terms of the agreement.
4. The treaty established a ceasefire between the two sides for ten years.

The terms of the treaty seemed unfavorable to many of the Prophet's companions, some of whom felt it was an unjust concession, if not an outright defeat. Umar ibn al-Khattab, in particular, struggled to understand the rationale behind accepting such heavy terms. Seeking clarification, he approached the Prophet and asked, "Are you not truly God's Messenger?"

The Prophet replied, "Yes, I am indeed God's Messenger."

Umar continued, "Are we Muslims not on the truth, and are our enemies, the polytheists, not on falsehood?"

The Prophet responded, "Yes, that is the case."

"Then why are we allowing our religion to be humiliated?" Umar questioned further.

The Prophet said, "O son of Khattab! I am the servant of God and His Messenger. I cannot act against God's commands. By accepting these terms of the treaty, I am not disobeying God. He will never let me be harmed."

Still seeking assurance, Umar asked, "Did you not promise us that God would grant us victory and that we would all go to the Kaaba and perform our pilgrimage together?"

The Prophet replied, "Yes, I did promise that. But did I ever say it would happen this year?"

Umar admitted, "No, you did not."

The Prophet then reassured him, "In that case, I repeat: You will surely go to Mecca and perform your pilgrimage around the Kaaba."[97]

Reassuring his companions of the long-term benefits, Muhammad signed the treaty in 628 CE, bringing an end to hostilities with the Meccans. This agreement was a significant milestone, as it marked the first time the Meccans officially recognized the Muslim community as an equal entity. Though the treaty initially seemed to put the Muslims at a disadvantage, it ultimately proved to be a strategic triumph.

By choosing peace over conflict, Muhammad created an opportunity to win over hearts and minds. The cessation of hostilities allowed Muslims to travel freely across Arabia, interact with non-Muslims, and spread the message of Islam through peaceful dialogue and engagement. This freedom greatly accelerated the spread of Islam. Notably, in the two years following the treaty, leading up to the conquest of Mecca, more

---

97. Suruç, *Kainatın Efendisi*, 579–580.

people embraced Islam than in the entire eighteen years of the Prophet's mission before the agreement.[98]

What is remarkable is that, on the way back to Medina, Muhammad received a revelation describing the treaty as a "clear victory" (*fathan mubinan*).[99] The revelation also assured the Prophet that his vision of visiting the Kaaba would come true: "God has truly fulfilled His Messenger's vision: 'If God wills, you will most certainly enter the Sacred Mosque in security, with the hair of your heads shaven or cut, without fear!'—God knew what you did not— and He has granted you a speedy victory."[100] This divine message reinforced the wisdom of the treaty and foretold the fulfillment of the Prophet's vision, offering hope and reassurance to the Muslim community.

Letters of Invitation to Islam

The peace agreement with the Quraysh provided the Prophet and his community the opportunity to turn their attention to other nations in the Near East and expand the reach of his message. Taking advantage of this period of stability, he sent letters to various kings and rulers in the region. Among the recipients were the emperors of Persia and Byzantium, the king of Abyssinia, and the ruler of Egypt. Each letter began with the Qur'anic phrase "In the name of God, the Most Merciful, the Most Compassionate." The Prophet's seal at the end of the letters bore the inscription "Muhammad, the Messenger of God." These letters firmly invited the rulers and their people—including Christians, Zoroastrians, and Jews—to accept Islam.

In his correspondence with Christian rulers, the Prophet frequently referenced a Qur'anic verse that underscored the potential for shared beliefs between Muslims and Christians: "Say, 'People of the Book, let us come to a common word between us: that we worship God alone,

---

98. Ibn Ishaq, *Life of Muhammad*, 507.

99. Qur'an 48:1.

100. Qur'an 48:27.

associate no partners with Him, and that none of us takes others as lords besides God.' If they turn away, say, 'Bear witness that we are Muslims [in submission to Him].'"[101] This verse has since become a key reference point for Muslim theologians engaging in interfaith dialogue with Christians and Jews, both historically and in contemporary discussions, emphasizing shared values and the call to monotheism.

The letters Muhammad sent to the rulers of the region underscored the universal scope of his mission.[102] They conveyed that he was not sent solely to the Arabs but to all of humanity. The Qur'an, revealed to him as the final divine message, built on and confirmed the revelations delivered through earlier prophets in Judaism and Christianity. Numerous Qur'anic verses emphasize the universal nature of the Prophet's message. For instance, one verse states, "Say [Muhammad], 'People, I am the Messenger of God to you all, from Him who has control over the heavens and the earth. There is no God but Him; He gives life and death. So believe in God and His Messenger, the unlettered prophet who believes in God and His words, and follow him so that you may find guidance.'"[103] Another verse highlights the Prophet's mission in relation to other religions: "It is He who has sent His Messenger with guidance and the religion of truth, to make it prevail over all [other] religions, however much the idolaters may hate it."[104] These verses reflect the comprehensive and inclusive nature of the Prophet's message, calling all people to the worship of one God and affirming the continuity of divine guidance through Islam.

The Conquest of Mecca

Although the peace agreement was originally intended to last for ten years, it was broken in less than two. The Meccans, along with their allied tribes, violated the terms by attacking a tribe allied with the Muslim community,

---

101. Qur'an 3:64.

102. See, Qur'an 7:158; 4:79, 170, 174; 9:33; 34:28; 22:67; 33:40.

103. Qur'an 7:158.

104. Qur'an 9:33.

killing its leader and several members. In response, the Prophet demanded that the Meccans pay blood money for the killings and warned that failure to comply would constitute a breach of the treaty and could result in war. When the Meccans refused, the Prophet began preparing for a decisive response. Quietly assembling an army of ten thousand, the Prophet marched toward Mecca. When news of the advancing Muslim army reached the Quraysh, they sent a delegation led by Abu Sufyan, one of the Prophet's staunchest opponents, to negotiate. To the astonishment of the Meccans, Abu Sufyan and his delegation embraced Islam after meeting with the Prophet. On returning to Mecca, Abu Sufyan urged his people to surrender peacefully, recognizing that resistance would be futile.

The Prophet instructed his commanders to avoid violence unless provoked, emphasizing a peaceful and measured approach. Other than minor skirmishes with a small group of Meccans, the Muslim army encountered little resistance and entered Mecca with minimal conflict. Once in the city, the Prophet made his way to the Kaaba and declared a general amnesty, forgiving even his bitterest enemies and those who had persecuted him and his followers. His extraordinary act of mercy and forgiveness echoed the words of the prophet Joseph in the Qur'an: "There is no reproach against you this day. God will forgive you. And He is the Most Merciful of the merciful."[105] This was a reference to Joseph forgiving his brothers who had betrayed and attempted to kill him. Not long after, the Meccans, including many of Muhammad's fierce enemies, embraced Islam.

The Prophet and his followers removed all the idols from in and around the Kaaba, restoring it to its original purpose. Built by Abraham, the Kaaba symbolizes monotheism—the worship of the one true God. By eliminating the symbols of polytheism, Muhammad restored the sacred monument to its intended mission. As the idols were being destroyed, the Prophet repeatedly recited a Qur'anic verse: "Say, 'The truth has come, and falsehood has vanished. Indeed, falsehood is bound to vanish.'"[106] This verse signifies the ultimate triumph of truth over

---

105. Qur'an 12:92.

106. Qur'an 17:81.

falsehood. The conquest of Mecca not only marked the end of hostilities between Muslims and the Quraysh but also laid the foundation for the political and spiritual unity of Arabia under the banner of Islam.

The Prophet's Farewell Sermon

After the conquest of Mecca, the Prophet and his companions returned to Medina to continue living there. That year, Gabriel recited the Qur'an with the Prophet twice, which Muhammad interpreted as a sign that his mission as God's messenger was nearing its end. In previous years, the archangel had recited the Qur'an with him only once a year during Ramadan. Consequently, the Prophet decided to fulfill his *hajj* duty, also known as his farewell pilgrimage, and traveled to Mecca with his companions. During this pilgrimage, Muhammad delivered his final universal message to the people as God's messenger. He urged those present to listen carefully and to relay his message to those who were absent, indicating that this might be his last year with them. Here are some of the major points from his sermon.

First, life and property are sacred trusts and must be respected as such. If someone is entrusted with goods, they should return them to their rightful owners: "Hurt no one so that no one may hurt you." Second, everyone will be held accountable. All people will appear before God on the day of judgment and be judged for their actions in this world. Third, avoid usury and beware of Satan's traps. Fourth, while men have certain rights concerning women, women also have rights over men. Treat women with respect and kindness, as they are men's partners and committed helpers. Fifth, worship God, perform the five daily prayers (*salat*), fast during Ramadan, give to charity (*zakat*), and undertake the pilgrimage (*hajj*) if you are able. Sixth, no one is superior to another because of their skin color or race: "All people are from Adam and Eve. An Arab has no superiority over a non-Arab, nor does a non-Arab have any superiority over an Arab; likewise, a white person has no superiority over a black person, nor does a black person have any superiority over a white person except through piety and good deeds."

The Prophet concluded his sermon with the following words:

> O People, no prophet or messenger will come after me, and no new faith will be born. Reason well, therefore, and understand the words I convey to you. I am leaving you with the Book of God (the Quran) and my Sunnah (the way of the Prophet). If you follow them, you will never go astray. All those who listen to me shall pass on my words to others and those to others again; and may the last ones understand my words better than those who listen to me directly. Be my witness, O God, that I have conveyed your message to your people.[107]

During the farewell pilgrimage, one of the last verses of the Qur'an was revealed: "Today I have perfected your religion for you, completed My blessing upon you, and have chosen for you Islam as your religion."[108] This was another indication that Muhammad was approaching the end of his mission as God's messenger. Muhammad conveyed God's message to the people and fulfilled his responsibility. Over 100,000 of his companions witnessed this fulfillment. By the time of his death, Muhammad had brought peace to Arabia, and nearly the entire region had embraced Islam.

The Prophet's Final Days

After the farewell pilgrimage, the Prophet returned to Medina with his companions. He began more often visiting the local cemetery (*Jannat al-Baqi'*), where many of his relatives and companions were buried, and would offer prayers for those who had passed away. In the meantime, the Prophet's health began to decline, and he became very ill. His wife Aisha reported, "I have never seen anyone suffering from an illness more severe than that of God's Messenger."[109] Despite his severe illness, the

---

107. Bünyamin Erul, "Veda Hutbesi," in *İslam Ansiklopedisi* (Türkiye Diyanet Vakfı, 2012), 42:591–593.

108. Qur'an 5:3.

109. *Sahih Muslim, kitab al-birr, bab thawab al-mu'min fima yusibuhu min marad.*

Prophet remained engaged with daily life. For instance, even in his final moments, he continued to clean his teeth with a *siwaq*, a tooth-brushing stick.[110] He maintained his five daily prayers and often inquired whether the people had completed their communal prayers at the mosque. He also reminded his companions to be mindful of others' rights.

On his deathbed, the Prophet was surrounded by his family, including his daughter, Fatima. Witnessing her father's pain, Fatima lamented and wept. The Prophet then comforted her, saying, "Your father will no longer suffer after today. The inevitable death, which no one can escape until the Day of Resurrection, has come for your father."[111] Muhammad also told his daughter that she would be the first to join him after he departed from this world. Indeed, Fatima, the Prophet's only surviving child, passed away six months after his death. Muhammad often invoked "to the highest companion," indicating his desire to be with God after departing this world. His last words, spoken while his head rested on his wife Aisha's chest, were "O God, pardon me and let me be united with You as the highest companion."[112] The Prophet's final prayer before his death was to be united with God and remain in God's presence.

Understandably, Muhammad's death was shocking news for his companions, who struggled to believe that he had died. His companion Umar even declared, "By God, God's messenger has not died." Umar continued, "By God, it never crossed my mind that he would die, and truly, God will resurrect him."[113] The Prophet's wife said, "I could not believe that the Messenger of God had passed away until I heard the sound of pickaxes" digging his grave.[114] Anas ibn Malik, another close

---

110. *Sahih al-Bukhari, kitab al-maghazi, bab marad al-nabiyy salla allahu 'alayhi wa sallam wa wafatihi.*

111. *Sahih al-Bukhari, kitab al-maghazi, bab marad al-nabiyy salla allahu 'alayhi wa sallam wa wafatihi* and *Sunan Ibn Majah, kitab al-janaiz, bab dhikri wafatihi wa dafnihi salla allahu 'alayhi wa sallam.*

112. *Sahih al-Muslim, kitab al-salam, bab istihbab ruqya al-marid.*

113. *Sahih al-Bukhari, kitab fadail ashab al-nabiyy salla allahu 'alayhi wa sallam, bab qawl al-nabiyy salla allahu 'alayhi wa sallam, "law kuntu muttakhizan khalila."*

114. Imam Malik, *al-Muwatta', kitab al-janaiz.*

companion, expressed his sorrow, saying, "On the day the Messenger of God entered Medina, everything was illuminated, and on the day he died, everything turned dark."[115]

It was finally Abu Bakr who stepped forward to remind everyone of the Qur'anic verses emphasizing Muhammad's mortality: "You [O Muhammad] will certainly die, and so will they."[116] Similarly, God said, "Muhammad is no more than a messenger: many were the messenger who passed away before him. If he died or was killed, would you revert to your old ways? If anyone did so, he would not harm God in the least. God will reward the thankful."[117]

The Prophet's body was washed and buried in the same place where he passed away, in accordance with a hadith in which he said, "No Prophet ever passed away without being buried where he died."[118] His bed was removed, and a grave was dug in its place.

The Messenger of God chose a life of simplicity over one of extravagance. Like other prophets before him, he fulfilled his mission of delivering the divine message without seeking anything in return and did not amass wealth and property as some leaders who held power did. As a result, the wealth he left behind was very modest. He left only a white mule, his weapons, and a piece of land he had received as charity.[119] However, the Prophet left behind a profound spiritual legacy, rooted in the Qur'an and his example (Sunna), that would continue to shape and inspire people's hearts and minds for centuries to come, which we will explore in the next chapter.

---

115. *Jami' al-Tirmidhi, kitab al-manaqib an rasul allahu salla 'alayhi wa sallam, bab fi fadli al-nabiyy salla allahu 'alayhi wa sallam.*

116. Qur'an 39:30.

117. Qur'an 3:144.

118. Imam Malik, *al-Muwatta', kitab al-janaiz.*

119. *Sahih al-Bukhari, kitab al-wasaya, bab al-wasaya* and *Sahih al-Muslim, kitab al-wasiya, bab tarq al-wasiyya liman laysa lahu shay'un yusi fihi.*

CHAPTER TWO

The Prophet's Spiritual Life and Character

Perhaps no story better illustrates the spiritual life of the Prophet than the following account. The Prophet's wife Aisha recounted that one night, as she and the Prophet were lying close together with his body touching hers, the Prophet asked, "Oh, Aisha, would you allow me to worship my Lord tonight?" Aisha replied, "Oh, Messenger of God, I love having you near me, but I also love that you worship your Lord." The Prophet then got up, performed ablution, and stood for prayer, where he began to weep. He cried until his beard became wet. Then, as he moved into prostration (*sujud*), he continued to cry until the ground beneath him was wet. Later, as he lay down on his side, Bilal, his companion, came to call for the morning prayer (*fajr*).[1] Seeing the Prophet in tears, Bilal asked, "Oh Messenger of God, why do you cry when God has forgiven all your past and future sins?" The Prophet responded, "How could I not cry? Tonight, God revealed the verse of the Qur'an: 'Indeed, in the creation of the heavens and the earth, and in the alternation of night and day, there are signs for those with understanding.'"[2]

This short account offers insights into the Prophet's spiritual life and character. He frequently withdrew from society for worship and contemplation, with night prayers serving as an essential part of his daily devotion. These prayers involved the recitation of Qur'anic verses and deep reflection. As part of his practice, the Prophet performed

---

1. The *fajr* prayer is observed from the break of dawn until just before sunrise.

2. *Sahih al-Bukhari, kitab al-tafsir, bab qawlihi "Inna fi khalqi samawati wa al-ard" al-ayah.* For the verse cited in this hadith, see Qur'an 3:190.

ablution—ritual washing—before prayer to attain a state of ritual purity. His prayer included standing in devotion, a fundamental posture in the Islamic prayer cycle (*salat*), which also incorporates prostration as an expression of humility and submission to God. The exchange between the Prophet and Aisha highlights his gentle nature and the balance between his personal life and his devotion to God. His request for permission to pray demonstrates his thoughtfulness, showing that even in acts of worship, he remained considerate of his loved ones. Aisha's response reflects her understanding of his spiritual priorities, emphasizing the harmony between love for one's spouse and love for God. Once the Prophet begins his prayers, his overwhelming emotion becomes evident. His weeping is not out of fear of God but out of reverence and gratitude. The fact that he cries so intensely—so much that his beard and even the ground beneath him become wet—reveals the depth of his connection with God. His worship is not a mere obligation but an expression of awareness of the divine. His companion Bilal's question, expressing wonder at why the Prophet wept despite being forgiven by God, reveals an important aspect of the Prophet's spirituality: His spirituality is not only about seeking forgiveness but also about maintaining an intimate and conscious relationship with God. The Prophet's response, citing Qur'an 3:190, emphasizes the importance of remembering God by reflecting on God's signs (*ayat*) in creation.

In this chapter, we will focus on the spiritual practices of the Prophet, their meanings, and how they are integrated into Muslim spirituality. Among the most important practices are the five daily prayers (*salat*), the night prayer (*tahajjud*), fasting, pilgrimage, charity, recitation of the Qur'an, the prayer of supplications (*du'a'*), contemplation (*tafakkur*), prayers that he performed during certain occasions, and remembering death and the finite nature of the world. Additionally, the chapter will discuss the character and some of the virtues of Muhammad, as they were integral to his spirituality. The Qur'an mentions that the Prophet had an outstanding character.[3] In a

---

3. Qur'an 68:4.

hadith, Muhammad said, "I was sent to perfect good character."[4] The Prophet's life serves as a practical example of virtues such as honesty, compassion, patience, humility, courage, and justice. His spiritual practices and moral conduct are inseparable, making him an ideal model for ethical living.

The Five Daily Prayers in the Prophet's Spirituality

The five daily prayers are one of the pillars of Islam and were among the most important of Muhammad's spiritual practices. They are commonly known as *salat* in Islamic literature, which has the connotation of *prayer* or *blessing*. *Salat*'s form and structure are based on the Prophet's practice. According to tradition, the method of performing the *salat* was taught to Muhammad by the archangel Gabriel. The companions around the Prophet and the generations after him have taken his model of establishing the *salat*. Muhammad said in a hadith, "Perform the *salat* the way you see me performing."[5]

Salat is performed five times a day: dawn (*fajr*), noon (*dhuhr*), late afternoon (*'asr*), evening (*maghrib*), and late evening (*'isha*). The times of the prayers are determined based on the position of the sun in the sky. The early morning prayer begins with the first light of dawn and ends at sunrise. The noon prayer begins when the sun is at its zenith or reaches the highest point in the sky and ends when the shadow of an object becomes equal to its actual length. The late afternoon prayer begins when the shadow of an object is equal to itself and ends just before sunset. The evening prayer begins right after the sunset when the sun disappears below the horizon and ends when the red twilight in the sky fades. The late evening prayer begins when the red twilight disappears and continues until before dawn.

---

4. Imam Malik, *al-Muwatta'*, kitab husn al-khuluq.

5. Sahih al-Bukhari, kitab al-adhan, bab al-adhan lilmusafir idha kanu jama'a wal'iqama wa kadhalika bi'arafa wa jam'in.

Each prayer consists of cycles (*rak'at*). The dawn prayer has two required cycles and two recommended cycles. The noon consists of four required cycles. There are also four before and two after the required part. The late afternoon prayer includes four recommended and four required cycles. The evening prayer consists of three required cycles followed by two recommended cycles. In the case of the late evening prayer, the believer offers four cycles of required prayer. Similar to the noon prayer, it also includes four recommended cycles before and two cycles after the required ones. Each cycle consists of the elements of standing, bowing down, standing upright, prostrating, and sitting. During each action, recitations from the Qur'an or certain supplications are recited, which are all in Arabic.

In the standing position, for example, the believer turns to the Kaaba with the intention of the prayer and starts the *salat* by invoking, "God is the greatest." Following an optional supplication, the first chapter of the Qur'an is recited: "In the name of God, the Compassionate, the Merciful! Praise belongs to God, Lord of the Worlds, the Compassionate, the Merciful. Master of the Day of Judgement. It is You we worship; it is You we ask for help. Guide us to the straight path: the path of those You have blessed, not of those who incur wrath, nor of those who are astray."[6] This chapter is believed to be the synthesis of the Qur'an and is one of the passages most recited by Muslims. It emphasizes that God is the Creator and the Most Merciful. Everything depends on God. Therefore, God is the only One worthy of being worshipped. Many hadiths and Qur'an commentaries highlight the merits of this chapter of the Qur'an. It is often recited at the beginning and end of virtuous activities and on the occasions of funerals, weddings, and the birth of a child. The chapter is also included as part of the invocations of the Sufi orders.

In the state of bowing, the believer recites, "Glory be to my Lord, the Most Great."[7] The believer then stands up, saying, "God hears those

---

6. Qur'an 1:1–7.

7. The phrase in Arabic is *subhana rabbiyal adheem*.

who praise Him" and "Our Lord, to you all the praise."⁸ While in prostration, the worshipper invokes, "Glory is to my Lord, the Most High."⁹ In the full sitting of the second cycle, the following prayer is invoked: "All glorifications, greetings, prayers, and good deeds are for God. Peace be upon you, O Prophet, and the mercy of God and His blessings. Peace be upon us and upon the righteous servants of God. I bear witness that there is no deity except God, and I bear witness that Muhammad is His servant and Messenger."¹⁰ It is believed that this prayer is based on the dialogue between Muhammad and God during the night journey (*mi'raj*). In this encounter, the Prophet addressed God by glorifying God, and God responded with words of peace, mercy, and blessing. Witnessing this divine favor, the Prophet expressed the wish for peace on all righteous servants of God. On hearing this dialogue, the angels proclaimed the testimony of faith (*shahada*).¹¹

Before starting the prayer, the believer should be in a state of minor ritual purity, which is known as *wudu* in Islamic literature. The practice of *wudu* was taught to the Prophet by the archangel Gabriel during the early days of revelation in Mecca. *Wudu* literally means *ablution* or *cleanliness*. The requirements of the ablution are outlined in the Qur'an: "You who believe, when you are about to pray, wash your faces and your hands up to the elbows, wipe your heads, wash your feet up to the ankles."¹² If a worshipper is in a state of major ritual impurity, which can be caused by sexual intercourse, seminal discharge, menstruation, and postnatal bleeding, then they are required to take a full bath (*ghusl*). In this case, all parts of the body are ritually washed. Ablution is a key

---

8. The Arabic versions of these phrases are *sami'allahu liman hamidah* and *rabbana wa laka al-hamd*.

9. The phrase is rendered as *subhana rabbi al-a'la*.

10. This supplication is known as *tahiyyat*. The prayer is recorded in most of the hadith collections with a slight variation.

11. Fahrettin Atar, "Teşehhüd," in *İslam Ansiklopedisi* (Türkiye Diyanet Vakfı, 2011), 40:563–564.

12. Qur'an 5:6.

aspect of Islamic spirituality and piety. It is not only a physical act of cleanliness but also spiritual cleanliness. In the process of the ablution, numerous prayers are invoked. The ritual purity prepares the worshipper for the right state of heart, mind, and body for the divine presence. It is traditionally recommended to be in a state of ritual purity not only for the prayer but also in other situations such as when studying, reciting the Qur'an, reading hadith, feeling angry, entering a mosque, washing and carrying the body of a deceased, and also before and after sleeping, during a pilgrimage, and so on.

The *Salat* in the Life of the Prophet

We are told in the Qur'an that the *salat* was part of the spiritual practices of previous religious traditions and prophets before Muhammad as a sign of their submission to God. The Qur'an mentions that Abraham performed *salat* solely for God and prayed to keep himself and his descendants among those who establish *salat*.[13] His son Ismail also instructed his people to perform the *salat* and give charity (*zakat*). For remembrance of God, God asked Moses to establish the prayer.[14] When the angels of God approached Zakariyya and gave him the good news of the birth of John (Yahya), he was in the middle of offering *salat* in the temple's sanctuary. We also know from the Qur'an that Mary's prayer involved elements of the *salat*, including bowing down and prostrating.[15] When the infant Jesus miraculously spoke supporting his mother, Mary, he made a reference to the *salat*, pointing out that God enjoined on him prayer and charity as long as he remained alive.[16] The Qur'anic account of the companions of the cave (*ashab al-kahf*), who are known as "the seven sleepers of Ephesus," also mentions the word

---

13. Qur'an 6:162; 14:40.

14. Qur'an 20:14.

15. Qur'an 3:43.

16. Qur'an 19:31.

masjid (literally *the place of prostration*), which indicates that the prayers of the Christian community at the time involved prostration.[17]

Traces of *salat* could still be observed in Arabia before the advent of Islam, albeit in altered forms. People were somewhat familiar with the practice, which was initially associated with worshipping God. However, in its modified form, it became intertwined with polytheistic practices. Some hadiths mention that a number of people performed *salat* during their visits to the Kaaba, following the tradition of Abrahamic monotheism (*Hanif*), and Muhammad was among them. It is also known that Muhammad frequently secluded himself in the Cave of Hira for worship and contemplation during the month of Ramadan.

The *salat* was part of the Prophet's spiritual practice from the early days of Islam. As mentioned earlier, Gabriel taught him how to perform both *salat* and ablution (*wudu*). The Prophet taught these practices to his wife Khadija and the companions who joined him. Initially, *salat* was performed twice a day—at dawn and in the evening—and in secret, away from the public eye. According to the Prophet's biography, one day Ali ibn Abi Talib, the Prophet's cousin who lived with him, saw Khadija and the Prophet performing *salat*. Curious, Ali asked what they were doing. The Prophet's explanation of the new revelation and this spiritual practice eventually led to Ali's conversion.

The Prophet's biography also recounts instances when the Meccans insulted and tortured him while he was offering prayers at the Kaaba. Due to these persecutions, the companions would gather with the Prophet at the house of one of his followers (*dar al-arqam*) to learn about the new religion and perform *salat* together. With the conversion of Umar ibn al-Khattab, Muslims gained more confidence and began publicly performing their *salat*, including at the Kaaba.

The *salat* also played a significant role in one of the most prominent events in the Prophet's life: the night journey and ascension to heaven (*isra and mi'raj*). When the Prophet was taken to Jerusalem during the night journey, he led the prophets who came before him in prayer, including Abraham, Moses, and Jesus. This moment not only

---

17. Qur'an 18:21.

signified that Muhammad was the inheritor of the divine laws revealed to previous messengers but also highlighted the *salat* as a shared spiritual practice among the prophets. The tradition further recounts that the Prophet ascended to heaven immediately after leading the prayer. Following this spiritual ascent, Muhammad experienced a direct encounter with God—perhaps the most profound moment in his life. This sequence of events underscores the centrality of *salat* in spiritual elevation and progress.

The night journey had several significant outcomes for the Prophet and the early Muslims, one of which was the establishment of the five daily prayers. The initial requirement had been fifty prayers per day. However, during the journey, the Prophet encountered Moses, who, on learning of the number of daily prayers, advised Muhammad to request a reduction from God, as it would be too burdensome for the community. Through a series of back-and-forth requests, the number was eventually reduced to five. This event offers several key insights. First, during a profound spiritual experience in the Prophet's life, he and his community were gifted the five daily prayers, one of the most spiritually rewarding rituals in Islam. Second, these five prayers, though few in number, are rewarded by God as if they were performed fifty times a day, reflecting both divine mercy and the immense spiritual significance of this practice.

During *salat*, the moment one is closest to God—according to Muhammad—is when the worshipper is in prostration. He encouraged making as many invocations as possible in this state. Prostration is an intense expression of complete submission to God, symbolizing the acknowledgment of our dependence on God. It is a declaration: "I am the servant; God is the Lord. I am weak; God is the Almighty. I am in need; God is the Sustainer." There is great spiritual power in recognizing and embracing one's weakness in relation to God.

The Prophet was deeply devoted to prayer and never abandoned it, even during battles, travels, or periods of illness. On the day he passed away, one of the last things he did was to establish his prayers. Because of these attributes, the five daily prayers became one of the most defining marks of a believer. The Prophet emphasized the importance of this ritual in numerous hadiths. In one of them, he stated, "*Salat* is the central pole of Islam,"[18] implying that a Muslim who neglects their prayers risks destabilizing their faith.

Salat is also a means of spiritual purification. The Prophet said, "Prayer is the key to heaven."[19] On one occasion, he illustrated the significance of the five daily prayers by asking his companions, "If one of you had a river flowing by your door and bathed in it five times a day, would any dirt remain on your body?" The companions replied, "No dirt would remain on that person." The Prophet then explained, "The five daily prayers function in the same way. Through them, God removes sins."[20] The Qur'an also highlights the importance of *salat*, describing it as a key attribute of the believers and stating that it prevents them from indecency and abomination.[21]

Spiritual Dimensions of *Salat*

Considering the form and content of *salat* based on the Qur'an and the Prophet's practice, many Muslim scholars have explored its spiritual dimensions. Said Nursi, for example, wrote extensively on *salat*, highlighting its profound spiritual aspects. First, Nursi emphasizes that the purpose of *salat* is to "glorify, exalt, and give thanks to God." This involves proclaiming "glory be to God" (*subhanallah*) through words and actions to acknowledge God's majesty and sanctify God. It also includes declaring "God is the greatest" (*Allahu akbar*) to recognize God's perfection and exalt God and expressing gratitude to God (*alhamdulillah*) with the heart, tongue, and body for God's beauty and

---

18. *Jami' al-Tirmidhi, kitab al-'iman, bab ma ja'a fi hurmati al-salat.*

19. *Jami' al-Tirmidhi, kitab al-thaharah, bab ma ja'a la tuqbalu salatu bighayri thuhurin.*

20. *Sahih al-Bukhari, kitab mawaqit al-salah, bab al-salawat al-khamsu kaffara.*

21. Qur'an 2:3; 29:45.

perfection. These three acts—glorification (*tasbih*), exaltation (*takbir*), and praise (*hamd*)—form the foundation of *salat*, which is why they are integrated into every movement and recitation within it.[22]

Second, the Prophet described *salat* as the spiritual ascension (*mi'raj*) of a believer. Through *salat*, the worshipper is graciously received into the presence of God five times a day. Nursi likens this experience to a soldier being granted an audience with a king. In *salat*, the servant transcends the constraints of the physical world, attaining the honor of standing in the divine presence, both spiritually and mentally.[23]

Third, commenting on the Qur'anic phrase that believers are "steadfast in prayer,"[24] Nursi explains that *salat* is the most comprehensive form of worship. He writes, "The specification of *salat* over other acts of worship indicates that it serves as a comprehensive index and exemplar of all virtuous deeds. Just as Surah *Al-Fatiha* [the first chapter of the Qur'an] is an index of the Qur'an and humanity is an index of the universe, *salat* reflects and encompasses all forms of worship." In this sense, *salat* represents the worship, both innate and voluntary, of all creatures. For instance, some angels bow in worship, others prostrate, and yet others stand; likewise, some stones prostrate, some trees stand upright, and some animals bow down in acts resembling worship.[25]

Nursi further emphasizes that *salat* incorporates elements of the core pillars of Islam. During prayer, the believer repeatedly proclaims the oneness of God and affirms Muhammad as God's messenger, thereby renewing the testimony of faith (*shahada*). Refraining from eating or drinking during *salat* reflects a form of fasting. Facing the Kaaba during prayer symbolically connects the believer to pilgrimage (*hajj*). Moreover, dedicating time to prayer can be likened to an act of charity (*zakat*), as it involves devoting oneself to spiritual well-being and worship.

---

22. Said Nursi, *The Words* (Söz Basim, 2012), 70–71.

23. Said Nursi, *The Rays* (Söz Basim, 2012), 279.

24. Qur'an 2:3.

25. Bediuzzaman Said Nursi, *İsaratul İ'caz* (Söz Basım, 2012), 70.

Additionally, humanity, as stewards of the earth, is seen as representing all creation in worship. Nursi reflects on the Qur'anic verse "Everything in the heavens and earth glorifies God," noting that all creation—angels, animals, and even inanimate objects—is engaged in glorifying God.[26] During the night journey (*isra* and *mi'raj*), the Prophet Muhammad is believed to have presented the prayers of all beings to God as their representative. The supplications (*tahiyyat*) he recited during this encounter are now included in the sitting position of *salat*, symbolizing this universal act of worship.

Communal Prayer: Worship in Unity

The Prophet's *salat* was remarkably communal. He not only strongly encouraged his followers to perform their prayers in congregation but also regularly led them in prayer. His final prayer was the dawn (*fajr*) prayer on the day he passed away, and he performed it with his companions in the mosque. In one hadith, he stated, "A prayer offered in congregation is twenty-seven times more rewarding than one performed individually."[27] In another narration, the Prophet said, "Whoever performs ablution (*wudu*) properly and then goes to offer the obligatory prayer, whether joining others in congregation or praying in the mosque, God will forgive their sins."[28]

From the early days of revelation, the Prophet prioritized communal prayer. He would initially pray together with his wife Khadija and later with the companions who embraced Islam. During the early period of persecution, the Prophet and his followers prayed communally in a companion's house, known as *Dar al-Arqam*. As Islam became more public, particularly after the conversion of Umar ibn al-Khattab, they began openly praying together, often at the Kaaba.

---

26. Bediuzzaman Said Nursi, *Emirdağ Lahikası II* (Söz Basım, 2012), 575–576.

27. *Sahih al-Bukhari, kitab al-adhan, bab fadl salat al-jama'a.*

28. *Sahih al-Muslim, kitab al-thahara, bab fadl al-wudu' wassalati 'aqiba.*

The mosques built during the Prophet's time are a significant testament to the communal nature of prayer in his spiritual practice. The Arabic word for mosque, *masjid*, literally means *place of prostration*. Before the Prophet's migration (*hijra*) to Medina, the Muslims in Medina designated a prayer space (*masjid*) for communal worship in Quba, a village several miles outside of Medina. When the Prophet arrived in Quba, he stayed there for a few days and, together with his followers, built a mosque known as Masjid Quba. The Prophet himself participated in its construction. Due to the sincerity and faith of those who built it solely for the sake of God, the Qur'an refers to this first mosque in Islam as a mosque "founded on piety."[29]

When the Prophet moved to Medina, one of his first actions was to build a mosque, which came to be known as Masjid al-Nabawi, or the Prophet's Mosque. This mosque became the center of all Muslim activities in Medina. The Muslim community performed its daily prayers in congregation at the mosque, and the Prophet himself regularly joined them and led the prayers. When the Prophet was not in the city, he would appoint one of his companions to lead the community in his place.

It is reported that even during battles, the Prophet prioritized offering prayers in congregation whenever possible. The Qur'an references the Prophet and his community performing prayers together, even in the midst of battle: "When you [Prophet] are with the believers, leading them in prayer, let a group of them stand up in prayer with you, taking their weapons with them, and when they have finished their prostration, let them take up their positions at the back. Then let the other group, who have not yet prayed, pray with you, also on their guard and armed with their weapons."[30] Commentaries on this verse explain that despite being engaged in combat, the Prophet and his

---

29. Qur'an 9:108. While some scholars interpret this verse as a reference to the Prophet's Mosque in Medina, the majority of them maintain that it refers to the first mosque built in Quba.

30. Qur'an 4:102.

companions offered their prayers in congregation, rotating in groups for safety. While one group performed its prayers, the other stood guard to protect the members. This practice demonstrates that even in the most challenging circumstances, the Prophet and his followers prioritized communally performing their daily prayers. They placed their spirituality and connection to God above even the most pressing worldly matters in their lives.

One of the most remarkable aspects of communal prayer is its emphasis on equality. During *salat*, Muslims stand shoulder to shoulder, worshipping one God without regard to rank, status, color, race, or ethnicity. United in devotion, they all face the Kaaba, bowing and prostrating together in humility before God. Due to the importance of communal prayers, mosques have become one of the most defining features of Islamic societies. In Muslim-majority countries, nearly every neighborhood has a mosque. Even in countries where Muslims are a minority, one of the first priorities for the community is often to establish a mosque as a center for worship and communal activities.

The Call to Prayer: The Mark of a Muslim Community

An important aspect of communal prayer is the call to prayer (*adhan*). As the Muslim community grew in Medina, the Prophet consulted with his companions about how to inform believers of the prayer times and invite them to participate in communal prayers. Other religious communities of the time had established methods for announcing prayer times and gatherings. For example, Christians used church bells, and Jews blew a trumpet-like horn.

While the Prophet was considering a suitable way for the call to prayer, one of his companions, Abdullah ibn Zayd, had a vision in which a wise person taught him the words for the call to prayer in Arabic, as follow:

God is the greatest, God is the greatest.
God is the greatest, God is the greatest.

I bear witness that there is no god but God.
I bear witness that there is no god but God.
I bear witness that Muhammad is the Messenger of God.
I bear witness that Muhammad is the Messenger of God.
Hasten to prayer.
Hasten to prayer.
Hasten to success.
Hasten to success.[31]
God is the greatest, God is the greatest.
There is no god but God.[32]

Abdullah shared his experience and what he had learned with the Prophet. The Prophet instructed his companion to deliver the call to prayer (*adhan*) accordingly.

The five daily prayers are performed at designated times, and the *adhan* serves as a notification, letting believers know when to join their fellow Muslims for communal worship. During the Prophet's time, the caller would climb to an elevated place to make the *adhan* audible over a wide area. To enhance the reach of the call, Muslim communities later began constructing minarets—tall towers that became an integral part of mosque architecture. Visible from a distance, minarets not only amplify the call to prayer but also symbolize the presence of Islam in the surrounding area.

For believers, the call to prayer (*adhan*) is a deeply spiritual moment. It reminds them that God is the ultimate source of power, that Muhammad is God's messenger, and that they should hasten to prayer, a means of peace and eternal salvation. When a Muslim hears the *adhan*, they repeat the words of the caller (*muadhdhin*) after them. However, in response to the phrases "hasten to prayer" (*hayya 'ala al-salah*) and "hasten to success" (*hayya 'ala al-falah*), they say instead,

---

31. In the morning call to prayer, the caller adds the phrase that "prayer is better than sleep" (*al-salatu khayrun min al-nawm*).

32. The call to prayer is in Arabic.

"There is no power or strength except by God" (*la hawla wa la quwwata illa billah*).

After the call to prayer, the Prophet recommended his followers to recite the following invocation: "O God, Lord of this perfect call and the ritual prayer to be performed, grant Muhammad every means and virtue that draws him closer to You. Elevate him to the Praised Station (*Maqam Mahmud*) that You have promised him."[33] The *adhan* is not only a spiritual reminder to remember God but also an encouragement to lead a worship-centered life, structured around the five daily prayers—performed individually and, if possible, in congregation.

The Friday Prayers: A Weekly Spiritual Renewal

Although performing the five daily prayers in congregation is strongly recommended by the Prophet, it is not obligatory; a believer may perform them individually as well. However, the weekly Friday congregational prayer (*salat al-jum'a*) is required to be performed in congregation.[34] The two most important elements of the Friday prayer are the sermon (*khutba*) and the two congregational cycles of prayer led by an imam, the person who leads the prayer.

The sermon typically begins with praising and glorifying God, followed by sending peace and blessings on God's messenger, Muhammad. The imam then delivers a sermon centered on a theme relevant to the community, often citing verses from the Qur'an. The sermon concludes with an invocation (*du'a'*). The Friday prayer is usually done around noon. The Prophet performed his first Friday prayer after his migration (*hijra*) to Medina and continued to lead this weekly congregational prayer for his community until his death.

Friday is the most sacred day of the week for Muslims, offering a unique spiritual opportunity. The sixty-second chapter of the Qur'an is

---

33. *Sahih al-Bukhari, kitab al-adhan, bab al-du'a' 'inda al-nida'.*

34. While the Friday prayer is required for all men who have reached puberty, it is not required for women.

named after this day. The time of the Friday prayer serves as a moment for Muslims to pause their business and worldly affairs and turn their attention to God, as highlighted in the Qur'an: "Believers! When you are called to the congregational prayer, hasten to the remembrance of God and leave off trade. That is better for you, if you only knew."[35] Leaving business for prayer is not just a physical act but also requires mental and spiritual focus. Unlike in Judaism and Christianity, the sacred day of the week in Islam is not considered a day of rest. Believers may resume their daily activities after completing their prayer. The Qur'an addresses this aspect: "And when the prayer is completed, disperse in the land and seek out God's bounty. Remember God often so that you may prosper."[36] This verse implies that Islam does not draw a strict division between sacred and profane. As long as the believer performs their prayers and remembers God, their other daily activities are also regarded as part of their worship and spirituality.

The Prophet encouraged his community to make the most of Friday due to its spiritual significance. In one narration, he said, "Whoever performs the major ritual purification [*ghusl*], attends the Friday prayer, performs the prescribed prayer, listens attentively and silently to the sermon until it concludes, and then joins the imam in prayer, will have their sins forgiven from that Friday to the next."[37] In another hadith, he stated, "There is a moment on Friday when, if a servant asks God for something, He will surely grant their request."[38] These examples highlight the importance of Friday in the Prophet's spirituality. It is a day of both communal and individual spiritual renewal. Many Muslims use this day to recite the Qur'an and give charity as part of their spiritual practices.

---

35. Qur'an 62:9.

36. Qur'an 62:10.

37. *Sahih al-Bukhari, kitab al-jum'a, bab la yafarraqu bayna isnayni yawma al-jumu'a.*

38. *Jami' al-Tirmidihi, kitab al-jum'a, bab ma ja'a fi al-sa'ati allati turja fi al-yawm jumu'a.*

The Night Prayer: "A Thankful Servant"

Besides his five daily prayers and the Friday congregational prayers, a hallmark of the Prophet's spirituality was his individual night prayers. The Messenger of God devoted much of his nighttime to worship. He would rise during the last third of the night to pray. This spiritual ritual of the Prophet is known as *tahajjud*. In a report, Muhammad's wife Aisha describes his night routine concerning sleeping and prayer as follows:

> After performing the late evening prayer, the Messenger of God (peace be upon him) would lie down and sleep for a while. Then, he would wake up and perform the night prayer [*tahajjud*] for as long as he wished. When the time of pre-dawn [*sahar*] arrived, he would perform the *witr* prayer and then return to his bed to rest. Upon hearing the call to prayer [*adhan*], he would immediately rise from his bed. If there was a need for a major ritual purification [*ghusl*], he would perform it; otherwise, he would perform ablution (*wudu*). He would then pray the two cycles of recommended prayer [*sunnah*] for the dawn prayer [*fajr*] and leave his home to perform the dawn prayer in congregation in the mosque.[39]

There are numerous narrations confirming the Prophet Muhammad's routine during the night. From these accounts, we learn that after the late evening prayer (*'isha*), the Prophet would go to bed, then rise from his sleep to perform the night prayer (*tahajjud*). He would return to bed again and later rise for the dawn prayer (*fajr*). One question often asked is how long he would pray during the night. The night prayer consists of at least two cycles, but the Prophet is reported to have performed up to thirteen cycles, including the *witr*

---

39. *Sunan al-Nasa'i, kitab qiyam al-layl, bab waqt al-witr* and *Sahih al-Bukhari, kitab al-tahajjud, bab man nama awwala al-layl wa 'ahya akhirahu.*

prayer, which concludes the night prayer.[40] Compared to his five daily prayers, the Prophet's night prayer was marked by prolonged postures in each cycle—standing, bowing, and prostrating. His recitations from the Qur'an were lengthy, and he frequently invoked God with supplications of praise and glorification.

The Qur'an references the night prayer in several verses, highlighting its significance. In some verses, God instructs Muhammad to rise at night and worship God.[41] For example, the Qur'an addresses the Prophet, "During the night, wake up and pray, as an extra offering of your own, so that your Lord may raise you to a [highly] praised status."[42] The Qur'an also describes night prayer as a key attribute of a faithful servant of God: "The servants of the Compassionate are those who walk humbly on the earth, and who, when the ignorant address them, reply, 'Peace'; those who spend the night bowed down or standing, worshipping their Lord."[43] In another verse, the Qur'an praises believers who forsake their beds at night to invoke God in fear and hope.[44] The Qur'an not only highlights night prayer as an essential aspect of the spirituality of the Prophet and his community but also acknowledges its significance among some members of the People of the Book (i.e., Jews and Christians): "There are some among the People of the Book who are upright, who recite God's revelations during the night and prostrating in prayer."[45] These verses collectively emphasize the importance of night prayer as a hallmark of devotion and humility, connecting it to a broader tradition of worship shared across faith communities.

---

40. *Witr* literally means *odd numbers*, such as 1, 3, and 5. Muhammad would conclude his night prayers with an odd number of prayer cycles.

41. Qur'an 17:79; 20:130; 50:40; 52:49; 73:1–7; 76:25.

42. Qur'an 17:79.

43. Qur'an 25:63–64.

44. Qur'an 32:16.

45. Qur'an 3:113.

The night prayer was the Prophet's sacred time alone with his Creator, a deep expression of thanks and gratitude to God. According to a hadith narrated by his wife Aisha, the Prophet would pray at night until his feet became swollen. When Aisha asked him, "O Prophet of God, why do you exert yourself in worship so much when God has forgiven your past and future sins?" he replied, "Should I not be a thankful servant of God?"[46]

In several narrations, the Prophet emphasizes the importance of the night prayer for one's spiritual growth. Highlighting its benefits, the Prophet said, "Every night, during the last third of the night, our Lord descends to the Heaven of this earth and says, 'Who calls upon Me that I might answer them? Who asks of Me that I might grant them? Who seeks My forgiveness that I might forgive them?'"[47] This narration teaches that during the night, God actively seeks out servants who turn to God, offering them the opportunity to seek God's help, forgiveness, and blessings. In another hadith, the Prophet said, "Perform the night prayer, for it was the practice of the righteous people who came before you. The night prayer draws you closer to God, serves as an expiation for sins, heals spiritual ailments, and acts as a deterrent against sin."[48] This narration links the night prayer to righteousness and obedience, portraying it as a means of purifying the self, strengthening one's connection to God, and avoiding sin.

From the early days of revelation, the night prayer was one of the most integral spiritual practices of the Prophet and his community. Subsequent generations of Muslims have continued to make the night prayer a cornerstone of their spiritual practice. In the stillness of the night, when the world retreats, believers rise to have personal time with their Lord. This practice serves as both a spiritual reset and preparation, helping believers reflect on the past day and spiritually fortify themselves for the day ahead.

---

46. *Sahih al-Bukhari, kitab al-tafsir, bab "liyaghfir laka allahu ma taqaddama..."*

47. *Sahih al-Bukhari, kitab al-da'wat, bab al-du'a' nisf al-layl.*

48. *Jami' al-Tirmidihi, kitab al-da'wat.*

Because of the significance of the night prayer in the Qur'an and the life of the Prophet, many Muslim scholars have made it a central element of their spirituality and teachings. The prominent Muslim thinker Imam al-Ghazali (d. 1111), for example, dedicated significant attention to the night prayer and related devotions in his monumental work *Ihya' 'Ulum al-Din*. Alongside highlighting the virtues of the night prayer, al-Ghazali offers practical advice to help believers rise for it. He suggests avoiding overeating and drinking, refraining from exhausting the body with tiresome actions during the day, taking a short midday nap, and abstaining from sins. He also emphasizes preparing the right internal state, as a heart free from hatred toward others and detached from excessive worldly concerns makes it easier to rise for worship. Al-Ghazali notes that a person consumed by worldly matters may struggle to rise for night prayer, and even if they do, their mind may remain preoccupied with worries and anxieties, distracting them from their devotion.

Al-Ghazali further recommends contemplating the realities of the hereafter—heaven, hell, and the day of judgment. A state of hope and fear about the eternal life can motivate a believer to stay awake for worship. However, for al-Ghazali, the highest and noblest internal state is a heart filled with love for God. He explains that worshippers must firmly believe that every moment of night prayer is an intimate conversation with God, who knows the state of their hearts. When a servant truly loves God, they naturally desire to be alone with God and find joy in this intimate communion. This delight in worship stems from sincere love for God, inspiring a longing for God's closeness and pleasure.[49] For a believer in such a state of heart, rising for night prayer is not a burden but a cherished opportunity—something they eagerly anticipate, as they yearn for this special moment with their Lord.

Prayer During the Solar and Lunar Eclipses

In addition to the night prayers, the Prophet turned to God in prayer on various other occasions, including during solar and lunar eclipses

---

49. Al-Ghazali, *Ihya' 'Ulum al-Din* (al-Quds, 2012), 1:591–595.

(*salat al-kusuf* and *salat al-khusuf*). In pre-Islamic Arabia, certain beliefs were associated with the sun and the moon, which were often considered sacred. Eclipses, in particular, were linked to events such as the birth or death of an important person. For example, the death of the Prophet's son, Ibrahim, at the age of about two coincided with a solar eclipse, prompting such associations. The Qur'an, however, frequently emphasizes that the sun and the moon are signs (*ayat*) of God's power and perfection, dismissing any notions of their independent sanctity.[50] One verse states, "Among His signs are the night and the day, the sun and the moon. Do not prostrate to the sun or the moon, but prostrate to God who created them, if it is He Whom you worship."[51] In another place, the Qur'an points out that the sun's course and the phases of the moon are determined by God. Each of them floats in its orbit because of their Creator's power and precise knowledge.[52] The Prophet's spiritual practices during eclipses reflect the Qur'anic emphasis on these celestial phenomena as reminders of God's greatness. Many hadith collections include chapters detailing the Prophet's prayers during solar and lunar eclipses, demonstrating their significance as moments of reflection and worship in Islamic spirituality.

It is reported that during an eclipse, the Prophet would lead the community in a special prayer consisting of two cycles, similar to the regular *salat*. Each action within the cycles—standing, bowing, and prostrating—was prolonged, accompanied by invocations of praise and glorification of God. The prayer would continue until the eclipse had passed. Following the prayer, the Prophet would address the community with a short sermon, saying, "The moon and the sun are among the signs of God's existence and power. They do not eclipse because of anyone's death or birth. When you see a lunar or solar eclipse, pray and supplicate until it clears."[53] The Prophet encouraged his followers to

---

50. Qur'an 6:77–78; 10:5; 36:38–40; 41:37; 74:32; 91:1–2.

51. Qur'an 41:37.

52. Qur'an 36:38–40.

53. *Sahih al-Bukhari, kitab al-kusuf, bab al-salati fi kusufi al-shams.*

use the occasion to remember God's greatness, pray, give charity, and free an enslaved person. Through this practice, the Prophet not only corrected the pre-Islamic misconceptions about eclipses being tied to events like births or deaths but also transformed these celestial occurrences into opportunities for worship, reflection, and good deeds. Today, Muslims around the world continue to observe this spiritual practice. For example, in preparation for the solar eclipse scheduled for Monday, April 8, 2024, many mosques planned congregational eclipse prayers followed by sermons, maintaining the tradition established by the Prophet.

The Prayer for Rain

Another occasion when the Prophet would pray with the community was during droughts. Through this collective act of worship, they would turn to God to seek mercy and ask for rain. Prayers for rain are an ancient practice observed in many religions, including Hinduism, Judaism, and Christianity. The Qur'an frequently references rain as a sign of God's power and mercy. It emphasizes that God sends rain in measured amounts and, through it, revives the earth: "It is God who sends the winds as glad tidings ahead of His Mercy. When they bear heavy clouds, We drive them to a lifeless land and then cause rain to fall, producing every type of fruit. Similarly, We will bring the dead to life, so perhaps you will be mindful."[54] This verse draws a parallel between the revival of the earth through rain and the resurrection of the dead in the hereafter. Just as rain gives life to barren land, God will bring the dead back to life. The Qur'an further points out that if water were to withdraw, only God could restore it.[55] When people are in desperate need of rain and on the verge of losing hope, the Qur'an reminds them of God's mercy: "It is He who sends down the rain after they have despaired and spreads His Mercy. He is the Protector and

---

54. Qur'an 7:57.

55. Qur'an 18:41.

the Praised."[56] Through these teachings, the Qur'an links rain not only to physical sustenance but also to spiritual lessons about hope, mercy, and the power of God. The prayer for rain (*salat al-istisqa*) reflects this understanding, turning a time of need into an opportunity for collective worship and trust in God's providence.

Considering the Qur'anic references that God has complete control over rain, the Prophet and his community turned to God during droughts to seek God's mercy. Hadith collections often include sections dedicated to the prayer for rain, detailing this practice of the Prophet. He would go out with his community, lead them in two cycles of prayer, raise his hands, and supplicate to God for rain. It is important to note that turning to God on such occasions is not solely for material gain; it is generally understood as an opportunity for spiritual growth, to remember God, and to seek God's forgiveness.[57]

This spiritual practice of the Prophet continues to be widely observed by Muslims. For example, 2014 was one of the driest years on record in California, prompting the state governor to declare a state of emergency. In response, many local Muslim communities performed the prayer for rain, following the Prophet's tradition. One such prayer was led by Hamza Yusuf Hanson, the president of Zaytuna College. This effort was not limited to the Muslim community; the Catholic Bishops' Conference also issued a call for prayers for rain, urging their fellow Christians to join in supplication. This shared act highlights how faith communities turn to divine mercy during times of crisis.[58]

The Prophet would also pray on various other occasions. One of his regular prayers was the forenoon prayer (*salat al-duha*), performed about forty minutes after sunrise. When he received good news or blessings from God, he would express his gratitude by offering two cycles of prayer

---

56. Qur'an 42:28.

57. Nursi, *The Words*, 425.

58. "California Bishops Pray for Rain as State's Drought Continues," CAN, January 12, 2014, https://www.catholicnewsagency.com/news/28761/california-bishops-pray-for-rain-as-states-drought-continues.

or performing the prostration of thanks (*sujud al-shukr*). On entering a mosque, the first thing he would do was perform two cycles of prayer. Similarly, when returning from a journey, he would go to the mosque and perform two cycles of prayer as an act of devotion and gratitude.

Fasting in the Prophet's Spirituality

The Prophet's spirituality extended beyond prayer. A central element of his spiritual practice was fasting, a ritual that long predates Islam. Abstaining from food and drink is an ancient practice observed in many religious traditions, including Hinduism, Buddhism, Jainism, Zoroastrianism, Judaism, and Christianity. Fasting has been practiced for various purposes, such as self-purification, repentance, gratitude, rites of passage, simplicity, protest, or even health and dietary reasons. The Qur'an affirms the universality of fasting, stating that it was prescribed not only for Muslims but also for the communities before them: "O you who believe, fasting is prescribed for you as it was prescribed for those before you, so that you may become mindful of God."[59]

The most significant form of fasting in the Prophet's life was the fast of Ramadan, which became obligatory for the Muslim community in the second year after the migration to Medina. Following the guidance of the Qur'an and the Prophet's example, Muslims around the world today fast during Ramadan, the ninth month of the Islamic lunar calendar. The daily fast begins at dawn (*fajr*) and concludes at sunset (*maghrib*). During the fast, believers abstain from food, drink (including water), and sexual activity. Muslims typically wake before dawn for a meal called *suhoor* and break their fast at sunset with a meal known as *iftar*, often starting with dates and water, following the tradition of the Prophet. The conclusion of Ramadan is marked by Eid al-Fitr, a major holiday in the Islamic calendar. As part of the celebration, the Muslim community gathers to perform two cycles of prayer (*salat al-eid*) in congregation, followed by a sermon delivered by the imam.

---

59. Qur'an 2:183.

In addition to the fast during the month of Ramadan, the Prophet fasted during the preceding month of Sha'ban, as well as six days of fasting in Shawwal (the month after Ramadan). He encouraged his followers to do the same, stating, "Whoever fasts during Ramadan and follows it with six additional days of fasting in Shawwal, it is as if they have fasted for the entire year."[60] Additionally, the Prophet regularly fasted at least three days each lunar month, with Mondays and Thursdays being his preferred days for fasting. He also observed fasting during the first ten days of Dhu al-Hijjah, the twelfth Islamic month, which coincides with the annual pilgrimage (*hajj*).

The Prophet's Spirituality in the Month of Fasting

The month of Ramadan was a period of intense devotion in the life of Muhammad. He would get up for the predawn meal (*suhoor*) and break his fast at sunset with dates or water, often doing so in the company of others. In addition to fasting, the Prophet would increase his recitation of the Qur'an. Each night during Ramadan, the archangel Gabriel would visit the Prophet, and together they would recite and review the Qur'anic verses that had been revealed up to that point. It is believed that during the final Ramadan before the Prophet's death, they conducted this review twice. This practice, known as *muqabala* (*comparative review*), continues to be widely observed among Muslims, especially during Ramadan. As part of this tradition, at least two individuals gather, taking turns to recite the Qur'an. While one recites, the other listens and follows along, ensuring accuracy and fostering a shared spiritual experience.

Another significant spiritual practice of the Prophet during Ramadan was the Tarawih prayer, a special prayer unique to this month. The Prophet would perform at least eight cycles of additional prayer following the late evening prayer (*'isha*). Unlike the daily prayer, the Prophet prolonged each action of the Tarawih with extended recitations

---

60. *Sahih Muslim, kitab al-siyam, bab istihbab sawm sitta ayyamin min shawwal itti-ba'an liramadan.*

from the Qur'an. Following the Prophet's example, Muslims today widely perform Tarawih prayers during Ramadan, often completing twenty cycles in congregation. During these prayers, one-thirtieth (a *juz'*, literally a *part*) of the Qur'an is recited each night, allowing the entire Qur'an to be completed by the end of the month. The person leading the prayer (imam) recites the Qur'an, while the congregation follows along, making it a communal act of devotion. The duration of the Tarawih prayer typically ranges from one to two hours, depending on the length of the recitation. In regions where Ramadan overlaps with the long summer days, Tarawih prayers may extend until shortly before midnight in some mosques, reflecting the dedication of the community to this special form of worship.

In addition to his special prayers, the Prophet would observe a spiritual retreat (*i'tikaf*) during the last ten days of Ramadan. In the final Ramadan before his passing, he spent two-thirds of the month in retreat, reflecting his heightened devotion. As part of *i'tikaf*, the Prophet would seclude himself in the mosque, dedicating his days and nights to prayer, worship, and reflection. This practice has its roots in the Qur'an, which traces it back to the traditions of Abraham and his son Ishmael.[61]

The Prophet's wife Aisha reported that the Prophet would intensify his devotion during the last ten days of Ramadan. What made this period particularly special was the belief that the most sacred night in the Islamic calendar, the Night of Power (*Laylat al-Qadr*), falls within this time. The Qur'anic chapter named after this night states that the Qur'an was revealed during it and describes it as being better than a thousand months.[62] According to Islamic tradition, righteous deeds and acts of worship performed on this night are considered spiritually equivalent to those performed over a thousand months. The Prophet encouraged his followers to spend this night in prayer and devotion. In one hadith, he said that whoever fasts during Ramadan and stands in prayer on the Night of Power with sincere faith will have all their

---

61. Qur'an 2:125.

62. Qur'an 97:1–5.

past sins forgiven.⁶³ Today, the Prophet's practice of spiritual retreat (*i'tikaf*) continues to be widely observed by Muslims worldwide. Many mosques, including those in the United States, organize retreats during Ramadan to help their congregations focus on worship, prayer, and spiritual reflection.

Spiritual Dimensions of Ramadan Fasting

Ramadan fasting is a time of spiritual renewal and an opportunity to strengthen one's relationship with God. Through fasting and spending nights in prayer and devotion, the worshipper is reminded that God alone is the ultimate Provider, with no partner or equal. Fasting serves as an act of gratitude, acknowledging the countless blessings one receives. It also humbles the believer, helping them recognize their dependence on God and their own weakness in relation to God's power.

In his treatise on fasting, Said Nursi highlights several of its virtues, emphasizing its profound spiritual and moral benefits:

> God Almighty has generously spread countless blessings across the earth for humanity. In return, He wants gratitude as the rightful acknowledgment of these blessings. The apparent causes and intermediaries of these blessings can be likened to tray-bearers; we pay them a price, express gratitude, and sometimes offer undue reverence, even though they do not truly deserve it. However, the True Bestower of Bounties is infinitely more worthy of gratitude than these intermediaries, which are merely means through which His blessings reach us. True gratitude to God lies in recognizing that all blessings originate directly from Him, valuing their significance, and acknowledging our dependence on His mercy.⁶⁴

---

63. *Sahih al-Bukhari, kitab fadl layl al-qadr, bab fadl layl al-qadr.*
64. Said Nursi, *Mektubat* (Söz Basım, 2012), 557.

Nursi highlights that when people receive a blessing or favor, they typically express gratitude by either paying a price or offering thanks. For instance, when purchasing an apple from a person or a grocery store, the payment itself can be seen as a form of gratitude. However, Nursi prompts us to reflect on a deeper question: What acknowledgment is due to God, the ultimate source of the apple? If we express thanks to the intermediary—the one who delivers the blessing—then it is only natural that we should offer even greater gratitude to the One who provides it. According to Nursi, fasting serves as a sincere way to express this gratitude to God:

> Fasting during Ramadan serves as a profound means to cultivate genuine, sincere, and all-encompassing gratitude. Throughout the rest of the year, many people, particularly those who live in comfort, often fail to appreciate the value of countless blessings because they rarely experience true hunger. When their stomachs are full—especially among the affluent—they may overlook the significance of even something as simple as a piece of dry bread. However, at the moment of breaking the fast, the act of tasting transforms that humble bread into a precious divine blessing for a believer. During Ramadan, individuals from all walks of life, from rulers to the impoverished, express a shared sense of gratitude by recognizing the true worth of these blessings.[65]

Nursi emphasizes that when people experience deprivation, they better understand the value of even the simplest provisions, such as a piece of bread. The act of breaking the fast becomes a moment of profound gratitude, uniting individuals across all social classes in recognizing and cherishing the divine blessings they often take for granted.

Fasting is also a form of purifying the self. It is a way to discipline oneself against unlimited desires and indulgences with patience. The self

---

65. Nursi, *Mektubat*, 557–558.

has the tendency to be heedless and forget its weakness and dependence. Nursi points to this aspect of the self below:

> In its heedlessness, the human soul forgets its true nature. It fails to recognize its profound powerlessness, neediness, and limitations—and even avoids acknowledging them. It does not reflect on its fragility, its susceptibility to transience and calamities, or the reality that it is made of perishable flesh and bones, destined to decay and disintegrate. Instead, the soul charges into the world with an illusion of invincibility, as though it possessed a body of steel and were immune to mortality. It pursues the world with insatiable greed, intense attachment, and fervent love, becoming ensnared by anything that brings pleasure or benefit. In doing so, it forgets its Creator, who sustains it with boundless compassion. It neglects to consider the ultimate purpose of its life and the reality of the hereafter, instead indulging in heedlessness, excess, and misconduct.[66]

Fasting serves as a wake-up call, shaking individuals out of their heedlessness to recognize their vulnerability, weakness, and dependence. It becomes a great reminder to seek refuge in divine mercy with a heart full of gratitude.

It is important to note that the experience of fasting extends beyond abstaining from food, drink, and sexual activity: It carries broader implications for one's spirituality. In this context, al-Ghazali identifies three levels of fasting, each reflecting a deeper dimension of spiritual practice. The first one is the fasting of an ordinary person, which involves refraining from eating, drinking, and having sexual relations. The second type of fasting is that, in addition to the first one, the worshipper keeps the ears, eyes, tongue, hands, feet, and other limbs away from sins. For example, fasting through the tongue means guarding the tongue against idle talk, lies, backbiting, gossip, obscene speech, harsh words, arguments, and speaking with ostentation. Fasting with

---

66. Nursi, *Mektubat*, 569.

the tongue also involves compelling the tongue to remain silent and engaging it in the remembrance of God and the recitation of the Qur'an. This constitutes the fast of the tongue. Fasting with your eyes constitutes guarding the eyes from looking at undesirable and inappropriate things, as well as avoiding anything that distracts the heart and diverts it from the remembrance of God. Al-Ghazali calls this type of fasting "the fasting of the righteous."[67]

The third type of fasting involves completely purifying the heart from worldly thoughts and distancing it from everything except God. This type is the fasting of those who are very close to God, of the prophets and the most righteous of the righteous. Al-Ghazali points out that this spiritual level in fasting cannot be explained in words; it can only be realized through practice. This state involves directing all of one's inspirations toward God and abandoning everything else for God's sake.[68] The Prophet Muhammad's fasting was the archetype of this spiritual state in fasting.

Fasting also carries significant social dimensions, fostering mindfulness of the plight of fellow human beings. It is reported that Muhammad was especially generous during the month of Ramadan and encouraged his followers to do the same.[69] As a result, Ramadan has become a season of sharing and care. Abstaining from food helps believers empathize with those who are poor and in need, inspiring acts of kindness and charity. A special charity (*sadaqa al-fitr*) is given during Ramadan, particularly before the Eid celebration, to support those in need and ensure everyone can partake in the holiday festivities. Additionally, if a believer is unable to fast due to old age or illness, they are encouraged to feed those who are poor for each day they cannot fast, further emphasizing the social and communal spirit of Ramadan.[70]

---

67. Al-Ghazali, *Ihya' 'Ulum al-Din*, 1:388–389.

68. Al-Ghazali, *Ihya' 'Ulum al-Din*, 1:389.

69. *Sahih al-Bukhari, kitab al-manaqib, bab sifat al-nabiyy salla allahu 'alayhi wa sallam.*

70. Qur'an 2:184.

Giving to Charity

The spiritual practices in the life of the Prophet were not limited to acts of physical worship. Giving to charity was a central aspect of his spirituality and teachings as well. Generosity and care for those in need were among Muhammad's most defining qualities. When the Prophet first received revelation and experienced doubt about his experience, his wife Khadija comforted him by reminding him of his noble character. She highlighted that he was not only kind to his relatives and neighbors but also devoted to helping those who were poor and needy, often opening the door of his home to them. Khadija's reassurance emphasized that God would not abandon or disgrace a person like Muhammad because of his remarkable generosity and compassion.

Generosity is a central theme in the Qur'an and is often described as one of the key attributes of believers.[71] The theological reasoning for giving lies in the understanding that God is the ultimate provider and the true owner of all wealth.[72] What a person possesses is considered a trust from God, and it should be used in accordance with God's will, which includes sharing it with those in need. The Qur'an highlights this attribute, stating that believers are those who "spend out of what God has provided for them."[73]

A remarkable feature of the Qur'anic approach is that charitable giving is often mentioned alongside prayer (*salat*) in the same verses, emphasizing its importance. The Qur'an uses various terms for charitable giving (e.g., *infaq* and *sadaqa*). Among these, a specific form of giving, rooted in the Qur'an and the teachings of the Prophet, is *zakat*. This obligatory charity requires all Muslims with sufficient financial means to give 2.5 percent of their wealth to those who are poor. The word *zakat* literally means *to purify*, signifying that through this act of giving, believers purify their wealth and themselves.

---

71. The Qur'an employs a number of terms for giving. Among them are *infaq*, *zakat*, and *sadaqa*.

72. Qur'an 24:33; 57:7.

73. Qur'an 2:3.

Zakat is one of the five pillars of Islam and is often discussed as part of Islamic worship and rituals. While the Prophet referred to the five daily prayers (*salat*) as the central pole of Islam, he described *zakat* as the bridge of Islam—a way to help fellow human beings safely and peacefully navigate the bridge of life. It symbolizes solidarity and mutual support between those who are rich and those who are poor, fostering a sense of compassion and social responsibility within the Muslim community.

The Prophet exemplified the Qur'anic teachings on charitable giving throughout his life. His companions often described him as the most generous of people. One report states that the Prophet was "more generous than a strong wind," meaning nothing could stop him from giving.[74] Whenever someone asked him for something, he would give without hesitation. If he had it, he never refused. He generously shared his food, clothing, and knowledge with others.

In a hadith narrated by his wife Aisha, a female companion once gave the Prophet a cloak she had made. The Prophet graciously accepted the gift and wore it. During a gathering, one of his companions admired the cloak and said, "This is beautiful. Would you give it to me?" The Prophet agreed. Shortly afterward, he went home and sent the cloak to the man.[75]

In another tradition narrated by Aisha, after the Prophet's family had slaughtered a goat, Aisha distributed most of the meat to those who were poor. When she informed the Prophet that only a small piece from the shoulder was left for them, he replied, "Everything remains except the shoulder piece."[76] This metaphor expressed the idea that what is given in charity is what truly lasts, as it returns as a spiritual reward. The Prophet embodied the Qur'anic message: "What is with you will

---

74. *Sahih al-Bukhari, kitab al-manaqib, bab sifat al-nabiyy salla allahu 'alayhi wa sallam.*

75. *Sunan ibn Majah, kitab al-libas, bab libas rasul allahi, salla allahu 'alayhi wa sallam.*

76. *Jami' al-Tirmidhi, kitab sifat al-qiyamah wa al-raqa'iq, wa al-wara'.*

vanish, but what is with God will endure. And He will certainly reward those who patiently persevere according to the best of their actions."[77] The Prophet was also known for his generous hospitality, often hosting those in need in his own home. He did not accumulate wealth, choosing instead to immediately distribute whatever he had. This is evident from what he left behind, as he passed away without material wealth, leaving only a legacy of generosity and selflessness.

In his teachings, the Prophet frequently emphasized the importance of giving. In one tradition, he stated, "One who sleeps with a full stomach while his neighbor is hungry is not one of us."[78] He strongly urged his companions to practice generosity, explaining that stinginess and faith cannot coexist in the same heart, implying that a true believer should always be charitable.[79] The Prophet himself would regularly supplicate, seeking refuge in God from stinginess.[80] In another teaching, the Prophet remarked, "A generous person is close to God, heaven, and people, and far from hell. Conversely, a stingy person is distant from God, heaven, and people but close to hell. In God's eyes, an ignorant yet generous person is better than a stingy pious one."[81] This highlights the idea that giving and caring for others are ways of being mindful of and drawing closer to God. The Qur'an identifies generosity as one of God's attributes (*al-Kareem*).[82] In a hadith, the Prophet stated that "God is generous and loves generosity."[83] By being generous, believers reflect this divine attribute in their lives, embodying God's qualities and bringing God's mercy and kindness into the world.

---

77. Qur'an 16:96.

78. *Sahih al-Bukhari, Al-Adab al-Mufrad, kitab al-jar, bab la yashba' duna jarihi.*

79. *Sunan al-Nasa'i, kitab al-jihad, bab fadl man 'amila fi sabilillahi 'ala qadamihi.*

80. *Sahih al-Bukhari, kitab al-da'wat, bab al-ta'awwudh min 'adhabi al-qabr.*

81. *Jami' al-Tirmidihi, kitab al-birr, bab ma ja'a fi al-sakha'.*

82. Qur'an 55:27; 96:3; 82:6.

83. *Jami' al-Tirmidhi, kitab al-'adab, bab ma ja'a fi al-nazafa.*

In the teachings of the Prophet, generosity is not limited to financial giving. One can be generous with time, knowledge, skills, and other resources. In fact, the Prophet said, "Even a smile is charity."[84] Because of the emphasis on giving in the Qur'an and the teachings of the Prophet, generosity and refraining from stinginess became central themes in Islamic literature. Hadith collections often include chapters not only on *zakat* but also on the importance of supporting those most vulnerable, including those who are poor, orphaned, and elderly. Additionally, a significant portion of jurisprudential works (*fiqh*) is dedicated to the obligations and recommendations surrounding charitable giving, including the eligibility of donors and recipients.

The theme of generous giving is also widely discussed in classical Islamic literature, where it is closely associated with a noble character. For example, one of the books in Imam al-Ghazali's *Ihya' 'Ulum al-Din* is devoted to the practice of *zakat*. In this book, al-Ghazali outlines the various types of giving and the requirements for fulfilling this spiritual obligation. This book is included in the section on acts of worship, alongside topics like the five daily prayers and fasting. In another part of his work, al-Ghazali addresses the problem of attachment to wealth and stinginess, offering insights and remedies for overcoming these tendencies.

Al-Ghazali explains that one reason people become overly attached to wealth, to the point of stinginess, is their love for material possessions. One remedy for this "sickness" is to reflect on the inevitability of death and the transient nature of worldly life. If a person knows they might die tomorrow, they are less likely to cling to their wealth. Another reason for attachment to wealth is concern for one's children and loved ones. People often accumulate wealth for their families, but al-Ghazali points to the Qur'anic teaching that God is the Creator and Sustainer of all, including children. He notes that many children who inherit nothing from their parents thrive, while those who inherit great wealth may misuse it, leading to harm for themselves and their parents.

---

84. *Jami' al-Tirmidihi, kitab al-birr, bab ma ja'a fi sana'i' al-ma'ruf.*

Al-Ghazali concludes that the wise recognize wealth as a means to fulfill basic needs, with the excess meant for charitable giving, which becomes a spiritual investment in the hereafter. Those who understand this know that giving wealth is far more beneficial, both in this world and in the next, than hoarding it. He advises that when one feels inclined toward generosity and good deeds, one should act immediately, as Satan continuously instills fear of poverty to deter people from giving.[85] Through these teachings, al-Ghazali and other scholars emphasize that generosity is not just an act of kindness but also a great spiritual practice that nurtures the soul and brings one closer to God.

In his classic work *Bustan*, the Persian poet Saadi Shirazi (d. 1291) dedicates a chapter to the theme of generous giving. I will conclude this section with a poem from Shirazi's book that beautifully encapsulates the prophetic teachings on giving and benevolence:

> If you are wise, focus on the eternal truth,
> For it lasts, while all else fades away.
> A person without knowledge, generosity, or faith
> Is human only in appearance.
> Those who bring peace to others
> Find peace themselves, even in their graves.
> Share your wealth and kindness now,
> For it will soon slip from your hands.
> Unlock your treasures today,
> For tomorrow, you may no longer hold the key.
> If you wish to avoid distress on Judgment Day,
> Remember those in distress today.
> Do not turn the poor away from your door,
> Lest you one day find yourself begging at another's.
> The one who helps those in need
> Understands they may one day need help too.

---

85. Al-Ghazali, *Ihya' 'Ulum al-Din*, 3:403–408.

Are you not also a seeker of grace?
Be grateful, and never turn away those who ask for your help.[86]

Pilgrimage: A Sacred Journey of Spiritual Reset

The Prophet also engaged in a spiritual practice that required dedication through both wealth and physical effort: the pilgrimage (*hajj*), one of the five pillars of Islam. *Hajj* was established as a requirement for the Muslim community during the Prophet's time in Medina. The Qur'an emphasizes its significance, stating that pilgrimage to the Kaaba is an obligation believers owe to God, provided they have the means to undertake it.[87]

Visiting designated sacred spaces has been part of religious rituals across many traditions, and pilgrimage as a spiritual practice is deeply rooted in history. In fact, many of the rituals associated with *hajj* predate Islam. Islamic tradition traces the origins of the Kaaba back to the time of Adam and Eve, with its reconstruction attributed to Abraham and his son Ishmael. The Qur'an describes the Kaaba not only as the first house of worship established for humanity but also as a place of blessing and guidance for all the worlds: "Indeed, the first house established for humanity was the one at Mecca. It is a blessed place; a source of guidance for all people."[88]

According to Islamic sources, Abraham and his wife, Sarah, were initially childless, with Sarah being beyond childbearing age. She gave Abraham her Egyptian handmaid, Hagar, as a second wife, and Hagar bore a son named Ishmael. Despite her age, Sarah also became pregnant and gave birth to Isaac. Not long after, God instructed Abraham to take Hagar and Ishmael to the valley of Mecca and settle there. Abraham left them in the area and continued on his prophetic journey. In the barren

---

86. Saadi Shirazi, *The Bustan of Saadi*, trans. A. Hart Edwards (Bibliotech Press, 2018), 34–35.

87. Qur'an 3:97.

88. Qur'an 3:96.

valley, Hagar and baby Ishmael were soon overcome by thirst. Hagar desperately searched for water, running back and forth between locations. God answered their pleas, causing a spring of water to gush forth from the sand at the touch of Ishmael's heel.[89] This water is known to Muslims today as the well of Zamzam. The water is considered sacred by Muslims. It has long been a tradition for Muslim pilgrims performing the annual pilgrimage (*hajj*) or lesser pilgrimage (*umrah*) to drink from the well and take some of the water home, often offering it to those who visit them.[90]

Abraham would occasionally visit his family, and during one of these visits, God commanded him and Ishmael to build a house of worship for God, known as the Kaaba. The Qur'an recounts that as they were constructing it, the father and son prayed as follows: "Our Lord, accept this service from us. You are the All Hearing, the All Knowing. Our Lord, make us submissive to You; make our descendants into a community devoted to You. Show us how to worship and accept our repentance, for You are the Ever Relenting, the Most Merciful. Our Lord! Raise from among them a messenger who will recite to them Your revelations, teach them the Book and wisdom, and purify them. Truly, You are the Mighty, the Wise."[91] In a report, the Prophet stated, "I am the fulfillment of my ancestor Abraham's prayer."[92] His lineage traces back to Abraham through his son Ishmael. Traditional Islamic sources frequently highlight Muhammad's noble ancestry, often listing his ancestors all the way back to Abraham.[93]

---

89. Lings, *Muhammad*, 1–3.

90. *Umrah* is a pilgrimage to Mecca that can be undertaken at any time of the year, unlike *hajj*, which has specific dates. Though it is not obligatory like *hajj*, *umrah* holds significant spiritual importance for Muslims and is often referred to as the "lesser pilgrimage."

91. Qur'an 2:127–129.

92. Ibn Ishaq, *Life of Muhammad*, 67–72.

93. Ibn Ishaq, *Life of Muhammad*, 3.

From its inception, the Kaaba has symbolized monotheism. God instructed Abraham to summon people from near and far to the pilgrimage.[94] The Kaaba thus became the focal point for pilgrimage and the worship of the one true God, attracting visitors from around the world. Jews, Abraham's descendants through Isaac, also visited this sacred site.[95]

However, over time, likely due to the influx of diverse people from across the region, the Kaaba also became a center of polytheism. According to Islamic tradition, this began when a Meccan merchant brought an idol to Mecca, leading to the area around the Kaaba being filled with idols. The Zamzam well eventually silted over and was forgotten, symbolizing a departure from Abraham's teachings.[96] Many tribes began to have their own idols, which became a unifying element for each tribe. These idols were seen as divine protectors and venerated at local shrines.[97] Among them, three idols—al-Lat, al-Uzza, and Manat—received special veneration, not only from the tribes in Mecca but also from Arabs in neighboring areas. Offerings to these deities were often made with the expectation of receiving favors in return: "I give you, lord, so you will grant me that favor."[98] As a result of these developments, those who worshipped only one God ceased visiting the Kaaba.[99]

With the new revelation of the Qur'an, the Prophet reinstated Abrahamic monotheism in Mecca and restored the pilgrimage rituals

---

94. Qur'an 22:27.

95. Lings, *Muhammad*, 4.

96. The well of Zamzam was rediscovered by Muhammad's grandfather Abd al-Muttalib through a vision before he was born.

97. Fred M. Donner, *Muhammad and the Believers* (Harvard University Press, 2012), 30.

98. Marshall G. S. Hodgson, *The Venture of Islam: Conscience and History in a World Civilization*, vol. 1, *The Classical Age of Islam* (University of Chicago Press, 1977), 156, 159.

99. Jonathan A. C. Brown, *Muhammad: A Very Short Introduction* (Oxford University Press, 2011), 5.

associated with the Kaaba, the sacred house dedicated to the worship of one God. The Prophet performed the annual pilgrimage (*hajj*) only once, following the Muslims' conquest of Mecca. This pilgrimage is famously known as the Farewell Hajj (*hajjat al-wada'*). The rituals practiced by Muslims during *hajj* today are based on the Prophet's example and include many reenactments of events from the life of Abraham. In addition to the annual *hajj*, the Prophet performed the lesser pilgrimage (*umrah*) several times. Unlike *hajj*, which is performed specifically during the twelfth month (Dhu al-Hijjah) of the Islamic calendar, *umrah* can be performed at any time of the year and is considered a recommended act of worship. In a hadith, the Prophet said that an *umrah* performed during the month of Ramadan is spiritually equivalent to the reward of the annual *hajj*.[100]

The *hajj* pilgrimage is an obligation for all Muslims who have reached puberty and possess the financial and physical means to perform it at least once in their lifetime. The first step of *hajj* is entering the state of *ihram* by donning the prescribed pilgrimage attire. Men wear two unstitched white cloths, while women wear modest clothing that covers their bodies except for the face and hands. In this state of *ihram*, pilgrims recite a supplication (*talbiya*) attributed to the Prophet: "Here I am, O God, here I am. Here I am, You have no partner, here I am. Verily, all praise, blessings, and sovereignty belong to You. You have no partner."[101] This supplication expresses the pilgrim's total devotion and submission to God in humility, preparing their mind and heart for a spiritually transformative journey.

The rituals of *hajj* are deeply symbolic and involve collective acts of prayer and supplication. Key rituals include walking between the hills of Safa and Marwah (*sa'i*), circling the Kaaba (*tawaf*), symbolically stoning the devil, sacrificing an animal, and, for men, trimming or shaving their hair. Each step of the pilgrimage is designed to draw the pilgrim closer to God and foster a spiritual renewal. The spiritual

---

100. *Jami' al-Tirmidhi, kitab al-hajj, bab ma ja'a fi 'umrati ramadan.*

101. *Sahih al-Muslim, kitab al-hajj, bab al-talbiya wa sifatiha wa waqtiha.*

pinnacle of *hajj* is the gathering of several million pilgrims at Arafat, a plain about twelve miles southeast of Mecca. At this sacred station, pilgrims turn to God in earnest prayer and supplication while listening to a sermon. This moment is followed by spending the night under the stars at Muzdalifah, an open area near Mecca.

This collective act of worship symbolizes the unity and equality of all humanity before God. The core message of the Prophet's sermon during his pilgrimage at Arafat emphasized this universal equality: "O people! Know that your Lord is one, and your ancestor is one. All humans are from Adam, and Adam was created from dust. An Arab has no superiority over a non-Arab, nor does a non-Arab have superiority over an Arab; a white person has no superiority over a black person, nor does a black person have superiority over a white person. Superiority in the sight of God is only through piety and righteousness [*taqwa*]."[102] This timeless message underscores the spiritual and social dimensions of *hajj*, where pilgrims stand together as equals before their Creator in humility, united by their faith.

Pilgrims from across the Muslim world have long been awed by the sight of the vast multitude at Arafat. Many have documented their observations of the *hajj*. Among them was Ibn Jubayr (d. 1215), who traveled to Mecca for *hajj* from medieval Spain. In his *hajj* account, he reflects on the remarkable gathering at Arafat, capturing the spiritual and communal essence of this overwhelming event:

> The morning of this Friday there was at Arafat an assemblage that can only be equaled by the Final Gathering. . . . Some truthful elders among the local population with experience of the Holy House said that they had never seen a more numerous crowd at Arafat, and my own opinion is that not since the time of Harun, who was the last Caliph to make the Hajj, has there been a similar gathering in Islam. After the two prayers of noontime and mid-afternoon had been combined this Friday, the faithful made their "standing" in adoration, in humility

---

102. Erul, "Veda Hutbesi," 42:592.

and in tears, begging the favor of the Most High. Cries of "God is great!" arose and a tumult of voices went up in invocation of God . . . The crowd remained there, their faces burned by the sun, until its orb had disappeared and the prayer of sunset had arrived.[103]

Ibn Jubayr vividly describes the spiritual and emotional intensity of the gathering of pilgrims at Arafat, comparing it to the assembly of humanity on the day of judgment in the hereafter.

Centuries later, Malcolm X (d. 1965) also found the Islamic *hajj* rituals, particularly the gathering at Arafat, extremely moving. In a letter written from Mecca in 1964 while performing *hajj*, he observed, "I have prayed on Mt. Arafat. There were tens of thousands of pilgrims, from all over the world. They were of all colors, from blue-eyed blonds to black skin Africans. But we were all participating in the same rituals, displaying a spirit of unity and brotherhood that my experiences in America had lead me to believe never could exist between the white and non-white. America needs to understand Islam, because this is the one religion that erases from its society the race problem."[104] For Malcolm X, who experienced racial discrimination and segregation in America, the Islamic pilgrimage served as a powerful example of unity transcending racial and cultural divides.

The prophetic practice of pilgrimage is regarded by Muslims as an invitation from God. It is an intense spiritual journey that calls believers to detach themselves from worldly attachments, including home, family, and daily routines. This journey requires a sacrifice of time, wealth, and physical effort. Pilgrims are expected to empty their hearts of all worldly concerns and entirely dedicate themselves to God, joining their fellow pilgrims in collective devotion. The *hajj* journey is often likened to preparing for death and the hereafter. Pilgrims are encouraged to

---

103. Ibn Jubayr, qtd in F. E. Peters, *The Hajj: The Muslim Pilgrimage to Mecca and to Holy Places* (Princeton University Press, 1994), 123.

104. Alex Haley, *Autobiography of Malcolm X* (Grove Press, 1965), 34–54.

write their wills before departing, seek forgiveness from those they may have wronged, and ensure all debts are paid. These actions reflect the humility and self-reflection inherent in the pilgrimage.

The major Muslim holiday Eid al-Adha coincides with the days of *hajj*. Following the example of the Prophet, Muslims begin the celebration with two cycles of prayer (*salat al-eid*) in congregation, followed by a sermon delivered by the imam. They then perform the ritual sacrifice of animals (*qurban*), distributing the meat to those in need. This act of sacrifice not only symbolizes a believer's piety and gratitude but also serves as a means of drawing closer to God.

Recitation of the Qur'an in the Prophet's Spirituality

Daily recitation of the Qur'an was a key aspect of the Prophet's spiritual practice. This recitation was (and still is) viewed as a form of worship and a great spiritual act. The Prophet frequently recited the Qur'an during prayers (*salat*). In communal prayers, he would typically recite shorter passages, but in his private devotions, especially during the night prayers, he would spend hours reciting the longer chapters of the Qur'an. His supplications, invocations, and remembrance of God often included verses from the Qur'an.

In several hadiths, the Prophet emphasized the benefits of reciting the Qur'an. In one of them, he mentioned, "Whoever recites a letter from the book of God will be credited with a good deed, and a good deed earns a ten-fold reward."[105] Another hadith states, "The one who recites the Qur'an aloud is like the one who gives charity publicly, and the one who recites it quietly is like the one who gives charity in secret."[106] The Prophet uses an analogy to underscore the significance of reciting the Qur'an and living according to its teachings: "The example of a believer who recites the Qur'an and acts on it, like a citron which

---

105. *Jami' al-Tirmidhi, kitab thawab al-qur'an, bab ma ja'a fiman qara'a harfan min al-qur'an ma lahu min al-ajr.*

106. *Jami' al-Tirmidhi, kitab thawab al-qur'an.*

tastes nice and smells nice. And the example of a believer who does not recite the Qur'an but acts on it is like a date which tastes good but has no smell. And the example of a hypocrite who recites the Qur'an is like sweet basil, which smells good but tastes bitter, and the example of a hypocrite who does not recite the Qur'an is like a colocynth which tastes bitter and has a bad smell."[107]

The recitation of the Qur'an is also regarded as a source of healing for both the body and the soul. This healing power of the divine words is emphasized in several verses of the Qur'an:

> People, there has come to you an advice from your Lord, a healing for what is in the hearts, and a guidance and a mercy for the believers.[108]
> We send down the Quran as healing and mercy for the believer.[109]
> It [the Qur'an] is guidance and healing for those who have faith.[110]

Because of the healing aspect of the Qur'an, Muhammad consistently encouraged his followers to seek healing through its verses. The Prophet's wife Aisha reported, "Whenever the Prophet became ill, he would recite Surat al-Falaq and Surat al-Nas [chapters 113–114] and then blow over his body. When he was seriously ill, I would recite these two chapters and rub his hands over his body, hoping for their blessings."[111] Following the Prophet's example, Muslims have long used the recitation of Qur'anic verses for both spiritual and physical healing.

---

107. *Jami' al-Tirmidhi, kitab al-amsal, bab ma ja'a fi masal al-mu'min al-qari' lilqur'an wa ghayri al-qari'.*

108. Qur'an 10:57.

109. Qur'an 17:82.

110. Qur'an 41:44.

111. *Sahih al-Bukhari: kitab fadail al-qur'an, bab fadl al-mu'awwidhat.*

It is reported that Muhammad not only recited the newly revealed revelations to his followers but also enjoyed listening to them recite the Qur'an. The Prophet encouraged his companions to both learn and teach the Qur'an, emphasizing its importance in several sayings. In one hadith, he said, "The best among you are those who learn the Qur'an and teach it."[112] In another hadith, the Prophet stated, "The one who recites the Qur'an beautifully, smoothly, and precisely will be in the company of the noble and obedient angels. As for the one who struggles, stammering or stumbling through its verses, they will receive twice the reward."[113] Abdullah ibn Masud, a close companion, recounted that the Prophet once asked him to recite the Qur'an for him. Abdullah replied, "Shall I recite the Qur'an to you when it was revealed to you?" The Prophet responded, "I like to hear the Qur'an from others." Abdullah then began reciting the fourth chapter of the Qur'an, Surat al-Nisa, until he reached the verse that says, "What will they do when We bring a witness from each community, with you [Muhammad] as a witness against these people?"[114] At that point, the Prophet said, "Stop here!" and his eyes were filled with tears.[115]

Due to its central role in the Prophet's spiritual practice, reciting from the Qur'an is one of the most important elements of Islamic worship and prayers. Qur'anic recitation permeates every aspect of Muslim life, from birth rituals to funerals and from weddings to business gatherings. Engaging with the words of God through recitation provides a direct connection to the divine. It serves as a form of remembrance (*dhikr*), supplication (*du'a'*), worship (*'ibadah*), and blessing (*baraka*). The recitation illuminates the hearts and minds of believers, strengthening their faith.

---

112. *Sahih al-Bukhari: kitab fadail al-qur'an, bab khayrukum man ta'allama al-qur'an wa 'allamahu.*

113. *Sunan Ibn Majah, kitab al-adab, bab thawab al-qur'an.*

114. Qur'an 4:41.

115. *Sahih al-Bukhari, kitab al-tafsir, bab "fakayfa 'idha ji'na min kulli ummatin bi shahidin wa ji'na bika 'ala ha'ulai' shahidan.*

Contemplating God's Creation

The Prophet not only recited the verses of the Qur'an but also regularly contemplated (*tafakkur*) and read the signs (*ayat*) of God in creation. Contemplation was a fundamental part of his spiritual practice. He frequently remembered God by reflecting on the wonders of creation. The Qur'an consistently invites people to contemplate and reflect on their own creation and the universe. Creation is seen as a manifestation of God's names and signs. It is a way to know God. This knowledge generates love for God.

Indeed, the very first revelation of the Qur'an urges people to ponder God's creation: "Read! In the name of your Lord who created: He created humans from a blood clot. Read! Your Lord is the Most Generous, Who taught by the pen, taught humanity what they did not know."[116] In this passage, the Qur'an introduces God to humanity through God's creation and attributes. The concept of reading extends beyond the revealed sacred text, the written Qur'an, to include the book of creation, the cosmic Qur'an. Humans are encouraged to read and reflect on both of these "books." In doing so, the attributes of God are emphasized.

As a demonstration of God's creative power, the Qur'an cites the creation of humans from a "blood clot" as an example. In other verses, the Qur'an provides further details about the stages of human creation by God: "Indeed, We created man from an essence of clay, then We placed him as a drop of fluid in a secure place, then We made that drop into a blood clot, and We made that form into a lump of flesh, and We made that lump into bones, and We clothed those bones with flesh, and later We made him into other forms. Glory be to God, the best of creators. After that you will surely die, and then, on the Day of Judgment, you will be resurrected."[117]

---

116. Qur'an 96:1–5.

117. Qur'an 23:12–14.

The creation of humans is an indication of God's control as well as God's boundless generosity in the universe. God teaches humans the meanings of their own creation as part of God's mercy.

The Qur'anic verses not only point to the creation of humans but also repeatedly bring up God's creation around us among God's signs so that people can know their Creator and contemplate God's creation. Many of the chapters of the Qur'an are named after things God created. For example, chapter 2, which is the longest, is titled "The Cow." Others are named "The Cattle," "The Thunder," "The Bee," "The Light," "The Spider," "The Mountain," "The Star," "The Moon," "The Human Being," "The Elephant," "The Ants," "The Iron," "The Sun," "The Night," "The Fig," "The Morning Brightness," "The Earthquake," and so on. In chapter 16, which is named after the bee, the Qur'an points to blessings from God: "It is God who sends water down from the sky and with it revives the earth when it is dead. Surely in this is a sign for those who listen. And surely in the cattle here is a lesson for you: We give you a drink from that which is in their bellies, between refuse and blood, pure milk, sweet to the drinker. From the fruits of date palms and grapes you take sweet juice and wholesome provisions. Surely in this is a sign for people who use their reason."[118] The Qur'an then illustrates the bee as the sign of God's power and knowledge: "And your Lord revealed to the bee, saying, 'Build yourselves houses in the mountains and trees and what people construct. Then feed on all kinds of fruit and follow the ways made easy for you by your Lord.' From their bellies comes a drink of different colors in which there is healing for people. There truly is a sign in this for those who think."[119]

The Prophet, often referred to as the "living Qur'an," fully embodied its teachings on contemplation in his daily life. He would reflect deeply on creation in relation to God, using this practice as a means of remembrance and gratitude. In one account, the Prophet

---

118. Qur'an 16:65–67.

119. Qur'an 16:68–69.

said, "An hour of contemplation (*tafakkur*) is better than a year of worship."[120] It is reported that the Prophet would frequently gaze at the sky and reflect on God's power over creation. On such occasions, he would say, "The stars are the guarantors of the sky, and when the stars disappear, the sky will meet the fate that has been promised [i.e., Judgment Day]."[121] These reflections illustrate the Prophet's deep connection with the natural world as a way of recognizing and honoring God's majesty and wisdom.

Muhammad frequently used examples from creation to illustrate God's attributes. For instance, speaking of God's mercy, the Prophet said, "When God created the heavens and the earth, He made one hundred units of mercy. Each unit is vast enough to encompass everything between heaven and earth. Of these, He placed one on earth, through which mothers show compassion for their children, and animals and birds show compassion for each other. On the Day of Resurrection, He will perfect and complete His mercy."[122] To help people understand God's mercy and compassion, the Prophet reflected on how these qualities are manifested in creation, particularly through mothers.

In another example, the Prophet compared the attributes of a Muslim to those of a bee: "By the One in whose hand is the soul of Muhammad, the believer is like a bee which eats that which is pure and wholesome and lays that which is pure and wholesome. When it lands on something, it does not break or ruin it."[123] Bees are key pollinators and play a fundamental role in biodiversity and ecosystems. They are known for their diligence and hard work, yet their efforts do not harm the environment. Reflecting on this aspect of bees, the Prophet Muhammad encourages believers to emulate them: to be

---

120. Bediuzzaman Said Nursi, *Tarihçe-i Hayat* (Söz Basım, 2012), 574.

121. *Sahih Muslim, kitab fada'il sahaba, bab bayan anna baqa'a al-nabiyy salla allahu 'alayhi wa sallam 'amanu liashabihi wa baqa'a 'ashabihi 'aman.*

122. *Riyad al-Salihin, kitab al-muqaddamat, bab al-rija'.*

123. *Musnad Ahmad*, 6872; *Hadislerle İslam* (Diyanet İşleri Başkanlığı, 2014), 1:611.

productive without causing harm. Bees take nectar only from pure and clean flowers. Similarly, believers should consume what is lawful (*halal*). What bees produce—honey—is pure and beneficial. In the same way, a believer's contributions to society should be positive and beneficial. When bees collect nectar, they land gently and leave the flower unharmed. Likewise, a believer's productivity and success should not come at the expense of harming the environment or depleting natural resources. The Prophet's teaching highlights that believers can learn from God's creation in nature by reflecting on it.

In another instance, the Prophet highlights the connection between the diversity in creation and humanity: "God created Adam from a portion of soil gathered from all parts of the earth. For this reason, the children of Adam reflect the diversity of the earth in both color and nature. Some are red, some white, some black, and some are a mix of these. Similarly, their characteristics vary: some are soft, others hard; some are good, while others are less so."[124]

This hadith echoes the Qur'anic verse that celebrates diversity as a sign of God: "And one of His signs is the creation of the heavens and the earth, and the diversity of your languages and colors. Surely in this are signs for those of sound knowledge."[125] Both the hadith and the verse emphasize that the richness of diversity among people and creation is a reflection of God's wisdom and a sign for those who reflect.

Many Muslim scholars incorporated the virtue of contemplation into their spiritual lives and teachings. Imam al-Ghazali, for instance, dedicates an entire book to the subject of contemplation (*kitab al-tafakkur*) in his monumental *Ihya' 'Ulum al-Din*. In this work, he explores the virtues of contemplation, its spiritual benefits, and practical methods for engaging in it. Al-Ghazali emphasizes that everything in creation is a manifestation of God's actions and attributes, reflecting God's wisdom, power, and majesty. He explains

---

124. *Sunan Abi Dawud, kitab al-sunna, bab fi al-qadar.*

125. Qur'an 30:22.

that when believers contemplate creation, they come to realize "not a single particle among the inanimate objects, plants, animals, celestial spheres, and stars in the heavens and on the earth moves on its own. It can only move with the permission of God. In its movement, there are countless wisdoms. All of these are signs testifying to God's oneness and indicating His majesty and greatness."[126]

Al-Ghazali also discusses contemplation of the creation of humans and the self. He points out that the creation of humans is one of God's greatest signs, as God formed humans from a drop of sperm, and within their creation lies innumerable wonders that reflect God's greatness—wonders so vast that a lifetime would not suffice to describe them all. Al-Ghazali asserts that reflecting on the self ultimately deepens one's knowledge of God, as self-awareness leads to a greater understanding of the Creator.

Reflecting on Qur'anic verses concerning human creation, al-Ghazali highlights the precision and wisdom with which human faculties and organs are designed. Regarding the ears, the nose, and the mouth, he writes:

> Then He fashioned the ears, placing in them a bitter fluid to preserve their ability to hear and to repel harmful creatures. He surrounded the ears with cartilage to gather sounds and deliver them to the eardrum. He created curves within the ears to detect the movement of harmful creatures attempting to enter. He made the ear canal long and winding so that if any creature tries to enter while the person is asleep, the person would wake up. Then He elevated the nose in the middle of the face and made its shape beautiful. He opened the nostrils and endowed them with the ability to smell so that one could distinguish foods by their scent. He created the nostrils to enable breathing, cooling the body's internal heat, and supplying air to

---

126. Al-Ghazali, *Ihya' 'Ulum al-Din*, 4:670.

the heart. Then He opened the mouth and placed within it the tongue as a means of speech, the interpreter of the heart, and an indicator of the meanings within. He adorned the mouth with teeth, which serve as tools for grinding, breaking, and cutting. He made their roots strong, their tips sharp, and their color white. He arranged them in neat rows, aligning them like pearls strung on a thread, equal and orderly in appearance.[127]

Al-Ghazali emphasizes that when believers closely observe the grace, generosity, power, and wisdom of God in creation, they will be filled with awe and amazement. He compares the spiritual practice of contemplation to admiring a beautiful piece of art. While observing the art, a person naturally admires the artist's skill and creativity. Similarly, when believers reflect on the wonders of creation, they are reminded of God's infinite power, wisdom, and compassion, deepening their gratitude and connection to the Creator.

Said Nursi also regards contemplation as a key aspect of spirituality and includes it among the four essential elements of spiritual formation. He points out that "believers should carefully read and study the lines of the book of the universe because they are letters to them from God."[128] This phrase from Nursi is a metaphorical expression emphasizing that the universe, with its intricate design and order, is a source of divine wisdom and guidance. By observing and reflecting on the "lines" or aspects of creation, one can perceive messages or lessons from the divine realm. In this regard, every entity in creation is a form of divine communication. Nursi explains that humans are endowed with the ability for both inward and outward contemplation. Through this practice, believers come to view all beings not as acting independently but as manifestations of God, their Creator. This reflective process leads them from observing creation to recognizing

---

127. Al-Ghazali, *Ihya' 'Ulum al-Din*, 4:673–674.

128. Nursi, *Mesnevi-i Nuriye*, 165.

the Creator, safeguarding them from heedlessness and fostering an awareness of God's presence.[129]

One of Nursi's major treatises, *The Supreme Sign* (*Ayat al-Kubra*), within his *Risale-i Nur* collection, illustrates the power of contemplation through the journey of an imaginary traveler who finds himself in the world. Nursi guides the traveler through and among different aspects of the universe—such as the heavens, atmosphere, earth, seas, rivers, mountains, plains, trees, plants, and animals—answering the traveler's questions about their Creator. Nursi describes the traveler's initial impressions and observations: "Every traveler who enters this world opens their eyes and wonders: Who is the master of this magnificent place? It appears to be a most generous banquet, a masterful exhibition, an impressive camp and training ground, an awe-inspiring realm of recreation, and a profound center of wisdom and instruction. They also ask: Who is the author of this great book and the sovereign of this majestic realm?"[130]

Through this narrative, Nursi highlights contemplation as a journey from the marvels of creation to the recognition of the Creator's majesty and wisdom.

For Nursi, a reflective person would be struck with awe and amazement by the beauty and generosity present in the world. This sense of wonder naturally sparks curiosity and prompts questions about the Creator, God. Take, for instance, the air. The reflective traveler observes,

> The air is employed with such wise and generous purposes in countless tasks that it seems as though each particle of that seemingly lifeless and unconscious air listens to, understands, and flawlessly executes the commands of the Sovereign of the Universe. Without neglecting a single duty, it fulfills its responsibilities with the power of that Commander, maintaining perfect order. It provides breath to all living beings on earth,

---

129. Nursi, *Sözler* (Söz Basım, 2012), 645.

130. Bediuzzaman Said Nursi, *Şualar* (Söz Basım, 2012), 147.

transmits essential elements such as heat, light, electricity, and sound, and serves as a medium for plant pollination. In all these comprehensive functions and services, it is guided by an unseen hand imbued with extraordinary wisdom, knowledge, and a profound love for life.[131]

Through these observations, the traveler concludes that the marvelous artistry evident in creation cannot be the product of random coincidence. The precise balance, meticulous order, and profound wisdom all unmistakably point to the all-powerful and all-knowing Creator, God.[132]

Be Like a Traveler: Remembering Death and the Hereafter

While contemplating the creation of God, the Prophet also often remembered the finite nature of the world. Reflecting on death and the hereafter was among his common spiritual practices. Human mortality and ultimate destiny are central themes in the Qur'an, which repeatedly reminds humanity that every soul will taste death, and none can escape it.[133] However, life extends beyond this world into the hereafter, where individuals will be held accountable for their deeds. Belief in the hereafter is a fundamental article of faith in Islam.

We have already discussed that the recitation of the Qur'an was an integral part of the Prophet's daily spiritual practice, forming a significant component of both his day and night prayers. Given that nearly one-third of the Qur'an addresses themes of death and the hereafter, its recitation served as a profound reminder of human mortality and the transient nature of this world.[134] The Prophet's daily supplications

---

131. Nursi, *Şualar*, 149.

132. Nursi, *Şualar*, 160.

133. Qur'an 62:8; 4:78; 3:185; 29:57; 21:35.

134. Nursi, *Şualar*, 246.

often referenced death and the hereafter. One of his most frequently recited prayers was "O God, grant us goodness in this world and goodness in the Hereafter, and protect us from the torment of the Fire."[135] Another supplication he frequently invoked was "O God, I seek refuge in You from weakness and laziness, from cowardice and the burdens of old age. I seek Your protection from the torment of the grave and the afflictions of life and death."[136] These prayers reflect the Prophet's balanced focus on life and death, as well as the interconnection between this world and the hereafter.

The Prophet's mindfulness of death extended to his prayers for specific occasions. For instance, before going to bed, he would say, "O God, in Your name I die and I live" and on waking, he would recite, "Praise be to God, who gave us life after causing us to die, and to Him is the resurrection."[137] Through these prayers, the Prophet transformed the act of sleeping into an opportunity to express gratitude to God, reflect on death, and remember the ultimate return to God. In a hadith, the Prophet remarked, "Sleep is the brother of death."[138] This connection between sleep and death is also highlighted in the Qur'an, which states, "He it is Who takes your souls by night, and He knows what you commit by day. Then by day He resurrects you, that a term appointed may be fulfilled. Then unto Him shall be your return, and He shall inform you of that which you used to do."[139] Here, sleep is likened to death and waking to resurrection. A similar analogy appears in the story of the People of the Cave. The Qur'anic message emphasizes that

---

135. *Sahih al-Bukhari, kitab al-da'wat, bab qawl al-nabiyy salla allahu 'alayhi wa sallam, "rabbana atina fi dunya hasana."* This prayer remains widely recited by Muslims during their daily prayers.

136. *Sahih al-Bukhari, kitab al-da'wat, bab al-ta'awwudh min fitnati al-mahya walmamat.*

137. *Sahih al-Bukhari, kitab al-da'wat, bab wad' al-yad al-yumna tahta al-khaddi al-'ayman.*

138. Khatib al-Tabrizi, *Mishkat al-Masabih, kitab ahwal al-qiyama wa bad' al-khalq.*

139. Qur'an 6:60.

just as God withholds ordinary consciousness during sleep and restores it daily, God has the power to withhold it permanently through death and restore it through resurrection in the hereafter.[140]

It is reported that when the Prophet rode his camel, he would say, "Glory be to Him who has given us control over this; we could not have done it by ourselves. And indeed, to our Lord do we return."[141] Through this invocation, the Prophet transformed the simple act of riding into an opportunity to glorify God, acknowledge human dependence on God's power, and reflect on the ultimate return to God through death. This practice elevated a mundane daily activity into a spiritual act, serving as a reminder of the transient nature of this world and the ultimate reality of the hereafter.

The Prophet's remembrance of death and the hereafter was not limited to supplications and invocations. He would often attend community funerals and visit those who were sick, both serving as poignant reminders of the finite nature of life in this world. Additionally, the Prophet frequently visited the local cemetery, where he would greet its inhabitants with the following words: "Peace be upon you, O believing and Muslim inhabitants of this abode. If God wills, we shall join you. I ask God for peace and well-being for us and for you."[142] Through these actions, the Prophet exemplified a deep awareness of human mortality and the inevitable return to God.

Following the Qur'anic injunctions, the Prophet frequently reminded his followers to reflect on death and the transient nature of this world. In one hadith, he said, "Remember death often, for it shatters the pleasures of worldly life."[143] When asked who the wisest person

---

140. Maria Massi Dakake, *Commentary on Surat al-An'am*, in *The Study Quran: A New Translation and Commentary*, ed. Nasr et al. (HarperOne, 2015), 460.

141. This supplication of the Prophet is based on the Qur'an 43:13–14. Also see *Sunan Abi Dawud, kitab al-jihad, bab ma yaqul al-rajul idha safar.*

142. *Sahih Muslim, kitab al-jana'iz, bab ma yuqal 'inda dukhul al-qubur wa du'a'i li'ahliha.*

143. *Sunan al-Nasa'i, kitab al-jana'iz, bab kathrati dhikr al-mawt.*

is, the Prophet replied, "The wisest person is the one who remembers death the most and prepares themselves for what comes after it."[144] In another report, he warned, "The unfortunate person is the one who forgets the reality that one day they will lie in a grave and face what comes after it."[145] The Prophet cautioned his followers about the dangers of becoming overly attached to the finite world at the expense of their relationship with God. He highlighted humanity's insatiable greed in a poignant metaphor: "If a human being were to possess two valleys filled with riches, they would still desire a third. The only thing that truly fills the stomach of the human being is soil."[146] He acknowledged that his community would also face tests related to wealth and worldly attachments, expressing concern that this would be a major challenge for them after his death.[147]

The Prophet used a vivid analogy to underscore the insignificance of this world compared to the hereafter: "This world compared to the Hereafter is like one of you dipping their index finger into the ocean and observing how little water clings to it."[148] This metaphor emphasizes the fleeting and limited nature of worldly life, represented by the drop of water, in contrast to the vast and eternal reality of the hereafter, symbolized by the ocean. It serves as a powerful reminder to prioritize eternal life over temporary pleasures and to focus on one's relationship with God rather than worldly attachments. The Qur'an also praises those who maintain this balance: "They are not distracted—either by buying or selling—from the remembrance of God, the performance of prayer, and the giving of alms."[149] This verse encourages believers to integrate

---

144. *Sunan ibn Majah, kitab al-zuhd, bab dhikr al-mawt wa al-isti'dad lahu.*

145. *Jami' al-Tirmidhi, kitab sifat al-qiyama.*

146. *Sahih Muslim, kitab al-zakat, bab law anna liibn adam wadiyayn liabtagha thalithan.*

147. *Jami' al-Tirmidhi, kitab al-zuhd, bab ma ja'a 'anna fitnata hadhihi al-'umma fi al-mal.*

148. *Sahih al-Muslim, kitab al-jannah wa sifat na'imiha wa ahluha.*

149. Qur'an 24:37.

their worldly responsibilities with their spiritual obligations. It reminds them that no matter how busy their lives may be, their connection to God should remain at the center of their priorities.

The Prophet strongly encouraged his followers to attend the funerals of fellow believers and actively participate in all aspects of the process. While this practice provides support to the community during a time of grief, it is also regarded as a spiritual act. In one report, the Prophet said, "Whoever washes a deceased person, shrouds them, embalms them, carries them, offers the funeral prayer for them, and does not reveal what they have seen, will be cleansed of their sins, as pure as the day they were born."[150] Due to the Prophet's emphasis on the importance of funerals, attending them is considered a religious duty in Islamic jurisprudence. Funerals are communal events in Muslim communities, serving not only as a means of collective support but also as an opportunity to reflect on death and the transient nature of worldly life.

Remembering death and the hereafter is a prominent theme in Islamic literature on spirituality. Many Muslim theologians have regarded death as a key means of cultivating spiritual character. Nursi, for instance, wrote, "If you seek advice, death is sufficient. Indeed, one who reflects on death is freed from the love of the world and works earnestly for their Hereafter."[151] Nursi saw death not only as a powerful reminder to detach oneself from worldly attachments but also as a means to achieve sincerity in faith. He explained, "One of the most effective ways to attain and preserve sincerity is through contemplation of death (rabıta-i mevt). Just as worldly ambitions undermine sincerity and lead a person toward hypocrisy and attachment to the world, contemplation of death fosters a disdain for hypocrisy and cultivates sincerity. This involves reflecting on death, recognizing the fleeting nature of this world, and thereby freeing oneself from the deceptions of the soul."[152] Sincerity (*ikhlas*) in this context refers to performing actions

---

150. *Sunan ibn Majah, kitab al-jana'iz, bab ma ja'a fi ghusl al-mayyit*.

151. Nursi, *Mektubat*, 399.

152. Bediuzzaman Said Nursi, *Lem'alar* (Söz Basım, 2012), 272.

purely for the sake of God without being driven by worldly desires or the approval of others. To Nursi, contemplating death was an impactful way to attain this state of sincerity.

In Sufism, contemplation of death is an integral part of the spiritual journey. As part of this practice, disciples often imagine themselves as deceased, envisioning their bodies being washed and placed in the grave.[153] This exercise is intended to transform the self, shifting its focus away from the love of the material world and toward the eternal realities of the hereafter.

Death is also viewed in Islamic tradition as a gateway to eternal life and a means of union with God. The Prophet's final words before his passing were "O God, pardon me and let me be united with You as the highest companion." For him, death was not an end but a transition to be united with the Highest Companion, God. For those in the right spiritual state, death is not a source of fear but an anticipated meeting with their Creator.

Al-Ghazali, in his writings on death and the hereafter, draws a connection between people's attitudes toward death and their spiritual state. He identifies three groups in this context: sinners, the repentant, and Gnostics (*'arifs*):

1. Sinners: These individuals are deeply attached to the world and detest the thought of death because it interrupts their pursuit of worldly pleasures and disrupts their comfort. They hate the reality of death, seeing it as an unwelcome intrusion.
2. Repentant: This group remembers death but does not wish for it. They view their remaining time in life as an opportunity to perform more acts of worship and good deeds to attain a higher spiritual rank before meeting their Lord.
3. Gnostics (*'arifs*): These individuals constantly reflect on death, seeing it as the means to meet their Beloved, God. For them, death is not a source of dread but an eagerly awaited moment of reunion with their Highest Friend, God. They are indifferent to when

---

153. Nursi, *Lem'alar*, 273.

death comes, as they perceive it as the ultimate union with their Creator.¹⁵⁴

Among those who embraced this last approach to death was Mawlana Jalaluddin Rumi. In his poetry, Rumi referred to the day of his death as the moment of union and meeting with God.¹⁵⁵ He called it his "Wedding Night" (*Şeb-i Arus*), and each anniversary of his passing continues to be commemorated under this name.

Al-Ghazali also mentions a fourth group whose spiritual rank surpasses even the Gnostics. These individuals have no desire for either life or death. They accept God's decree with complete contentment and submission, leaving the matter entirely to God's will. For them, the essence of devotion lies in completely surrendering to God's plan, trusting in God's wisdom and timing.¹⁵⁶

Invocations in the Prophet's Spirituality

No discussion of the Prophet's spirituality would be complete without mentioning his supplications (*du'a's*). Muhammad was constantly mindful of God in every aspect of his life, offering daily invocations for nearly every good deed. He would express words of repentance (*tawba*) and seek refuge in God (*istighfar*) as many as seventy times a day. One of his frequent prayers was "O God, You are my Lord. There is none to be worshiped besides You. You have created me, and I am Your servant. I strive to abide by Your covenant and pledge as best I can. I seek refuge in You from the evil that I committed. I fully acknowledge Your favor upon me, and I fully confess my sin. So [please] forgive me, for there is none to forgive sins except You."¹⁵⁷

---

154. Al-Ghazali, *Ihya' 'Ulum al-Din*, 4:693.

155. Jalaluddin Rumi, "On the Day of My Death," in *Diwan-e Kabir*, trans. Ibrahim Gamard, Dar al-Masnavi, https://www.dar-al-masnavi.org/gh-0911.html.

156. Al-Ghazali, *Ihya' 'Ulum al-Din*, 4:693.

157. *Sahih al-Bukhari, kitab al-da'wat, bab ma yaqul idha asbaha*.

Another common supplication of the Prophet was:

> O God, forgive my mistakes, my ignorance, my extravagance in my affairs, and that which You are better aware of than I. O God, forgive the sins which I have done in seriousness and in jest, inadvertently and advertently; for I am indeed guilty of all that. O God, forgive that which I have committed in the past and that which I will commit in the future, that which I have done in secrecy and that which I have done openly and that which You are better aware of than I. You are the One Who brings matters forth and You are the One Who delays them, and You have Absolute Power over all things.[158]

Muhammad also frequently prayed, "O God, I ask You for Your love, the love of those who love You, and the deeds that will cause me to attain Your love. O God, make Your love more beloved to me than my own self, my family and cold [thirst-quenching] water."[159]

Muhammad offered supplications to God in all aspects of his daily life: when he ate and drank, when he went to sleep and woke up, when he entered and left his house, and when he got dressed. After eating, he would pray, "Praise be to God who feeds us, gives us drink, and has made us among those who submit to Him."[160] Before going to bed, his prayer was "In Your Name, my Lord, I lay myself down; and in Your Name, I rise. If You take my soul, have mercy on it, and if You return it to me, protect it as You protect Your righteous servants."[161] In times

---

158. *Sahih al-Bukhari, kitab al-da'wat, bab qawl al-nabiyy, salla allahu 'alayhi wa sallam, "Allahummaghfir li ma qaddamtu wa ma akhkhartu."*

159. *Jami' al-Tirmidhi, kitab al-da'wat, 'an rasul salla allahu 'alayhi wa sallam.*

160. *Sunan Abu Dawud, kitab al-ad'ama, bab ma yaqul al-rajul 'idha da'ima.*

161. *Sahih Muslim, kitab al-dhikr wa al-du'a' wa al-tawba al-istighfar, bab yaqul 'inda al-nawm wa 'akhdh al-madja'.*

of distress, he would often pray, "O Ever Living and Self-Sustaining Sustainer, I seek relief in Your mercy."[162]

Moderation in Spirituality

While remembering God and being mindful of Him were central to the Prophet's spirituality, he also practiced moderation in his spiritual practices. He encouraged his companions to be balanced in their worship and prayer, cautioning them against neglecting their familial responsibilities. Muhammad discouraged them from devoting all their time to worship and prayer, advising them to remain attentive to the needs of their family and fellow humans.

For instance, when the Prophet learned that Abdullah ibn Amr, one of his companions, had decided to spend his nights in prayer and his days in fasting, Muhammad advised him against such extreme devotion. He reminded Abdullah that his body, wife, and children also had rights over him, suggesting that excessive worship could negatively affect their well-being.[163] On another occasion, a group of men visited the Prophet's house, eager to learn more about spiritual practices. They felt their own efforts were insufficient and wanted to exceed even the Prophet's devotion. One of them declared, "I will pray throughout the night for the rest of my life." Another said, "I will fast every day of the year without breaking it." The third vowed, "I will avoid women and never marry." The Prophet responded, "I am more mindful of God than any of you. I fast and break my fast, I pray and I sleep, and I marry women."[164] He advised them to follow his example of balanced devotion.

Due to the Prophet's example, neither complete asceticism nor celibacy has ever been required for spiritual progress in Islam. In fact, many Muslim sages renowned for their piety and devotion were married and held professions, fully participating in everyday life. Ideal spirituality

---

162. *Jami' al-Tirmidhi, kitab al-da'wat 'an rasul salla allahu 'alayhi wa sallam.*

163. *Sahih al-Bukhari, kitab al-sawm, bab haqq al-ahl fi al-sawm.*

164. *Sahih al-Bukhari, kitab al-nikaah, bab al-targhib fi al-nikah.*

does not require a complete separation from the world. The Prophet not only advocated for moderation in spiritual practices but also stressed the importance of engaging in practices that align with human nature and can be maintained consistently. He advised, "Take up good deeds only as much as you are able, for the best deeds are those done regularly, even if they are few."[165] This teaching is reflected in several Qur'anic verses: "God wants ease for you, not hardship" and "God does not burden any soul with more than it can bear."[166]

Muhammad's Simplicity and Humility

As emphasized in the Introduction, good character is regarded as an integral aspect of a believer's piety. The Prophet's spirituality was closely intertwined with his moral character, which was evident in his exemplary personality. Muhammad lived a life of humility, residing in a simple clay house until his death. He would sleep on a straw mat, which would leave marks on his body. On one occasion, his close companion Umar saw the marks on his body and became emotional, shedding tears as he said, "O Messenger of God, the emperors of Byzantium and Persia enjoy luxurious lives, yet you, the Messenger of God, live like this." Umar implied that the Prophet deserved a more comfortable life. The Prophet replied, "Wouldn't you prefer that this world be theirs and the hereafter ours?"[167]

Muhammad ate very little, often having just dates and water for his meals. At home, he took part in household chores, including cleaning and sewing his own clothes. When a companion asked the Prophet's wife Aisha about his activities at home, she responded, "He did what any of you would do in your home. He mended sandals, patched garments,

---

165. *Sunan Ibn Majah, kitab al-zuhd, bab al-mudawama 'ala al-'amal.*

166. Qur'an 2:186.

167. *Sahih al-Bukhari, kitab al-tafsir, bab tabtaghi mardata azwajik.*

and sewed."[168] He hardly had two pairs of clothes, which he would wash himself.

Despite being the Messenger of God and the leader of his community, Muhammad remained profoundly humble in all aspects of his life. As both the Prophet and the leader of his society, he was accessible to everyone, including children, women, the elderly, and people with disabilities. Anas ibn Malik, a companion who served the Prophet for many years, narrated, "Even a little girl could take the Prophet's hand and lead him wherever she wished."[169] The Prophet was so accessible to his community that, at times, people unintentionally violated the proper etiquette in their interactions with him. Some would enter his home without permission and linger longer than was appropriate, while others would address him without the proper respect. In response, the Qur'an provided guidance to the believers on maintaining appropriate manners when interacting with the Prophet. For example, it states, "O believers! Do not enter the Prophet's dwellings for a meal unless you are invited. Do not come too early and wait for the meal to be prepared. But if you are invited, then enter at the proper time. Once you have eaten, disperse and do not stay for casual conversation. Such behavior offends the Prophet, though he is too shy to ask you to leave. But God is not shy of the truth."[170] Another verse advises believers on how to conduct themselves in the Prophet's presence: "O believers! Do not raise your voices above the voice of the Prophet, nor speak loudly to him as you do to one another, lest your deeds become void while you are unaware."[171] These verses emphasize the importance of showing respect and maintaining proper decorum in the Prophet's presence, highlighting the need for reverence and etiquette in interactions with him.

Muhammad consistently cared for the most vulnerable in the community and accepted invitations from people regardless of their status,

---

168. *Al-Adab al-Mufrad, kitab al-tasarruf al-'am, bab ma ya'mal al-rajul fi baytihi.*

169. *Sahih al-Bukhari, kitab al-adab, bab al-kibr.*

170. Qur'an 33:53.

171. Qur'an 49:2.

whether they were free or enslaved. On one occasion, the Prophet was walking with a nobleman who was considering becoming Muslim but was still uncertain. As they walked to the Prophet's house, an elderly woman stopped Muhammad, and he took the time to attentively listen to her and offer his help. When they arrived at the Prophet's home, the nobleman observed the simplicity of the surroundings. There was only a cushion, and the Prophet invited his guest to sit on the floor. The man's admiration for Muhammad's compassion and humility grew, and he ultimately embraced Islam.[172]

The Prophet would visit sick people in his community and attend funerals. When someone addressed him with grand titles like "our master" or "the best of us," he would respond, "O people, be mindful of God. Let not Satan deceive you. I am Muhammad, the son of Abdullah, the servant and messenger of God. I do not want to be placed in any position higher than what God has assigned to me."[173] He was also adamant about ensuring that he was not regarded as a divine figure. He instructed his companions, "Do not exaggerate in praising me as Christians do with Jesus, the son of Mary. I am merely the servant of God. Therefore, call me the servant of God and His messenger."[174] On one occasion, while leading a daily prayer, he inadvertently performed five cycles instead of the usual four. When his followers asked if he had added to the prayer, he replied, "I am a human being like you. Like you, I remember and forget."[175] This was a clear acknowledgment from the Prophet that making mistakes, even during rituals, is part of human nature, and he was no exception.

Due to his simplicity and humility, it was often difficult for strangers to distinguish Muhammad from his companions in a gathering. On one occasion, a man came to visit the Prophet while he was sitting among his

---

172. This was the story of Adiyy ibn Hatim. See Suruç, *Kainatın Efendisi*, 145–146.

173. *Musnad Ahmad*, 12579.

174. *Sahih al-Bukhari, kitab 'ahadith al-anbiya', bab khalq adam salawat allahi wa dhurriyyatihi.*

175. *Sahih Muslim, kitab al-masajid, bab al-sahw fi salat wa al-sujud lahu.*

companions in the mosque in Medina. The visitor couldn't recognize the Prophet and asked, "Who among you is Muhammad?"[176] Muhammad did not want to be treated like a king. On another occasion, a man who came to see the Messenger of God was so nervous in his presence that he began to shiver. The Prophet comforted him, saying, "Calm down! I am not a king. I am just the son of a woman from the tribe of Quraish who used to eat dried meat."[177] Muhammad also discouraged his companions from showing him excessive reverence. In one case, while he was leaning on his staff and speaking to them, they stood up out of respect. The Prophet then said, "Do not stand up for people as foreigners do to venerate one another."[178] Another striking example of the Prophet's humility was reported by his companion Abdullah ibn Masud. During the first major battle with the Meccans, the Battle of Badr, the Muslim community had limited resources, including transportation. Three men would share a single camel, taking turns to ride while the others walked. On the day of the battle, the Prophet was sharing a camel with two companions. When it was their turn to ride and his turn to walk, they offered to let him continue riding, saying, "We will walk and let you ride." The Prophet responded, "You are not stronger than me, and I am not less in need of reward than you."[179] Here, the Messenger of God emphasized that he was fully capable of walking, and though he was the Prophet, he still sought spiritual rewards from God for his good deeds.

The Prophet lived a life much like any other member of his community. He experienced moments of joy and sadness, and there were times when he felt upset or angry. He was engaged in the everyday matters of life, had friends, was married, and had children and grandchildren. Like many people, he sometimes not only had conflicts with his spouses

---

176. *Sahih al-Bukhari, kitab al-'ilm, bab ma ja'a fi al-'ilm.*

177. *Sunan Ibn Majah, kitab al-ad'amah, bab al-qadid.*

178. *Sunan Abi Dawud, kitab al-adab, bab fi qiyam al-rajul lirrajul.*

179. *Musnad Ahmad*, 3901.

but also found joy and peace with them.[180] Still, despite his simplicity and humility, no leader was obeyed the way the followers of the Prophet obeyed him.

Muhammad's Mercy and Compassion

The Qur'an repeatedly refers to God as the Most Compassionate (*al-Rahman*) and the Most Merciful (*al-Rahim*). God says in the Qur'an, "My mercy encompasses my wrath."[181] God's mercy infuses the world,[182] and Muhammad is a central manifestation of this mercy. Muhammad exemplified the virtues of mercy and compassion in the highest form, with the Qur'an referencing him as a "mercy to the world."[183] His firm commitment to his mission stemmed from his deep compassion for people. At a time when humanity was shrouded in darkness, his teachings became a beacon of light, bringing hope and peace to many.

Muhammad emphasized God's compassion and forgiveness toward God's servants. He viewed the compassion in creation as the manifestation of God's mercy. In one narrative, the Prophet observed a woman who had been separated from her child. She was embracing and feeding every child she encountered on the street. The Prophet asked his companions, "Would this woman ever throw her child into the fire?" They replied that she would never do so. The Prophet then said, "Understand that God's mercy and compassion for His servants are far greater than this woman's compassion for her child."[184]

In several hadiths, the Prophet encouraged his followers to show compassion toward all creation, saying, "If you are merciful, God will be merciful to you. Show mercy to the creatures on earth, and those in

---

180. *Hadislerle İslam*, 6:279.

181. Qur'an 7:156.

182. Qur'an 30:50.

183. Qur'an 21:107.

184. *Sahih al-Bukhari, kitab al-'adab, bab rahmah al-walad wa taqbilihi wa mu'anaqatihi*.

heaven will show mercy to you."[185] On one occasion, a Bedouin saw the Prophet kissing his grandsons and remarked, "We don't kiss or hug our children." The Prophet responded, "What can I do if God has removed mercy from your heart?"[186] Even during prayers, Muhammad urged his followers to consider the most vulnerable people among them. He advised those leading the five daily prayers to keep them brief, noting that in the congregation, there might be weak, elderly, and sick people. However, when believers pray on their own, they are free to extend their prayers as long as they wish.[187] If the Prophet heard a child crying while leading the prayer, he would shorten it out of consideration.

The Prophet's mercy extended not only to humans but also to all living creatures, including animals. In a hadith, he stated, "Whoever shows mercy even to a sparrow, God will be merciful to him on the Day of Judgment." Another hadith reads, "A good deed done to an animal is like a good deed done to a human being, and an act of cruelty to an animal is as bad as cruelty to a human being." When one of the Prophet's companions asked if there would be any reward for caring for animals, Muhammad replied, "There is a reward for serving any living being."[188] On one occasion, the Prophet observed a woman who, despite having committed many sins, showed mercy to a thirsty dog by giving it water. He said that this act of kindness would lead her to paradise. In another instance, he warned that someone who killed a cat would face punishment in hell.

Muhammad's Patience and Forgiveness

Muhammad not only exemplified mercy and compassion but also embodied the virtue of patience throughout his life. Raised as an

---

185. *Jami' al-Tirmidhi, kitab al-birr wa al-salah, bab ma ja'a fi rahma al-muslimin.*

186. *Sahih al-Bukhari, kitab al-adab, bab rahmah al-walad wa taqbilihi wa mu'anaqatihi.*

187. *Sahih al-Bukhari, kitab al-adhan, bab idha salla linafsihi fayudawwil ma shaa.*

188. *Sahih al-Bukhari, kitab al-masaqah, bab fadl saqi al-ma'.*

orphan, he knew the struggles of poverty and endured the loss of most of his children. After receiving revelation, he faced isolation, insults, attacks, and persecution. He was even expelled from his homeland. Despite these hardships, he responded with firm patience. He also encouraged his companions to practice patience, living out the Qur'anic teaching to "endure patiently whatever befalls you."[189]

Muhammad's virtue of patience was paired with forgiveness. He was known as the most forgiving among his followers. The Qur'an encourages those who have been wronged to forgive, saying, "But if you overlook their offenses, forgive them, and pardon them, then truly God is Forgiving, Merciful."[190] The Qur'an also teaches that "the recompense for an evil act is an evil like it. But whoever forgives and seeks reconciliation, his reward is with God. Indeed, He does not love the wrongdoers."[191] Muhammad lived by this principle throughout his life. His wife Aisha reported that Muhammad never responded to evil with evil; he was forgiving and did not dwell on people's shortcomings.[192] In another hadith, she mentioned that the Prophet never punished anyone over personal grievances.[193] Even when he triumphed over his opponents, he forgave those who had persecuted him and forced him from his homeland, praying to God to guide his enemies rather than seeking their destruction.

Muhammad's Courage

For Muslims, the Prophet Muhammad is considered the ultimate embodiment of courage. Courage is a fundamental virtue emphasized across various religious traditions and philosophies. It is often defined

---

189. Qur'an 31:17.

190. Qur'an 64:14.

191. Qur'an 42:40.

192. *Jami' al-Tirmidhi, kitab al-birr wa al-silah, bab ma ja'a fi khuluqi nabiyy salla allahu 'alayhi wa sallam.*

193. *Sahih al-Bukhari, kitab al-hudud, bab kam al-ta'zir wa al-'adab.*

as mental or moral strength to venture, persevere, and withstand danger, fear, or difficulty. Aristotle described courage as the marker of moral excellence, a balance between recklessness and cowardice. In Islam, courage is seen as a reflection of integrity and a commitment to standing for justice. The Qur'an highlights courage as a key characteristic of believers. For example, one verse states, "Those whose faith only increased when people said, 'Fear your enemy: they have gathered a great army against you,' and who replied, 'God is sufficient for us: He is the best protector.'"[194] This verse implies that the believers were not intimidated by their enemy's great army due to their courage and unwavering faith in God.

Despite facing marginalization, persecution, attacks, and intimidation, the Prophet remained steadfast in his mission. Rather than staying in the safety of the rear, he fought alongside his companions, risking his life and sustaining injuries in battle. His cousin and companion Ali reported, "When the danger intensified and the battle raged, we would seek protection by the Messenger of God. None of us would be closer to the enemy than him."[195]

One notable instance of the Prophet's courage occurred during his journey to Mecca when he and Abu Bakr were hiding from their pursuers in a cave. As the enemy approached the cave entrance, Abu Bakr became anxious, fearing they would be discovered. The Prophet reassured him, saying, "Do not worry, God is with us." The Qur'an mentions this occasion: "Even if you do not help the Prophet, God helped him when the disbelievers drove him out: when the two of them were in the cave, he [Muhammad] said to his companion, 'Do not worry, indeed God is with us,' and then God sent down His tranquility upon him, supported him with forces invisible to you, and thwarted the disbelievers' plans. God's plan is higher: God is Mighty and Wise."[196]

---

194. Qur'an 3: 173.

195. *Musnad Ahmad*, 1347.

196. Qur'an 9:40.

Another example of his courage was when he was resting under a tree and awoke to find one of his fierce enemies standing over him with a drawn sword. The enemy asked, "Who will save you from me now?" The Prophet calmly responded, "God." His firm faith and composure intimidated the enemy, causing him to drop his sword. The Prophet then took the sword, asked him the same question, and when the man pleaded for forgiveness, the Prophet graciously forgave him and let him go.[197]

Muhammad, the Model of Justice and Equality

Embodying the Qur'anic teaching that piety is the standard for "being superior in the eyes of God,"[198] Muhammad discouraged his followers from discriminating against anyone based on race, rank, or gender. In pre-Islamic Arabian society, people were often judged by their physical strength, and women were considered weaker and therefore inferior to men. Forced marriages were common, polygamy was widespread, female infanticide was prevalent, and women had no rights to own property or receive an education. Muhammad transformed society, elevating the status of women and challenging these norms. Despite slavery being deeply entrenched during his time, Muhammad urged his followers to "dress their slaves in the same clothing they wear and feed them the same food they eat."[199] He also emphasized that slaves should be treated as equals before God, standing shoulder to shoulder in the same prayer line. When a prominent companion discriminated against a Black Ethiopian follower, Muhammad rebuked him for exhibiting the attitudes of *jahiliyya*, or the ignorance of the pre-Islamic period.[200]

---

197. *Sahih al-Bukhari, kitab al-jihad, bab man 'allaqa sayfahu bilshajari fi al-safar 'inda al-qa'ilah.*

198. Qur'an 49:13.

199. *Sahih al-Bukhari, kitab al-iman, bab al-ma'asi min 'amr al-jahiliyya.*

200. *Sahih al-Bukhari, kitab al-iman, bab al-ma'asi min 'amr al-jahiliyya.*

In a short period, Muhammad succeeded in reforming Arabian society in many ways. Before his time, Arabs strictly adhered to tribal norms. Muhammad introduced laws and justice that applied to everyone. He emphasized that even if an injustice went unnoticed by others, accountability still exists, as God always knows what is in a person's heart.[201]

Conclusion

The Prophet was a living embodiment of the Qur'an, with a spiritual life deeply rooted in its teachings. He modeled a life of piety that is pleasing to God. Key aspects of his spirituality included the five daily prayers, night prayers, fasting, pilgrimage, contemplating God's creation, reciting the Qur'an, offering supplications, remembering death and the afterlife, and reflecting on the transient nature of the world. While Muhammad had his personal religious practices, his spiritual life was communal. His spirituality was closely linked to his noble personality, characterized by simplicity, humility, generosity, forgiveness, justice, and patience. Muhammad's spiritual example also helped form a devout community of companions, which will be the focus of our next chapter.

---

201. Qur'an 3:29.

CHAPTER THREE

The Prophet's Spiritual Companions

After the Prophet Muhammad, the most important and respected individuals in Islamic tradition are his companions, known as *sahaba* (singular *sahib*). The root of the word (*sahiba*) means *to be or become a companion, associate, or friend*. As a term, it refers to any Muslim who met the Prophet Muhammad in person. By the time of his death, the Prophet had thousands of followers.[1]

The earliest companions of Muhammad were particularly renowned for their extraordinary sacrifices, firm commitment to his teachings, and exemplary embodiment of his spiritual practices. They not only followed the Prophet's example but also transmitted his teachings and practices to subsequent generations. Both the Qur'an and collections of hadith frequently highlight the virtues, dedication, and piety of the Prophet's companions. Reading the stories of the companions plays a vital role in the spiritual formation of Muslims. Moreover, Islamic tradition includes terms for those who had close ties to the companions: *Tabi'un* (literally *the followers* or *successors*) refers to Muslims who met the companions, while *tabi'u al-tabi'in* (*the successors of the successors*) refers to those who met the *tabi'un*. Any individual who was close to the Prophet or his companions holds a highly esteemed position among Muslims, and following their example is considered an essential element of spiritual practice.

---

1. There is no consensus among scholars regarding the exact number of the Prophet's companions. However, historical accounts indicate that more than 10,000 companions accompanied him during the conquest of Mecca. Additionally, it is reported that over 100,000 Muslims performed the pilgrimage with the Prophet during his Farewell Hajj.

In this chapter, we will explore the lives of some of the Prophet's earliest and closest companions, their dedication to the faith, and their reception in Islamic tradition. The Prophet cared deeply for his companions, guiding them through his living example and making every effort to ensure they would have a good life both in this world and in the hereafter. The Qur'an, for example, describes this aspect of the Prophet's character: "A Messenger has come to you from among yourselves. Your suffering distresses him; he is deeply concerned for you and full of kindness and mercy towards the believers."[2] The Prophet visited his companions when they were ill, attended their funerals, and was attentive to their concerns. He frequently sought their counsel and turned to them during difficult and stressful times. Whenever he met his companions, he would hug them and offer a prayer (*du'a'*) for them. Muhammad also expressed his love for the followers who would come after him. In a report, he said in the presence of his companions, "I wish I could meet my brothers." The companions asked, "Are we not your brothers?" The Prophet replied, "You are my companions, but my brothers are those who have faith in me without having seen me."[3] The Prophet was referring to the future generations of Muslims who, despite not witnessing him firsthand, would believe in his message and hold deep love for him.

The Qur'an on the Virtues of the Prophet's Companions

The companions were not only praised by the Prophet but also frequently acknowledged in the Qur'an for their commitment to the new faith and their exemplary character. The Islamic scripture, for example, describes the companions as "the best community ever raised

---

2. Qur'an 9:128.

3. *Musnad Ahmad*, 12579.

for humanity" and those who "promote what is right, prevent what is wrong, and believe in God."⁴

One of the most powerful examples of the companions' love and dedication to the Prophet is the story of the *muhajirun*, the "emigrants" who migrated from Mecca to Medina to freely practice their faith. These companions of the Prophet endured persecution and torture for their faith and spiritual practices. They left everything behind and migrated to Medina to follow Muhammad's message, driven by their devotion to God and their love for God's messenger. The Qur'an points to their sacrifices, promising them a great reward in the hereafter: "As for those who emigrated in God's cause after being wronged, We shall give them a good home in this world, but the reward of the Hereafter will be far greater, if they only knew it."⁵

In another verse, the Qur'an recognizes the offerings made by the "helpers" (*ansar*) in Medina, who warmly welcomed the emigrants from Mecca and generously shared what they had with their fellow believers. The Qur'an describes the helpers as follows: "Those who were already firmly established in their homes [in Medina], and firmly rooted in faith, show love for those who migrated to them for refuge and harbor no desire in their hearts for what has been given to them. They give them preference over themselves, even if they too are in need: those who are saved from their own souls' greed are truly successful."⁶ According to hadith reports, this verse was revealed following an incident in Medina. The Prophet entrusted a poor man from the *muhajirun* to one of the *ansars*. When the companion brought the poor man to his home, he asked his wife if they had any food. She replied, "We have nothing except the children's food." He then said, "Put the children to sleep, and bring me the food. When you serve it, turn off the lamp." This way, the guest would not understand that the host family is in a difficult situation. The companion offered all they had to their guest. The

---

4. Qur'an 3:110.

5. Qur'an 16:41.

6. Qur'an 59:9.

next morning, he brought the man back to the Messenger of God. The Prophet said, "Truly, the dwellers of the heavens are amazed at what you two have done." It was after this that the verse was revealed.[7] The Qur'an praises the believers with this spirit, giving as those "who give from what they love."[8]

In another passage, the Qur'an celebrates both the emigrants and the helpers: "As for the foremost—the first of the Emigrants and the Helpers—and those who follow them in righteousness, God is pleased with them, and they are pleased with Him. He has prepared for them Gardens beneath which rivers flow, where they will dwell forever. That is the ultimate triumph."[9] Here, the revelation assures both groups of their blessed status, even stating that heavenly rewards are stored up for them.

The Qur'an also emphasizes the companions' spiritual practices, including their devotion to prayer: "Muhammad is the Messenger of God. And those with him are firm against the disbelievers and compassionate with one another. You see them bowing and prostrating in prayer, seeking God's bounty and pleasure. The signs of their devotion are evident on their faces from the marks of prostration."[10]

Here the companions are said to have visible marks of their piety on their bodies, with "signs of their devotion ... evident on their faces" from their repeated prostrations on the ground during prayer. Some scholars interpret the mark on their faces as a reflection of the beauty radiating from them, referencing the hadith of the Prophet: "Whoever prays much at night, his face will be beautiful by day."[11] This mark is also understood as a distinguishable sign on the faces of believers on

---

7. Joseph E. B. Lumbard, *Commentary on Surat al-Hashr,* in *The Study Quran: A New Translation and Commentary,* ed. Nasr et al. (HarperOne, 2015), 1353.

8. Qur'an 2:177; 76:8.

9. Qur'an 9:100.

10. Qur'an 48:29.

11. Joseph E. B. Lumbard, *Commentary on Surat al-Fath,* in *The Study Quran: A New Translation and Commentary,* ed. Nasr et al. (HarperOne, 2015), 1256.

the Day of Resurrection. Another interpretation suggests "it is a light upon their faces, resulting from their humility."[12]

Who Were the First Followers of the Prophet?

Most of the Prophet's early followers were young, with only a few over the age of thirty. Some came from prominent families, while others were from humble backgrounds. However, due to their young age, many were dependent on their families and faced persecution from their own relatives. Among the first fifty Muslims, about 30 percent were women, and 30 percent were slaves, both men and women. Below are portraits of some of Muhammad's early companions.[13]

Khadija bint Khuwaylid

Khadija was a highly respected and successful businesswoman in Mecca. Before the beginning of Muhammad's prophethood, she employed him to manage her trade caravans. Impressed by his success and character and encouraged by those in her circle, Khadija proposed marriage to Muhammad. Khadija was fifteen years older than Muhammad, and together they had six children.

When Muhammad received his first revelation, Khadija wholeheartedly supported him. Her immediate response was "I testify that you are the Messenger of God." Khadija became the first Muslim and the Prophet's earliest follower. She and the Prophet often prayed together, whether at home, at the Kaaba during quiet moments, or on the outskirts of Mecca. Khadija sacrificed everything to support the Prophet, standing by him against the oppression of the Meccans. This support came at a cost. When their opponents boycotted the followers of Islam, she used all her wealth to support the community. Due to her

---

12. Lumbard, *Commentary on Surat al-Fath*, 1256.

13. For a study on the demography of the first Muslims, see Abdurrahman Kurt, "Demografik Değişkenler Açısından İlk Müslümanlar," *Uludağ İlahiyat Fakültesi Dergisi* 18, no. 2 (2009): 27–41.

devotion and spirituality, it is reported that the archangel Gabriel asked the Prophet to convey God's greetings, along with his own, to Khadija and to share the good news of her reward: a beautiful mansion in heaven. Gabriel said, "When she comes to you, offer her greetings from her Lord, the Exalted and Glorious, and from me, and give her glad tidings of a palace of jewels in Paradise, where there is neither noise nor toil."[14] In another tradition, the Prophet stated, "Maryam bint Imran was the best woman of her time, and Khadija is the best woman of our time."[15]

The year of Khadija's death is remembered as the Year of Sadness in the Prophet's life, as her passing left an indelible mark on him. Because of Khadija's sacrifices for Islam during difficult times, the Prophet remembered her with profound love and gratitude throughout his life. This devotion was so strong that his wife Aisha would sometimes become upset and ask why he often spoke of an old woman who had passed away. The Prophet would explain that when no one else believed in his message, it was Khadija who sincerely accepted it; she supported him when others rejected him, and when no one else contributed to the cause of Islam, it was Khadija who generously gave her wealth and resources. Additionally, Khadija was the mother of his children. For these reasons, she held a special place in the Prophet's heart, and to him, she was the best of all women.

Khadija's legacy endures today among Muslim women who admire her example and devotion. Her influence is so great that *Khadija* remains one of the most popular names for Muslim women.

Abu Bakr

Abu Bakr was the first male adult to embrace Islam and played a significant role in influencing other key figures to convert as well. Abu Bakr was a merchant who dedicated his entire fortune to supporting the early Muslims. Many slaves were facing severe torture and persecution from

---

14. *Sahih al-Muslim, kitab al-fada'il wa al-sahaba, bab fada'il Khadija.*

15. *Sahih al-Bukhari, kitab 'ahadith, al-'anbiya'.*

their owners for following Muhammad's message, and Abu Bakr used his wealth to buy their freedom. Among those he liberated were Bilal ibn Rabah and his mother. The Prophet held Abu Bakr in deep affection and saw him almost every day.

Due to his unconditional support for the Prophet, especially during challenging times, Abu Bakr is known among Muslims as *al-Siddiq*, meaning *the truthful*. This title was particularly associated with the Prophet's ascension to heaven (*mi'raj*). When news spread that Muhammad claimed to have taken a miraculous journey from Mecca to Jerusalem and then to heaven, many people doubted him, and even some of his followers were perplexed. His opponents used this event to discredit him. However, Abu Bakr immediately and unhesitatingly affirmed his belief in the Prophet's words, saying, "If Muhammad said it, then it is true." This firm and immediate endorsement of the Prophet's message earned him the title of "al-Siddiq."[16]

When the Prophet decided to emigrate from Mecca to Medina, he invited Abu Bakr to join him on the journey. To evade their enemies, they hid together in a cave. As their Meccan pursuers drew closer to the cave's entrance, Abu Bakr grew anxious, but the Prophet reassured him. The Qur'an refers to this moment: "Remember when the disbelievers drove him out, the second of the two. When they were in the cave, he said to his companion, 'Do not worry; truly, God is with us.' Then God sent down His tranquility upon him and supported him with forces you did not see."[17] Due to his companionship with the Prophet during this critical moment, Abu Bakr is known as the companion of the cave (*yari gar*) in Turkish and Persian literature.

Abu Bakr is also well-known for his piety. On one occasion, he asked the Prophet if the late evening prayers could be held earlier so they could devote more time to night prayers. In another instance, the Prophet asked his companions, "Who among you is fasting today? Who has attended a funeral prayer? Who has fed a poor person? Who has

---

16. Ibn Ishaq, *The Life of Muhammad*, 181.

17. Qur'an 9:40.

visited a sick person?" Abu Bakr answered affirmatively to each question. The Prophet then remarked, "Whoever does these deeds will enter heaven."[18]

When the pilgrimage to Mecca became obligatory for the Muslim community in the ninth year of their time in Medina, the Prophet appointed Abu Bakr to lead the pilgrimage.[19] In the final days of the Prophet's life, as he fell ill, he asked Abu Bakr to lead the community in prayer. After the Prophet's death, many companions were overwhelmed with the reality that the Prophet, too, was mortal. Abu Bakr addressed them and reminded them of the Qur'anic teaching: "If anyone worshiped Muhammad, know that he has died. But those who worship God know that God is eternal."[20]

After the Prophet's death, Abu Bakr became his first successor (r. 632–634) and is widely recognized as one of the four "rightly-guided" caliphs (*al-khulafa al-rashidun*). Abu Bakr also played a crucial role in the preservation of the Qur'an. During his reign, many of the Prophet's companions who had memorized the Qur'an (*huffaz*) died in wars, making the preservation of the Qur'anic verses a pressing concern. Under his leadership, all the verses of the Qur'an were collected into a single volume. Additionally, some of the hadiths attributed to the Prophet were narrated by Abu Bakr.

Due to his significant role in the early years of Islam, Abu Bakr and his virtues are frequently highlighted in Islamic literature. A poem by the Prophet's poet, Hassan ibn Thabit, describes Abu Bakr with these words:

> If you remember a truthful person and saddened
> Then remember your brother Abu Bakr for his noble deeds
> He was the best of creation after the Prophet
> The most just and pious.

---

18. *Sahih al-Muslim, kitab fada'il al-sahaba, bab min fada'il 'abi bakr al-siddiq.*

19. Ibn Ishaq, *The Life of Muhammad*, 617.

20. Qur'an 3:144.

He was truthful to the cause that he shouldered
He was the first to accept the message of the Prophet
He stood by the Prophet in the most dangerous times,
When the enemies surrounded the mountain and climbed it,
He was the second of the two in the cave at the top of the mountain.

When people witnessed his love for the Prophet,
They realized that no one could match this hero![21]

Abu Bakr's legacy is celebrated among Muslims today. He is remembered as a pious, righteous, truthful, and generous companion of the Prophet. Having memorized the entire Qur'an, he embodied its teachings and followed the Prophet's example in his life. Several major Sufi orders trace their spiritual lineage and connection to the Prophet through Abu Bakr, including the Naqshbandi order, the most influential Sufi order in Islamic history. Abu Bakr is buried beside the Prophet in Medina, and today, when Muslims visit Muhammad's tomb, they also pay their respects at Abu Bakr's grave. The interiors of many mosques built during the Ottoman period and in modern Türkiye feature the calligraphic names of the Prophet's companions, with Abu Bakr's name being the most prominent.

Ali ibn Abi Talib

Ali ibn Abi Talib was the Prophet's cousin, as well as one of his earliest followers. Shortly after the first revelation, Ali saw the Prophet and Khadija praying together and asked what they were doing. Muhammad explained the new revelation he had received. Ali, unsure of what to make of it, mentioned that he needed to consult his father, Abu Talib. Since the message had not yet been made public, Muhammad asked Ali either to accept it or to keep what he had seen to himself. The next day,

---

21. Jamal al-Din Abi al-Faraj Ibn al-Jawzi, *Sifat al-Safwa*, ed. Khalid Mustafa Tartusi (Dar al-kitab al-arabi, 2012), 1:94–95.

Ali returned to the Prophet and said, "God did not ask my father when He created me, so I do not need to ask my father to worship God."[22] Ali was around ten years old when he accepted Islam, making him the first child to become a follower of the Prophet. He would go on to become one of the most influential figures in Islamic history.

In a powerful testament to his sacrifice, loyalty, and bravery, Ali played a crucial and risky role in the Prophet's emigration from Mecca. Concerned about the growing influence of Islam and Muhammad's presence in Mecca, the Prophet's opponents plotted to assassinate him while he slept. On learning of the plan, Muhammad decided to emigrate to Medina, but needed a strategy to ensure his safe escape. He turned to Ali, asking him to sleep in his bed to create the illusion that Muhammad was still in the house. Without hesitation, Ali agreed, fully aware of the life-threatening risk. That night, Muhammad successfully fled unnoticed. When the assassins stormed the house, they discovered Ali in the bed instead of the Prophet.[23] Ali later joined Muhammad in Medina.

Several hadiths and events highlight the special relationship between the Prophet and Ali. In one hadith, the Prophet said, "I am the house of wisdom, and Ali is its gate."[24] In another, he stated, "For whoever I am his *mawla* (close friend), then Ali is his *mawla*."[25] During a major expedition, the Prophet left Ali in Medina to represent him. When Ali expressed his disappointment about not participating, the Prophet reassured him, saying, "You are to me as Aaron (Harun) was

---

22. Ibn Ishaq, *The Life of Muhammad*, 114–115, and Suruç, *Kainatın Efendisi*, 166.

23. Ibn Ishaq, *The Life of Muhammad*, 222–223.

24. *Jami' al-Tirmidhi, kitab al-manaqib*. In another version of this narration, the Prophet is reported to have said, "I am the city of knowledge, and Ali is its gate." For a detailed analysis of this hadith, see Seyit Avci, "'Ben ilim şehriyim, Ali de onun kapısıdır' hadisi üzerine," *Marife* 3 (2004): 371–381.

25. *Jami' al-Tirmidhi, kitab al-manaqib, bab manaqib Ali ibn Abi Talib*. The word *mawla* also carries the connotations of *leader, protector,* and *master*.

to Moses (Musa), except that there is no prophet after me."[26] Ali also served as one of the Prophet's scribes, being one of the few followers who knew how to read and write. Ali later married the Prophet's daughter Fatima, the Prophet's only surviving child, through whom his lineage would continue. Following the Prophet's death, it was Ali who washed and prepared his body for the funeral prayer and burial. He became the fourth successor (*khalifa*) after the Prophet.

Ali is known for his sound judgment, deep knowledge, piety, and sincere faith. Because of his status as an important pious figure, several collections of supplications are attributed to him, one of which is *al-Jawshan al-Kabir* (*The Great Armor*), an invocation that includes 1,001 names and attributes of God. This prayer is particularly known for its protective qualities, thus providing the prayer its name. Each section begins with the Qur'anic phrase "in the name of God, the Most Merciful, the Most Compassionate" in Arabic, which is known as *basmala*, and concludes with a phrase glorifying God and seeking His mercy. The first section of the *Jawshan* begins as follows:

> In the Name of God, the Merciful, the Compassionate
> O God! I call upon You by Your Names:
> O God; Most Merciful;
> All-Compassionate;
> All-Knowing;
> Forbearing;
> Mighty;
> All-Wise;
> Pre-eternal;
> Everlasting;
> Most Generous
> Glory be to You, free from all faults and without partner!

---

26. *Sahih al-Bukhari, kitab al-maghazi, bab ghazwa tabuk wahya ghazwa al-'usra* and *Jami' al-Tirmidhi, kitab al-manaqib*.

There is no god but You!
Grant us mercy, mercy, and deliver us from the Hellfire![27]

Many Muslims in the Shiite community and Türkiye recite the *Jawshan* daily. Invoking the divine names and attributes is a central element of Islamic spirituality, serving as a means of remembering God. In several hadiths, the Prophet emphasizes the spiritual rewards of learning and reflecting on God's names.[28] The Qur'an also highlights that God remembers those who remember God.[29] In many Sufi orders, invoking specific names of God is an integral part of a disciple's daily rituals. It is widely believed that remembering God through God's names brings peace and tranquility to the hearts of believers. Al-Ghazali wrote a book on the names of God, in which he explains their meanings and spiritual significance.[30] He underscores the importance of embodying these divine attributes in one's life. For example, since God is the Just, believers are encouraged to strive for justice in their actions. Similarly, as God is the Most Generous, people are urged to emulate God's generosity, and because God is the Compassionate, they should demonstrate mercy and kindness in their lives. Through this practice, believers seek to align their character with the divine attributes, deepening their spiritual connection with God.

Another supplication attributed to Ali is *Qasida al-Jaljalutiya* (the Unique Praise), a mystical prayer that praises God through God's names. In one section, Ali addresses God with these words:

In an ocean of dangers, keep me safe and guide me to a peaceful shore.

---

27. For a collection of invocations that also includes *Jawshan*, see *Mealli Büyük Cevşen* (Hayrat Neşriyat, 2015), 50–97.

28. *Sahih al-Bukhari, kitab al-da'wat, bab lillahi miatu ismin ghayra wahidin.*

29. Qur'an 2:152.

30. Al-Ghazali, *The Ninety Nine Beautiful Names of God*, trans. David B. Burrel and Nazih Daher (Islamic Text Society, 2007).

You are my refuge, and with Your help, all difficulties can be overcome!

Bless us with Your mercy like a shower of rain,
Even if people are excessively sinful, You are still their only hope.[31]

Because of its spiritual significance, many scholars, including Al-Ghazali and Ibn Arabi (d. 1240), wrote commentaries on Ali's *Jaljalutiyya*. It is reported that Ali learned both the *Jawshan* and *Jaljalutiyya* prayers from the Prophet.[32]

One of the most renowned works attributed to Ali is *Nahjul Balagha*, a collection of his sermons, letters, and well-known sayings and statements. Below are a few excerpts from *Nahjul Balagha*:

> The sin that displeases you is better in the view of God than the virtue that makes you proud.[33]
>
> Contentment is wealth that does not diminish.[34]
>
> If you are met with a greeting, give better greetings in return. If a hand of help is extended to you, do a better favor in return, although the credit will remain with the one who was the first.[35]

---

31. For *Qasida al-Jaljalutiya*, see *Mealli Büyük Cevşen*, 238–250.

32. Ahmed Ziyâeddin Gümüşhanevî (d. 1894), a prominent Ottoman Sufi scholar, included al-Ghazali's commentary on the *Jaljalutiyya* in his *Mecmuatü'l-Ahzab*, a collection of invocations recited within Sufi orders. Through Gümüşhanevi's work, some of the supplications attributed to Ali spread throughout the Ottoman Empire. Another late Ottoman scholar who incorporated both the *Jaljalutiyya* and *Jawshan* prayers into his daily invocations was Bediuzzaman Said Nursi (d. 1960). In his *Sikke-i Tasdik-i Gaybi*, Nursi frequently referenced the works of Imam Ali, as well as al-Ghazali's commentary on the *Jaljalutiyya*.

33. Ali ibn Abi Talib, *Nahjul Balagha*, ed. Yasin T. Al. Jiouri (Tahrike Tarsile, 2009), 840. I revised the translation for more accessibility.

34. Ali, *Nahjul Balagha*, 841.

35. Ali, *Nahjul Balagha*, 842.

The people of the world are like travelers who are being carried while they are asleep.[36]

Each breath taken by a man is a step towards his death.[37]

Remove evil from the chest of others by eradicating it from your own.[38]

One who is not saved by patience will be finished by impatience.[39]

Some people worship God out of their desire (to worship Him). Such is the worship of traders. Some people worship God out of fear of Him; such is the worship of slaves. And some people worship God to thank Him; such is the worship of the free.[40]

If a person has a good idea about you, make his idea come true.[41]

People are enemies of what they do not know.[42]

Backbiting is the tool of the helpless.[43]

Ali holds a significant place in Sufism, being the second most important spiritual figure after the Prophet. Major Sufi orders link the lineage of their founders to the Prophet Muhammad, and some of them make this connection through Ali. For example, the spiritual lineage of the guides

---

36. Ali, *Nahjul Balagha*, 842.

37. Ali, *Nahjul Balagha*, 842.

38. Ali, *Nahjul Balagha*, 865.

39. Ali, *Nahjul Balagha*, 865.

40. Ali, *Nahjul Balagha*, 871.

41. Ali, *Nahjul Balagha*, 873

42. Ali, *Nahjul Balagha*, 921.

43. Ali, *Nahjul Balagha*, 927.

in the Qadiriyya, one of the most influential Sufi orders, founded in the twelfth century, traces back to the Prophet through Ali.

Ali is also a significant figure in Rumi's *Masnavi*. Some of the titles Rumi uses for Ali include *the brave lion (haydar-e karrar)*, *the chosen one (murtaza)*, *the lion of God (asadullah)*, *the lion of truth (shir-e haq)*, and *the divine lion (shir-e rabbani)*. In the opening lines of one of his narratives about Ali, Rumi emphasizes Ali's sincerity:

> Learn how to act sincerely from Ali
> Know that the Lion of God (Ali) was purged of (all) deceit.[44]

When asked by his enemy why he put down the sword, Ali answered (in Rumi's words):

> He said, "I am wielding the sword for God's sake
> I am the servant of God, I am not under the command of the body
>
> I am the Lion of God, I am not the lion of passion
> My deed bears witness to my religion.[45]

Throughout the text, Rumi highlights Ali's virtues, such as his knowledge, piety, devotion, trust in God, humility, courage, sincerity, compassion, generosity, and commitment to justice.

In discussing Ali's sincere faith, Rumi shares a story: During a fierce battle, Ali, well-known for his unmatched bravery and strength, faced a formidable enemy warrior. After an intense struggle, Ali subdued his opponent and was prepared to deliver the final blow. However, in a final act of defiance, the defeated warrior spat in Ali's face. While such an

---

44. Jalaluddin Rumi, *The Mathnavi of Jalalu'ddin Rumi*, trans. Reynold A. Nicholson (Cambridge University Press, 1926), book 1, 3700–3724.

45. Rumi, *The Mathnavi of Jalalu'ddin Rumi*, book 1, 3775–3799.

act could have easily incited anger in most, Ali responded differently. He paused and lowered his sword. The astonished warrior, expecting death, was puzzled by Ali's sudden change in behavior. He asked why Ali had hesitated to kill him, especially when victory was already his. Ali responded with profound wisdom and humility: "I was about to kill you for the sake of God and in defense of justice. But when you spat in my face, my intention was momentarily tainted by personal anger. I refuse to let my actions be driven by ego or personal vendetta; I want them to be solely for the sake of God. That's why I spared your life, to ensure my intention remained pure."[46] This response truly affected the enemy warrior, who recognized the depth of Ali's character and the purity of his actions. Moved by Ali's nobility and the truth in his behavior, the warrior eventually accepted Islam.

Sumayya bint Khabbat

Sumayya was a slave in Mecca of Yemeni origin. She, along with her husband, Yasir, and their son Ammar was among the first to embrace Islam. Sumayya and her husband accepted Islam through Ammar. However, when their master, Abu Jahl, discovered that they had become followers of Muhammad, they were subjected to public torture. It is said that when the Prophet saw them enduring such severe torture, he would say, "O family of Yasir, be patient. Good news to you, your place is in Paradise."[47] Sumayya and Yasir were eventually tortured to death, becoming the first martyrs of Islam.

Their legacy lived on through their son Ammar, who became an influential figure in early Islamic history. Ammar endured severe persecution and torture at the hands of the Meccans. On one occasion, when he could no longer bear their relentless oppression, he was coerced into speaking in favor of their deities and against the Prophet to save his life.

---

46. Jalaluddin Rumi, *The Mathnavi of Jalalu'ddin Rumi*, trans. Reynold A. Nicholson (Cambridge University Press, 1926), book 1, 3923–3974.

47. *Musnad Ahmad*, 439.

After his release, Ammar rushed to the Prophet and tearfully explained what had happened. The Prophet reassured him that as long as his heart remained steadfast in faith, the words uttered under duress would not harm his belief, given the life-threatening circumstances. This reassurance was later affirmed by a Qur'anic revelation, which stated that those whose hearts are filled with faith but are forced to renounce their religion under coercion will not be held accountable for their words.[48] Ammar went on to become one of the most significant companions of the Prophet, participating in many battles alongside him. During the caliphate of Umar, Ammar served as the governor of Kufa. He also transmitted over sixty hadiths from the Prophet, which are preserved in the collections of hadith literature.

Uthman ibn Affan

Uthman was a respected merchant in Mecca and one of the earliest converts. His father passed away before the advent of Islam, and after Uthman became Muslim, he was tortured by his uncle for his faith. Due to the intense persecution in Mecca, he was among the Muslims who emigrated with his family to Abyssinia (modern-day Ethiopia). A year later, Uthman returned to Mecca after receiving false information that the situation for Muslims had improved. He later emigrated to Medina with many other companions.

Uthman married the Prophet's daughter Ruqayya, who bore Uthman a son named Abdullah, who died at a young age. In Medina, when Ruqayya fell ill, the Prophet excused Uthman from participating in the first major battle with the Meccans, the Battle of Badr, asking him to stay by Ruqayya's side. While the community returned to Medina celebrating their victory, they were also met with the sad news of Ruqayya's passing. After her death, the Prophet married his other daughter, Umm Kulthum, to Uthman. Because of his marriage to the Prophet's two daughters, Uthman became known as "the holder of two lights" (*dhu al-nurayn*).

---

48. Qur'an 16:106.

During the Hudaybiyya treaty, Uthman served as the messenger for the Muslim community, negotiating with the Meccans. Throughout his life, Uthman generously supported the Muslim community with his wealth, particularly during difficult times. After the Prophet's death, Uthman became the third caliph. It was under his leadership that the Qur'an was standardized. In Islamic literature, Uthman is also remembered for his piety and spirituality, and he was committed to following the Prophet's example. It is said that whenever Uthman saw a funeral procession approaching, he would stand up, and when asked why, he would reply, "I saw the Prophet doing the same."[49]

Some Sufi orders trace their spiritual lineage back to Uthman, and he is frequently celebrated in Sufi literature. It is said that the heart of Uthman's spirituality was his devotion to reciting the Qur'an. Al-Ghazali notes that Uthman had the habit of reciting the entire Qur'an once a week.[50] Uthman once remarked, "If our hearts were pure, we would never tire of the words of our Lord. I do not want a single day to pass without reciting the Qur'an."[51] In fact, he was killed by a rebellious group while reciting the Qur'an.[52] In his sermons, he often reminded people of death and the hereafter. In one of them, he said,

> O son of Adam, the angel of death, who is tasked with taking souls, will not leave you and go to others. As long as you are in this world, he will follow you. Sometimes you may think he has left you and gone to others, but you should be vigilant. Be prepared for death. Do not be heedless, for the angel of death is never unaware of you. O son of Adam, if you forget yourself and do not take precautions against your own soul, no one else will take precautions for you or against your soul. You will

---

49. *Musnad Ahmad*, 495.

50. Al-Ghazali, *Ihya' 'Ulum al-Din*, 1:456–457.

51. Ahmad Ibn Hanbal, *Kitab al-Zuhd*, ed. Muhammad Ahmad 'Isa (Dar al-Ghad al-Jadid, 2005), 154–155.

52. Ibn Hanbal, *Kitab al-Zuhd*, 154.

certainly appear before God. Take the necessary measures for yourself. Do not leave the precautions needed to restrain your soul to someone else. That is all."[53]

It is reported that Uthman's last sermon included the following remarks:

> God has given you the world so that you may earn the Hereafter, not to become attached to it! The world is transient, while the Hereafter is everlasting. Let not the fleeting pleasures of this world deceive you and keep you away from the Hereafter. Strive to prefer the eternal over the temporary. Worldly life will one day come to an end, and everyone will return to the presence of God. Seek the protection of God, for entering His protection and fearing Him is both a shield against calamities that may come from Him and a means to attain His pleasure. Do not forget God in your dealings with others. Do not separate from your community. Do not form groups and turn your backs on one another.[54]

Today, Uthman is remembered among Muslims for his dedication to the cause of Islam, along with his piety, sincerity, humility, modesty, and generosity.

Umar ibn al-Khattab

Umar initially was one of the Prophet's most determined opponents. Disturbed by how Islam was dividing families, he decided to kill the Prophet. However, on his way, he discovered that his sister and brother-in-law had also embraced Islam. He diverted to his sister's house and, on

---

53. Ibn Kathir, *al-Bidaya wa al-Nihaya*, ed. Abdullah ibn Abdulmuhsin al-Turki (Dar Hijr, 1998), 10:390.

54. Ibn Kathir, *al-Bidaya wa al-Nihaya*, 10:391.

entering, heard the recitation of the Qur'an, which deeply moved him. This first encounter with the revelation ultimately led to his conversion.

Umar was a prominent figure in the Quraysh tribe and became a Muslim in the sixth year of the Prophet's mission. With Umar's conversion, the Prophet and his companions openly proclaimed their message and practices. After the emigration to Medina, the Prophet married Umar's daughter, Hafsa, who had been widowed in Medina. Following the death of her father, it was Hafsa who safeguarded the revealed verses of the Qur'an in her home. Umar later became the second caliph after the Prophet's death and is recognized for his justice. During his reign, Islamic territories significantly expanded.

In Islamic literature, Umar is commonly referred to by the title *Faruq*, meaning *the one who distinguishes between truth and falsehood*. He is also known for his sense of justice. Like other companions, Umar was totally committed to following the Prophet's teachings. It is said that he lived a few miles from the Prophet's house in Medina, and he and his neighbor would take turns visiting the Prophet. One day, Umar would visit, and the next day, his neighbor would go, ensuring they both stayed informed of any new revelations or teachings, which they would then share with each other.[55] Umar also served as one of the Prophet's scribes and was acknowledged for his sound judgments. In a few instances when disagreements arose, Umar's position was confirmed by subsequent revelations. Due to Umar's sound judgments on matters of faith and his strong commitment, the Prophet praised him in a tradition, saying, "If God were to send a Prophet after me, it would be Umar."[56]

Umar was renowned for his simplicity and piety. It is said that the seal Umar used bore the inscription "O Umar, death is sufficient advice for you."[57] Another account mentions that Umar hired someone to knock on his door daily and remind him of death by saying, "O

---

55. Mustafa Fayda, "Ömer," in *İslam Ansiklopedisi* (Türkiye Diyanet Vakfı, 2007), 34:44.

56. *Jami' al-Tirmidhi, kitab al-manaqib, bab fi manaqib Umar ibn al-Khattab.*

57. Fayda, "Ömer," 34:46.

Umar, there is death." After some time, Umar told the person that his services were no longer needed. When asked why, Umar replied, "I now see white hairs in my beard. They are enough to remind me of my approaching death."[58] On one occasion, he arrived at the mosque a bit late and explained to the community that he only had one set of clothes, which he had washed, waiting for them to dry before coming.[59]

In his *Masnavi*, Rumi highlights Umar's simplicity, despite his position as the leader of the community. One day, a Byzantine ambassador came to Medina to visit Umar and inquired about his palace. The people replied that Umar had no palace and lived in a humble shelter, just like those who were poor. A woman directed the ambassador to where Umar was at that time. The ambassador found him sleeping alone under a tree without any protection. Despite Umar's simplicity, the ambassador was unexpectedly overcome with nervousness and began trembling. Rumi describes the ambassador's reaction as follows:

> He came and stood there at some distance from him:
> he looked at Umar and began to tremble.
>
> A fear came on the envoy from that sleeper,
> an ecstasy of sweetness on his soul.
>
> Though love and fear are mutual contradictions,
> he saw the two united in his heart.
>
> He said, "I have seen many kings,
> been honored and exalted before sultans.
>
> I never had a fear or dread of kings,
> but fear of this man robbed me of my wits.

---

58. Şemseddin Ahmed Sivasi, *Menâkıb-ı Çehâr-Yâr-ı Güzîn* (Milli Gazete, 2005), 165.

59. Ibn Hanbal, *Kitab al-Zuhd*, 151.

> I have gone through forests full of lions and panthers,
> they did not turn my face another colour.
>
> I've often been in battle in the fray,
> when things were at their worst I was a lion.
>
> I've often dealt and suffered heavy blows
> I was a braver heart than all the rest.
>
> This sleeping man lies defenseless on the ground.
> I shake in all my seven limbs-why so?"[60]

Rumi suggests that the ambassador was overwhelmingly affected by Umar's spiritual presence and piety. The man's trembling was not due to Umar's worldly authority but rather his deep spirituality and devotion to God.

While Islamic literature often emphasizes Umar's piety and simplicity, the virtue most closely associated with him is justice. Love for the Prophet and his companions is a central theme in the works of Ahmed Yesevi (d. 1166), an influential Sufi master who played a significant role in the spread of Islam in central Asia. In his *The Book of Wisdom* (*Divan-i Hikmet*), Yesevi particularly highlights Umar's justice, with each line of the poem ending with "the Just Umar":

> The second companion is the Just Umar,
> The friend in faith is the Just Umar.
>
> Observing the law (*sharia*) and following the path,
> The one who knows the truth is the Just Umar.
>
> A shining light who never abandons Islam,
> He never commits to anything unjust—the Just Umar.[61]

---

60. Rumi, *The Masnavi of Rumi*, 1:94–102.

61. Hoca Ahmed Yesevi, *Divan-ı Hikmet* (Ahmet Yesevi Universitesi, 2016), 126–127.

Umar's example of justice is often cited in modern times to advocate for justice and equality in Muslim societies. An illustrative example is the poem "The Old Woman and Umar" ("Kocakarı ve Ömer"), written by the prominent Turkish poet Mehmet Akif Ersoy, who also authored the lyrics of the Turkish national anthem ("İstiklal Marşı"). In the poem, Akif tells the story of an old woman struggling to feed her grandchildren after their parents' death. One day, Umar, accompanied by one of the Prophet's companions, comes across the scene. The children are crying, and the woman is trying to comfort them. When asked why the children are crying, the woman explains that they are hungry and haven't eaten for two days. Unaware that she is speaking to the caliph himself, the woman complains about the caliph, cursing him for being indifferent to their plight. When it is suggested that the caliph might not be aware of her situation, she replies that he is responsible for all his subjects and should know their circumstances. In Akif's poem, she laments:

> If a sheep is taken by a wolf from the banks of the Tigris River, Divine justice will hold Umar accountable for it.
> If an old woman has no one to care for her, Umar is responsible for her.
> If an orphan sheds tears of suffering, Umar is responsible for him.[62]

Umar's legacy continues to inspire Muslims, particularly for his courage and commitment to justice. Today, many scholars and intellectuals cite Umar as the ideal example of a just ruler. On hearing the news of Umar's death, the Prophet's companion Umm Ayman mourned, saying, "Today, Islam is weakened."[63] Her words encapsulate the profound impact Umar had on the Muslim community. Like Abu Bakr, Umar was also buried beside the Prophet.

---

62. Mehmet Akif Ersoy, *Safahat* (Bağcılar Belediyesi, 2014), 73–79.

63. Bünyamin Erul, "Ümmü Eymen," in *İslam Ansiklopedisi* (Türkiye Diyanet Vakfı, 2012), 42:317.

Zayd ibn Haritha

Zayd was among the earliest Muslims, often recognized as the fourth person to accept the Prophet's message, following Khadija, Ali, and Abu Bakr. Originally bought as a slave by Khadija's nephew, Zayd was given to Khadija as a gift. After the Prophet married Khadija, Zayd became part of their household and was later adopted as a son by the Prophet. It is said that when Zayd's biological father and uncle discovered his whereabouts, they sought to take him back. The Prophet gave Zayd the choice to leave, but Zayd chose to stay with him. Notably, Zayd is the only companion mentioned by name in the Qur'an.[64]

Zayd married Zaynab bint Jahsh at the Prophet's recommendation. However, their marriage did not succeed, and they eventually divorced, despite the Prophet's efforts to help them reconcile. Following a Qur'anic revelation, the Prophet married Zaynab. This event led to a significant reform in cultural practices: An adopted child was no longer considered equivalent to a biological child. Previously, adopted children were referred to by the name of their adoptive parent. After this reform, they would be identified by their biological father's name. For instance, Zayd was originally known as Zayd ibn Muhammad, but after the reform, he was referred to as Zayd ibn Haritha.

Zayd later married Umm Ayman, a significant figure in the Prophet's life. Umm Ayman, originally from Ethiopia (Habesha), had served in the household of the Prophet's grandfather. After his death, she remained with the Prophet and cared for him from birth. Umm Ayman was with the Prophet and his mother, Amina, during their visit to relatives in Medina. On their return journey to Mecca, Amina fell ill and passed away. Umm Ayman comforted the six-year-old Muhammad and brought him back to Mecca, playing a crucial role in his upbringing. She was also among the first women to embrace Islam. Due to her nurturing care, the Prophet fondly referred to her as "my mother after my mother." From his marriage to Umm Ayman, Zayd had a son named Usama. Umm Ayman participated in many battles

---

64. Qur'an 33:37.

alongside the Prophet, tending to those wounded. Due to the Prophet's deep respect for Umm Ayman, his companions Umar and Abu Bakr often visited her after the Prophet's death.

Zayd was the one who accompanied the Prophet on the journey to the city of Taif, where they sought refuge. During this difficult time, Zayd tried to shield the Prophet from the people of Taif's attacks. Zayd also became an influential military commander, leading numerous expeditions. His son, Usama, also became a key companion of the Prophet. The Prophet appointed Usama as the commander of a significant military expedition, a decision that sparked criticism among some followers, questioning how the son of a freed slave could be given such a role. The Prophet responded that they had similarly criticized his father, Zayd, and emphasized that both Usama and Zayd were fully qualified to lead the Muslim army.[65] Zayd ultimately died while serving as a commander during one of these expeditions.

Abu Ubuyda ibn al-Jarrah

Abu Ubayda was one of the earliest followers of the Prophet. He accepted Islam through the influence of Abu Bakr, despite facing strong opposition from his father. When the situation in Mecca became unbearable, he joined the other early converts in emigrating to Abyssinia. During a battle against the Meccans, Abu Ubayda found himself facing his own father, who attacked him despite the son's attempts to avoid the confrontation. In the end, Abu Ubayda was forced to fight and ultimately killed his father. The Qur'an addresses this difficult situation with the verse: "[Prophet], you will not find people who truly believe in God and the Last Day giving their loyalty to those who oppose God and His Messenger, even though they may be their fathers, sons, brothers, or other relations: these are the people in whose hearts God has inscribed faith, and whom He has strengthened with His spirit. He will let them enter Gardens graced with flowing streams, where they will stay: God is well pleased with them, and they with Him. They are on God's side,

---

65. Ibn Sa'd, *Kitab al-Tabakat al-Kubra*, 2:170–171.

and God's side will be the one to prosper."⁶⁶ This verse emphasizes the importance of loyalty to God and the Prophet over familial ties. Abu Ubayda was also one of the companions who memorized the entire Qur'an.

Salman al-Farsi

Salman was one of the first Persian followers of the Prophet. Raised as a Zoroastrian, Salman encountered Christianity and, despite his family's opposition, converted to the faith. He fled his hometown of Ramhormoz, located in present-day Iran, and traveled to Damascus and Mosul before settling in Asia Minor. During this time, he learned from a Christian priest about the impending arrival of a new prophet in the Hijaz region. Salman embarked on a quest to find this prophet, paying an Arab merchant to guide him across the desert. On reaching the vicinity of Medina, he was sold to a Jewish merchant, who brought him to the city. After learning about the Prophet and observing the characteristics described by the Christian monk, Salman became Muslim. The Prophet and his companions supported his quest for freedom.

Salman suggested digging a trench around the city to defend against the Meccan siege during the Battle of Trench. He was well-versed in several languages, including Greek and Hebrew. It is also reported that he translated the first chapter of the Qur'an (*al-Fatiha*) into Persian during the Prophet's time. Additionally, Salman served as the Prophet's barber.

Bilal ibn Rabah

Bilal, an Ethiopian slave, was owned by a staunch opponent of the Prophet. He embraced Islam through the influence of Abu Bakr. When his master discovered Bilal's conversion, he subjected Bilal to severe torture in the streets of Mecca. It is reported that Bilal was forced to lie under the scorching sun with a heavy rock placed on his chest in an

---

66. Qur'an 58:22.

attempt to make him renounce his faith. Despite this, Bilal remained steadfast and refused to abandon his new religion. His suffering deeply affected the Prophet and his companions. Eventually, Abu Bakr purchased Bilal's freedom, releasing him from his master's cruelty. Bilal later gained prominence as the Prophet's *muezzin*, being one of his closest companions. The Prophet referred to Bilal, known for his deep piety, as a person of paradise.

After the Prophet's death, Bilal stopped calling the *adhan* (the call to prayer) due to his grief and love for Muhammad. Unable to bear the loss, Bilal left Medina and relocated to Damascus.[67] When he eventually resumed calling the prayer years later, the community was deeply moved, as the last time Bilal did the call to prayer was before the Prophet's death.[68] The role of the *muezzin* became closely associated with Bilal in Islamic tradition.

Aisha Bint Abu Bakr

Aisha, the daughter of Abu Bakr, was the Prophet's wife, a close companion, and arguably one of the most influential women in Islamic history. Due to her close relationship with Muhammad, Aisha became a key authority on the Prophet's life, particularly regarding his personal and spiritual aspects. Due to her youth and keen intellect, Aisha also became a prominent authority on Islamic teachings. Many leading male companions would frequently seek Aisha's counsel on the Prophet's practices, and she was not hesitant to correct them when necessary. For example, al-Zarkashi, a fourteenth-century scholar of hadith, compiled a book featuring 220 hadiths narrated by Aisha, highlighting instances where she "refuted, corrected, contradicted or further explained hadiths

---

67. *Hadislerle İslam*, 6:438.

68. *Hadislerle İslam*, 6:439.

that were being circulated by other, invariably male, companions of the Prophet."⁶⁹

For example, on one occasion, Abu Hassan al-A'raj reported that two men came to Aisha and said, "Abu Hurayra narrates that the Prophet, peace and blessings be upon him, said: 'Verily, omens are in women, animals, and houses.'" The implication of this statement is that bad luck or misfortune can occur because of women, animals, and houses. Aisha was upset by this and responded, "By the One who revealed the Quran to Abu al-Qasim [Muhammad], that is not correct. The Prophet was actually quoting the people of ignorance who believed omens were found in women, houses, and animals." She then recited the Qur'anic verse "No affliction occurs in the earth or within yourselves except that it is written in a book"⁷⁰ Aisha, referencing this verse from the Qur'an, reminded her audience of the concept of divine predestination and God's all-encompassing knowledge. She emphasized that all events, whether on a global scale or in personal lives, are part of a preordained plan recorded by God. Thus, life's occurrences, whether positive or negative, cannot be attributed to superstitions or the notion of bad luck associated with women.

Aisha was a devout and pious woman dedicated to the Prophet. She would lead the women in prayer when they were among themselves. Aisha frequently fasted and spent much of the night in prayer alongside the Prophet. Despite being Muhammad's wife, Aisha had a modest life and lived in a simple room attached to the Prophet's Mosque (Masjid al-Nabawi). She was known for her generosity and care for orphans.

Aisha also went through some trials during her time with the Prophet. She often accompanied him to wars and on expeditions. On one occasion, while the army was taking a break, Aisha went out at night to relieve herself. When she returned, she realized that she had lost her necklace. She went back to search for it, but the army had moved on,

---

69. Sofia Abdur Rahman, *Gendering the Hadith Tradition: Recentering the Authority of Aisha, Mother of the Believers* (Oxford University Press, 2024), 2–3.

70. *Musnad Ahmad*, 26088.

mistakenly believing she was with them on her camel litter. One of the male companions, who was lagging behind, saw her and accompanied her. Hypocrites within the army spread false rumors that Aisha committed indecency, and some Muslims joined them in spreading these rumors. When the rumors reached the Prophet, he was extremely saddened and consulted some of his close companions for advice. Initially unaware of what was happening, Aisha eventually learned about the accusations and went to her parents. This situation continued for a month until a revelation came, confirming Aisha's innocence.[71]

Fearing that the rumors might have influenced the Prophet's view of her, Aisha sought refuge in God, much like the prophet Jacob (Yakub) did. The Qur'an recounts Jacob's response to the false claim that his son Joseph had been killed by a wolf, based on a bloodstained shirt. When Joseph's brothers showed their father his shirt, deceptively stained with blood, Jacob replied, "No! Your souls have enticed you to do wrong. But patience is most fitting. And God is the One whose help I seek against what you describe."[72] Despite the distressing period she endured, Aisha found great solace and honor in the revelation that confirmed her innocence.

The Qur'anic revelation also established ethical guidelines regarding rumors about fellow Muslims: "When you heard the falsehood, why did believing men and women not think well of their own people and say, 'This is clearly a lie'?"[73] Additionally, the revelation mandated that accusations of sexual misconduct must be supported by four eyewitnesses. According to this principle, even if an accusation of adultery is truthful, it is deemed invalid if it lacks the required four witnesses.[74]

It is reported that some of the Muslims who were involved in spreading the rumors had been regular recipients of charity from Aisha's father, Abu Bakr. In response to their involvement, Abu Bakr decided

---

71. Qur'an 24:11–22.

72. Qur'an 12:18.

73. Qur'an 24:12.

74. Qur'an 24:13.

to stop the charity. However, the subsequent revelation instructed him to forgive and continue his support: "Those who have been blessed with wealth should not swear off giving to relatives, the poor, or those who have emigrated for God's sake. Let them pardon and forgive. Do you not wish for God to forgive you? God is Most Forgiving and Merciful."[75] This was a significant test for Abu Bakr, as God was asking him not only to forgive those who had slandered his daughter but also to continue financially supporting them. Abu Bakr chose to maintain his support. Many Muslim scholars view this verse as a source of hope, highlighting God's mercy even toward those who commit slander.[76]

The Prophet passed away in Aisha's lap and was buried in the room where he and Aisha lived. At the time of his death, Aisha was still very young. The Qur'anic injunction prohibited the Prophet's wives from remarrying after his death.[77] Consequently, Aisha remained a widow for the rest of her life, and her influence continued to be significant.

After the assassination of the third caliph, Uthman, by a mob, Ali succeeded him as the fourth caliph and immediately set out to identify Uthman's killers. Aisha, the Prophet's influential wife, along with key companions such as Talha ibn Ubaydullah and Zubayr ibn Awwam, demanded immediate retribution for Uthman's death. However, with an entire group of rebels claiming responsibility, Ali felt it was wiser to focus on identifying and punishing the actual perpetrators rather than blaming the whole group. This more cautious approach led Aisha and her supporters to become impatient and rebel against Ali, who ultimately defeated them. Many Muslims died in this first civil war, including the Prophet's close companions Talha and Zubayr. The war is known as the Battle of the Camel, during which the camel Aisha rode into battle died in the fighting. The key role of Aisha in the battle

---

75. Qur'an 24:22.

76. Caner K. Dagli, "*Commentary on Surat al-Nur*," in *The Study Quran: A New Translation and Commentary*, ed. Nasr et al. (HarperOne, 2015), 873.

77. Qur'an 33:6, 53.

indicates her influence among the major companions of the Prophet after his death. Some scholars view her actions as an effort to seek justice.

As we will see in the next chapter, Muhammad's private life became as important as his public life for Muslims in practicing their religion. We probably do not know about any other historical figure on such an intimate and detailed level—information that his wives played a key role in revealing. The Prophet educated his wives about the most intimate issues, and the community—especially Muslim women—learned from them. Aisha, for example, narrated many hadiths, or reports attributed to the Prophet; she is among the top four contributors of Muhammad's narrations. This is partly because of her youth and partly because of her good memory. Many companions and successors sought Aisha's advice concerning matters of jurisprudence as well as hadiths from the Prophet. Aisha transmitted more than two thousand of the three thousand hadiths attributed to his wives.[78] She remains a role model for Muslims due to her intellectual contributions to Islamic hadith scholarship, teachings, devotion, and courage. Many Muslim women admire and follow her example.

Conclusion

Muhammad cherished his companions, spending time with them, seeking their advice, and addressing any issues they faced. In return, the companions held the Messenger of God in high regard and were willing to sacrifice anything, even their lives, for the cause of Islam. The transformative impact of the Prophet's message was profound on them. Their foremost goal was to please God and God's messenger, and they strived to model their lives after the Prophet's spirituality, character, and conduct. Following the Prophet's death, the companions dedicated themselves to preserving his spirit, upholding his teachings, and passing them on to future generations. This is the focus of our next chapter.

---

78. Muhammad Zubayr Siddiqi, *Hadith Literature: Its Origin, Development, and Special Features* (Islamic Text Society, 1993), 18.

CHAPTER FOUR

Following the Prophet

In 2022, the Muslim community of Knoxville, Tennessee, invited its members to spend the final days and nights of Ramadan at their mosque, offering a detailed schedule for the observances. The daily program began at 3:30 a.m. and concluded at midnight, including individual invocations and supplications, the five daily congregational prayers, Qur'an recitation, night prayers (*tahajjud*), and *tarawih* prayers, a special prayer specific to Ramadan performed after the late evening prayer (*'isha*). The center's initiative thus facilitated the practice of *i'tikaf*, a spiritual tradition of the Prophet Muhammad, who would retreat to the mosque during the last ten days of Ramadan.[1] By participating in *i'tikaf*, community members honor and continue this spiritual legacy, entirely dedicating themselves to God by detaching from worldly distractions. *I'tikaf* serves as a spiritual reset and renewal.

Today, mosques around the world, including those in the United States, open their doors to allow congregants to fulfill this prophetic tradition, serving as a way to follow the Prophet. Many Muslim countries also designate specific mosques for *i'tikaf* during Ramadan. For instance, in Ramadan 2024, the Ministry of Religious Affairs in Türkiye designated 4,665 mosques for *i'tikaf*, with 285 in Istanbul and 107 in Ankara alone.[2] In the same year, an organization in Saudi Arabia arranged an *i'tikaf* retreat for 5,000 participants at the Prophet's

---

1. "Itikaf Spiritual Retreat," Muslim Community of Knoxville, https://muslimknoxville.org/programs/ramadan1443/itikaf/.

2. "81 Il ve Ilcelerde Itikafa Girilecek Camiler-2024," *Diyanet Haber*, February 4, 2024, https://www.diyanethaber.com.tr/81-il-ve-ilcelerinde-itikafa-girilebilecek-camiler-2024.

Mosque (Masjid al-Nabawi) in Medina.³ This spiritual practice is just one example of how Muslims have been following the Prophet.

In this chapter, we will examine the importance of following the Prophet, commonly referred to as the *Sunna*, which literally means *path* or *custom*. As a term, it signifies the example, precedent, and practice of Muhammad, the Messenger of God. We will also explore hadith literature, a primary source of the Prophet's Sunna. The sayings, actions, approvals, and disapprovals of the Prophet are primarily preserved in hadith collections.

If You Love God, Follow the Prophet

From the early days of Islam, Muslims have been very keen on following the way of the Prophet (the Sunna). The idea of following the Prophet is grounded in the Qur'an, which repeatedly instructs Muslims to follow and obey Muhammad. Obedience to the Messenger of God is, in essence, obedience to God. The Qur'an states that if someone loves God, they should follow the Prophet: "Say (O Prophet, to the people), 'If you love God, follow me, and God will love you and forgive your sins. And God is Forgiving and Merciful.'"⁴ Several principles can be derived from this verse. First, if believers have faith in God, they also love God. If they love God, they will naturally love what God loves. Therefore, those who love God will also love God's messenger. Out of their love for God, they will obey the Messenger and strive to emulate his example.

Mirroring is a natural part of human behavior. People often emulate and mimic the actions of those they love and admire. This mirroring creates bonds and connections between the one who mimics and the one being mimicked. For Muslims who truly love the Messenger of God, it is natural for them to remember the Prophet's spirit, emulate his example, and follow his spiritual path. Moreover, the verse teaches that

---

3. "Hidayah Launches Itikaf Program" *Saudi Press Agency*, https://spa.gov.sa/en/N2077955.

4. Qur'an 3:31.

one can attain God's love by following the Prophet. In other words, God loves those who obey and follow God's prophet. Just as people naturally mimic their loved ones, they also long to be loved and feel love. The most precious love in Islam is the love that comes from God, and this love is attained by following the prophetic example, the Sunna.

The Qur'an not only associates following the Prophet with obedience to God but also refers to him as the best model for believers: "The Messenger of God is an excellent model for those of you who put your hope in God and the Last Day and remember Him often."[5] The implication of this verse is that the believers should take the Prophet's words and actions as a model in conducting their life because "to live in accord with the Prophetic model is to live in constant remembrance of God."[6]

Another verse emphasizes that the Prophet had an outstanding character.[7] When his wife Aisha was asked about it, she answered that his character was the Qur'an. He was the embodiment of the teachings of the Qur'an.[8] The Prophet himself also emphasized the importance of following his example. In a report, he said, "I have left two things by which, as long as you hold to them, you will not go astray: the Book of God and my Sunna."[9] In another tradition, he said, "The one who does not follow my way is not from me."[10]

Following the Prophet's Smile

Muhammad's companions sought to emulate every aspect of his life because following the Prophet's example was a sign of their love for

---

5. Qur'an 33:21.

6. Joseph E. B. Lumbard, *Commentary on Surat al-Ahzab*, in *The Study Quran: A New Translation and Commentary*, ed. Nasr et al. (HarperOne, 2015), , 1025.

7. Qur'an 68:4.

8. *Sahih Muslim, kitab salat al-musafirin wa qasruha, bab jami'i salat al-layl wa man nama 'anhu aw marida*.

9. Malik bin Anas, *al-Muwatta', kitab al-qadr*.

10. *Sahih al-Bukhari, kitab al-nikah, bab al-targhib fi al-nikah*.

God and God's messenger. For instance, it is reported that the Prophet once acquired a gold ring and began wearing it. His companions, following his example, also started wearing gold rings. However, one day, the Prophet climbed the pulpit (*minbar*) in the mosque, glorified God, and said, "I have had this gold ring, but I will not wear it anymore." He then removed the ring from his finger and threw it away. Without hesitation, his companions followed his lead and also discarded their rings.[11]

In another example, it is reported that years after the Prophet's death, a riding animal was brought to Ali ibn Abi Talib. When he placed his foot in the stirrup to mount the animal, Ali said, "In the Name of God." Once he had settled himself on the animal's back, he recited, "All praise belongs to God Who has made this subservient to us, for we did not have the strength to overpower it; and to our Lord shall we return." He then recited three times, "Praise be to God alone and God is the greatest." Afterward, Ali said, "You are far removed from imperfection, O God! I have wronged myself, so forgive me, for none but You can forgive sins." Then he smiled. Someone asked, "Why have you smiled, O Leader of the Believers?" Ali replied, "I saw the Messenger of God (peace and blessings be upon him) doing what I have done."[12] In riding his animal, Ali was emulating all the steps the Prophet would take, including the exact moment he would smile. These two examples demonstrate how the Prophet's companions loved him and were committed to following every aspect of his living example, both during his lifetime and after his death.

Using the Prophetic Example to Understand the Qur'an

Muslims have frequently looked to the prophetic example to understand the word of God, the Qur'an, as well. As the living embodiment

---

11. *Sahih al-Bukhari, kitab al-iman wa al-nudhur, bab man halafa 'ala al-shay' wa in lam yuhallaf.*

12. *Musnad Ahmad*, 753.

of the Qur'an, Muhammad served as the model for how to put its message into practice. Many aspects of the Qur'an are nearly impossible to fully grasp without the Prophet's guidance. For example, while the Qur'an instructs believers to pray, fast, give charity, and perform pilgrimage, it does not provide specific details on how these key Islamic rituals should be carried out. We learn the elements of these rituals through the living example of Muhammad. The Prophet explained and demonstrated them through his words and actions. Muslim scholars have written extensive volumes on rituals and transactions based on the Prophet's example.

A case in point is the five daily prayers. The scripture instructs Muslims to "establish the prayer" but does not provide detailed answers to questions such as: What are the requirements for the prayers? How should the prayers be performed? How often should they be offered? Under what circumstances can prayers be combined? What are the essential elements of the prayers? What should be recited during them? Therefore, Muslims have turned to the Sunna of the Prophet to fulfill this fundamental Qur'anic practice. While the five daily prayers have their foundation in the Qur'an, their form, structure, and elements are primarily based on the prophetic example. Thus, following the Sunna is essential for performing Islamic rituals.

We also see the Prophet's role in fasting. While the Qur'an instructs believers that "fasting is prescribed" for them during the month of Ramadan, it does not provide all the details regarding the practice. Again, the ambiguous aspects are clarified through the Prophet's example. For instance, regarding the time when fasting should begin and end each day, the Qur'an states, "Eat and drink until the white thread of dawn becomes distinct from the black. Then fast until nightfall."[13] It is reported that one of the Prophet's companions understood the verse literally, keeping black and white threads to distinguish them during the night. When the Prophet learned about this, he explained

---

13. Qur'an 2:187.

that the verse actually referred to "the darkness of the night and the whiteness of the day."[14]

One can also consider other examples, such as how to deal with crimes like theft. The Qur'an states, "As for the male thief and the female thief, cut off their hands as a recompense for what they have earned, as an exemplary punishment from God. Truly God is Mighty, Wise."[15] But what constitutes theft? Such questions are directly addressed in the Sunna of the Prophet. Based on the practices of the Prophet and his companions, it has been held that certain conditions must be met for punishment to be applied. Most legal authorities, relying on a prophetic hadith and the precedent set by the early caliphs, maintained that the punishment for theft should be enforced only when a substantial amount or a highly valuable item is stolen.[16] For example, during the caliphate of Umar, the punishment for theft was not applied to those who stole out of hunger during a famine.[17] This approach would later be reflected in Islamic law as well.

Following the prophetic example is also crucial for understanding the dietary laws in the Qur'an. For instance, several verses of the Qur'an prohibit believers from consuming the meat of animals already found dead (i.e., carrion).[18] Instead, the animal must be slaughtered according to specific guidelines, including the invocation of God's name before

---

14. *Sahih al-Bukhari, kitab al-tafsir, bab kawlihi "wa qulu wasrabu hatta yatabayyana lakum al-ghayd al-abyad..."*

15. Qur'an 5:38.

16. The minimum value for which the penalty may be applied is typically cited as three dirhams (three grams of silver) or, more commonly, one quarter of a dinar (one gram of gold) or its equivalent in goods. Maria Massi Dakake, *Commentary on Surat al-Mai'dah*, in *The Study Quran: A New Translation and Commentary*, ed. Nasr et al. (HarperOne, 2015), 295.

17. Ali Bardakoğlu, "Had," in *Islam Ansiklopeidisi* (Türkiye Diyanet Vakfı, 1996), 14:550.

18. Qur'an 2:173; 5:3.

the act of slaughter.[19] However, fish is an exception to this rule, based on reports from the Prophet.[20] Additionally, while the Qur'an forbids the consumption of pork, the Prophet extended this prohibition to include the meat of any predatory animal with fangs and birds with talons.[21] Consequently, the meat of animals such as cats, dogs, lions, bears, wolves, owls, eagles, and hawks is considered unlawful based on the Prophet's hadiths. Due to the Prophet's essential role in interpreting the Qur'an, one scholar remarked that "the need of the Qur'an for the Sunna is greater than the need of the Sunna for the Qur'an."[22]

What Does It Mean to Follow the Sunna?

While the Sunna of the Prophet is central to understanding the Qur'an and living an Islamic life, many scholars have sought to distinguish between Muhammad's teachings as a Prophet and his daily habits and cultural practices as a human being. For example, Imam al-Ghazali emphasizes the need to differentiate between following the Prophet's example and simply imitating him. Showing reverence toward the Prophet does not necessarily mean trying to emulate every aspect of his behavior. To illustrate his point, al-Ghazali offers the following example: "Respecting a king means obeying his commands and prohibitions. It does not mean sitting with crossed legs just because he did or sitting in a chair simply because he sat in a chair."[23] Al-Ghazali criticizes scholars who argue that following the Sunna means imitating (*tashabbuh*) every action of the Prophet.

---

19. Qur'an 6:121.

20. *Sunan ibn Majah, kitab al-ad'amah, bab al-kabid al-tihad.*

21. *Sahih al-Muslim, kitab al-sayd wa al-zabaih, bab tahrim 'akl kulli dhi nabin min al-siba' wa kulli dhi mighlabin min al-dayr.*

22. Quoted in *Hadislerle İslam*, 1:54. This statement is attributed to Muslim scholar Makhul al-Shami (d. 718).

23. Al-Ghazali quoted in *Islam Through Hadiths* (Presidency of Religious Affairs, 2020), 1:150.

Indeed, the essence of the Sunna is not about replicating the Prophet's outward appearance. For instance, eating exactly what the Prophet ate is mere imitation; however, consuming lawful (*halal*) food, avoiding waste, and adhering to the Prophet's manners, such as eating with the right hand and not overeating, are true examples of following the Sunna. The Prophet wore clothes that were appropriate for the customs and climate of his time and place. Simply wearing the same clothes as the Prophet is imitation, but practicing modesty, preferring clean clothing, and avoiding extravagance in dress are aspects of the prophetic example.[24]

This is why scholars have classified the Sunna of the Prophet into different categories. For example, some scholars divided the Sunna into actions that involve religious duties required of believers. In this category, examples include communal prayers and the call to prayer (*adhan*). Not following this type of Sunna is considered reprehensible (*karaha*). The other categories pertain to the actions of the Prophet as a human being, such as his style of dress, eating habits, and personal preferences, which are not part of religious obligations. When Muslims emulate these actions out of love and reverence for the Prophet, they are spiritually rewarded by God, but not performing them is not considered a misdeed or sin.[25]

Transmitting the Sunna of the Prophet

If the Sunna of the Prophet is central to understanding the message of the Qur'an and living a God-centered life, how was it transmitted and preserved, and how do we know about it? During Muhammad's life, the transmission of his Sunna was not an issue. The Prophet did not live in isolation; he was integrated into the community. Whenever Muhammad received a revelation of the Qur'an, he would embody its message in his actions, setting a precedent for how to live a life pleasing

---

24. *Islam Through Hadiths*, 1:151.

25. *Islam Through Hadiths*, 1:152.

to God. Every member of the community had access to him, interacting with the Prophet at the mosque, in his home, in the neighborhood, in the market, and during travels and expeditions. The entire city was like a school, with the Prophet as the teacher and every member of society as a student. This school was open to everyone. In fact, when the women of Medina expressed concern that the Prophet was less accessible to them than to the male companions, they approached him and said, "Teach us from what God has taught you." In response, the Prophet designated a day specifically to teach and educate them.[26]

The Prophet's companions closely followed his example, observing his actions and listening to his words with great care. It is reported that when they listened to the Prophet, they were so attentive as if they had birds perched on their heads.[27] As mentioned in the previous chapter, some companions took turns to ensure they missed nothing the Prophet said or did. Those who lived far from the Prophet would rotate their visits. This way, they did not miss any of Muhammad's daily teachings.

After the Prophet's death, the community, especially his close companions, themselves became the living embodiment of the Sunna. They carried forward the spirit of the Prophet in their actions, as if he were still with them. They focused on what he had done and said. Initially, the teachings of the Prophet were primarily transmitted orally and through communal practice. The oral reports attributed to the Prophet are known as *hadith* (plural *ahadith*). *Hadith* literally means *speech* or *report*, and as a term, it refers to a narrative record of what Muhammad said, did, and approved or disapproved of. Below are a few examples:

> Narrated by Umar ibn al-Khattab: "I heard God's Messenger (pbuh) say, 'The reward of deeds depends upon the intentions,

---

26. *Sahih al-Bukhari, kitab al-'itisam bilkitab wa al-sunnah, bab ta'lim al-nabiyy salla allahu 'alayhi wa sallam ummatahu min al-rijal wa al-nisaa'.*

27. *Sunan Abi Dawud, kitab al-tib, bab fi al-rajul yatadawa.*

and every person will receive the reward according to what they have intended.'"²⁸

It is narrated by al-Mughira: "The Prophet (pbuh) used to offer night prayers until his feet became swollen. Someone said to him, 'God has forgiven your past and future faults.' To that, he replied, 'Shouldn't I be a thankful servant of God?'"²⁹

It is narrated by the Prophet's wife Aisha: "God's Messenger (pbuh) used to offer the morning prayer (*fajr*), and some believing women, covered with their veiling sheets, would attend the prayer with him. Then, they would return to their homes without being recognized."³⁰

In the first hadith, the Prophet emphasizes the importance of intention in deeds. The second hadith highlights how central the night prayer was to the Prophet's spirituality. In the third hadith, we see that women would attend the morning prayer with the Prophet in the mosque, and the Prophet did not object to their participation.

Sacred Narrations (Hadith al-Qudsi)

In some instances, we find reports attributed to God in terms of their meaning but expressed in the words of the Prophet Muhammad. These reports are known as *sacred narratives* (*hadith al-qudsi*). For example, the Prophet said in a narration, "God has recorded the good deeds and the bad ones. Then He explained it, saying: If a person intends to do a good deed but does not carry it out, God records it as a full good deed. If he intends it and then performs it, God records it as ten good deeds, up to seven hundred times, or even more. However, if a person intends to do a bad deed but refrains from doing it, God records it as a full good

---

28. *Sahih al-Bukhari, kitab bad'u al-wahy, bab kayfa kana bad'u al-wahy.*

29. *Sahih al-Bukhari, kitab al-tafsir, bab "li yaghfir laka allahu ma taqaddam min thanbik."*

30. *Sahih al-Bukhari, kitab al-salat, bab fi kam tusalli, al-mar'atu fi al-siyab.*

deed. But if he intends it and goes through with it, God records it as one bad deed."³¹ In another example of a sacred narration emphasizing God's forgiveness, the Prophet says what God said to him: "O son of Adam, as long as you call upon Me and ask of Me, I will forgive you for what you have done, and I will not mind. O son of Adam, even if your sins were to reach the clouds of the sky, and you then sought forgiveness from Me, I would forgive you. O son of Adam, if you were to come to Me with sins as great as the earth, and you faced Me without associating any partner with Me, I would bring you forgiveness as great as that."³²

Transmission of the Sunna in Writing

It is reported that the Prophet had discouraged his companions from writing down the hadiths due to concerns that they might be mixed with Qur'anic revelation. This concern persisted among some companions even after the Prophet's death. For example, there was a suggestion to collect all hadiths during the caliphate of Umar, but it was not realized for the same reason—there was fear that people might prioritize the hadith collections over the Qur'an. However, there are also reports that the Prophet granted special permission to some of his companions to write down hadiths. For example, it is reported that Abu Hurayra, who transmitted more hadiths from the Prophet than any other companion, said that the only person who narrated more hadiths than him was Abdullah ibn Amr because, unlike Abu Hurayra, he would write them down.³³

There were several reasons to write down the hadiths. First, after the death of the Prophet, Islam spread to various regions, and the companions moved to different cities that became part of the Islamic world. While they shared the reports from the Prophet and embodied

---

31. *Sahih Muslim, kitab al-iman, bab 'itha hamma al-'abdu bihasanatin kutibat wa 'itha hamma bisayyi'atin lam tuktab.*

32. *Jami' al-Tirmidhi, kitab al-da'wat.*

33. *Hadislerle İslam*, 1:62–63.

his teachings in their lives, it is unlikely they always precisely quoted Muhammad. Instead, they often conveyed their understanding of the hadith in their own words. This led to diverse understandings and interpretations of the Prophet's reports. Such divergence was not new; it existed even during the Prophet's lifetime. For instance, during one of the expeditions, the Prophet instructed his companions to perform their prayer on reaching their destination. However, on the way, some companions were concerned that the time for the prayer might expire, so they wanted to pray before they arrived. Other companions disagreed, insisting on following the Prophet's command to pray at the destination. When the Prophet heard of their disagreement, he confirmed that both approaches were valid.[34] Although they had heard the same statement from the Prophet, they had two different interpretations. Similar disagreements regarding the implications of hadiths continued after the Prophet's death. Writing down the reports would help better navigate the disagreements on hadith and their interpretations.

Second, the early Muslim community was embroiled in several civil wars after the death of the Prophet. Knowing the respect and reverence that the words of the Prophet carried, individuals fabricated hadiths to justify their political views, mobilize people, and gain support. This situation made the study of hadith more urgent. As a result, Muslim scholars developed the field of hadith scholarship to assess the authenticity of reports about the Prophet's sayings and actions. Many scholars embarked on journeys to collect hadiths, write them down, and classify them according to their degree of authenticity.

Muslim scholars developed a number of criteria to evaluate the authenticity of a hadith. One of the most important principles in this science was the reliability of the chain of transmission (*sanad*). They assessed the chain of transmission based on several criteria: Is the chain that dates back to the Prophet complete (*muttasil*)? Who are the narrators? Are they reliable in terms of character, memory, and piety? Based

---

34. *Sahih al-Muslim, kitab al-jihad wa al-siyar, bab man lazima 'amr fadakhala 'alayhi 'amr akhar.*

on their assessment and critique, scholars categorized hadith narratives into four broad groups: authentic (*sahih*), good (*hasan*), weak (*da'if*), and fabricated (*mawdu'*). Hadiths classified as authentic and good are integral to Islamic teachings and legal rulings. Although scholars generally avoided using weak hadiths as evidence, they occasionally referred to them, particularly for moral and spiritual encouragement. Fabricated hadiths, however, were categorically rejected by scholars.

Scholars further classified authentic hadiths into subcategories. For example, for a hadith narration to be considered authentic, scholars usually outlined five conditions. First, the hadith should be reported through an unbroken chain of narration dating to the Prophet (*ittisal al-isnad*). Each narrator must have met and received the hadith they are narrating directly from the previous narrator. Second, the narrators in the chain should be trustworthy and just individuals known for their good character and integrity. This criterion is known as '*adl* (literally *justice* or *just*) in the hadith literature. Third, the report should be transmitted with accuracy and precision (*dabt*). There are two components of this condition: If the narrator is reporting from memory, it should be memorized and preserved accurately. If the narrator wrote down the hadith, it should be free of errors. The important part is that the narrator must possess all the qualities required to accurately and precisely transmit the hadith from the previous narrator. Fourth, the hadith must not be anomalous or irregular (*shadh*), meaning it should not contradict a more reliable narration. Finally, the hadith must not be defective (*mu'allal*). This type of hadith may initially appear authentic; however, a close examination by an expert may uncover a subtle flaw in the chain or content of the narration. Once such a defect is identified, the hadith loses its authentic status.

Scholars also classified hadiths into two categories based on the number of chains of narration. One of them is known as *mutawatir* hadith. This type is reported by a large number of narrators across the first three generations of Muslims, making it impossible for them to have fabricated it. The chain and content of a *mutawatir* hadith are not based on individual memory but on the collective memory of a group of people. Examples of *mutawatir* narrations include the transmission of the Qur'an, reports about the form of the five daily prayers and fasting, the prohibition of interest (*riba*), and the Prophet raising his hands while making supplications (*du'a'*). The hadiths that did not meet the standard of *mutawatir* narration are called *ahad* (literally, *individuals*). The number of hadiths classified as *mutawatir* ranges between one hundred and three hundred. This is why most hadiths in the collections fall under the category of *ahad*. Scholars further categorized *ahad* hadiths based on the number of people involved in their transmission: hadiths that are transmitted by many people (at least three), are well-known, and are widely corroborated, especially by the second and third generations of Muslims after the Prophet (*mashhur*); hadiths that are uncommon and narrated by at least two narrators (*'aziz*); and hadiths that are strange (*gharib*) and reported by only one narrator.

One of the earliest hadith classifications was done by Imam Malik (d.795). In his *Muwatta'*, he collected hadith narrations based on the communal practices of the people of Medina (*'amal ahl al-Medina*). In addition to narrations attributed to the Prophet, Imam Malik included the opinions of the Prophet's companions and the generation that followed them (*tabi'un*, or *successors*). The book is organized according to different topics of jurisprudence, thus combining hadith scholarship with legal principles. Here is an example of a hadith recorded in Imam Malik's *Muwatta'* with a complete chain dating back to the Prophet (*muttasil*): "Malik related from Ibn Shihab, from Said ibn al-Musayyab, from Abu Hurayra, that the Messenger of God, may God bless him and grant him peace, said, 'A strong person is not one who throws his adversaries to the ground. A strong person is one who contains himself when he is angry.'"[35] Here are the narrators in the chain of transmission: The chain begins with the Prophet Muhammad (571–632). His close companion Abu Hurayra (603–679) heard it directly from the Prophet. Said ibn al-Musayyab (637–715) then heard the hadith from Abu Hurayra and transmitted it to Ibn Shihab al-Zuhri (671–742).

---

35. Imam Malik, *al-Muwatta'*, *kitab husun al-khulq*.

Finally, Imam Malik (711–795) heard the hadith from al-Zuhri and recorded it in his *Muwatta'*.

Hadith Collections: The Codification Stage

The study of hadith reached its peak in the ninth century (the third century of Islam), a period known as the golden age of hadith scholarship. During the Prophet Muhammad's lifetime, his companions directly interacted with him, learned his teachings, and practiced them in their daily lives. After the Prophet's death, the companions not only continued to transmit hadith through their living example by adhering to his teachings but also began collecting them. In the final stage, scholars rigorously scrutinized the reported hadith and classified them based on their authenticity. This phase of hadith scholarship is referred to as the *codification stage*. By the mid-eleventh century, it is generally believed that all hadith reliably attributed to the Prophet had been documented and codified.[36]

One of the most reliable collections of hadith was compiled by Imam al-Bukhari. Born in 810 CE in Bukhara, present-day Uzbekistan, he lost his father during childhood and was raised by his mother. Al-Bukhari began studying Islamic sciences with local scholars in his early years. In his mid-teens, he traveled to Mecca with his mother and brother to perform the pilgrimage. Afterward, he chose not to return to Bukhara, instead dedicating himself to the study of hadith with scholars in Hijaz and other major centers of Islamic learning.

During his stay in Hijaz, al-Bukhari traveled to Baghdad at least eight times. On each visit, he sought the company of Ahmed ibn Hanbal (d. 855), a prominent hadith scholar and compiler of *al-Musnad*. Al-Bukhari greatly benefited from his knowledge. The pursuit of hadith scholarship led al-Bukhari to travel extensively to other major cities of the Muslim world, including Basra, Balkh, Damascus, Homs, Kufa, Merv, Egypt, and Nishapur. He passed away in Samarkand in 870 CE.

---

36. Jonathan A. C. Brown, *Hadith: Muhammad's Legacy in the Medieval and Modern World* (Oneworld, 2009), 42.

It is reported that al-Bukhari learned and recorded hadiths from more than a thousand scholars. He reviewed approximately 600,000 hadiths to select the most reliable ones. His anthology, *Sahih al-Bukhari*, includes around 7,275 hadiths (with repetitions), of which about 4,000 are unique, and 2,600 have a complete chain of narration (*muttasil*). Al-Bukhari's collection is organized into 97 books, each focusing on a specific theme or subject. These books are further divided into chapters. The themes cover a wide range of topics, including revelation, belief, ablution (*wudu*), knowledge, prayers, fasting, pilgrimage, sales and trade, partnership, peacemaking, marriage, divorce, hunting, medicine, inheritance, and more.

Al-Bukhari's *Sahih* became the most significant source of Islamic knowledge after the Qur'an. No book, apart from the Qur'an, has received as much attention as al-Bukhari's work. *Sahih al-Bukhari* was read not only with the intention of earning spiritual rewards but also with hopes of relief from material and spiritual hardships and illnesses and for the fulfillment of various aspirations. It was not uncommon to read *Sahih al-Bukhari* before embarking on a journey or before going to war for victory.[37] Many Muslim rulers organized sessions for reading the entire *Sahih*, often concluding with public celebrations.[38] This special regard for Al-Bukhari's work was not only a means to learn about the Prophet's Sunna and strive to embody it but also a way of seeking the Prophet's blessings through his recorded traditions.

Another major hadith collection was compiled by Imam Muslim, who was born in 821 CE in Nishapur, a city located in northeastern Iran today. From his mid-teens, he embarked on a journey to study hadith, traveling to major centers of Islamic scholarship, including Khurasan, Rayy, Hijaz, Iraq, Damascus, and Egypt, where he studied with renowned hadith scholars. Among his teachers was Imam al-Bukhari, with whom he had the opportunity to study directly. As a result of his extensive travels

---

37. Brown, *Hadith*, 40.

38. M. Yasar Kandemir, "al-Camiu's Sahih," in *İslam Ansiklopedisi* (Türkiye Diyanet Vakfı, 1993), 7:117.

and studies, Imam Muslim collected approximately 300,000 hadiths that he heard firsthand from hadith scholars. After meticulously examining each narration for authenticity, he selected only over 7,000 hadiths (including repetitions) for his collection.

The collections of al-Bukhari and Muslim are together known as the *Sahihayn* (literally, *the two authentic books*) because of the rigorous standards of authenticity applied in their compilation. Both scholars ensured that only hadiths meeting the highest criteria of reliability were included in their works, making these collections the most authoritative sources of hadith in Sunni Islam. In addition to al-Bukhari and Muslim's collections, four other hadith collections became prominent in the Sunni tradition. They are the *Jami'* of Imam al-Tirmidhi (d. 883), the *Sunan* of Muhammad ibn Yazid b. Majah (d. 886), the *Sunan* of Abu Dawud al-Sijistani (d. 888), and the *Sunan* of Ahmad ibn Shu'ayb al-Nasa'i (d. 915). These collections are collectively known as *the six books* (*kutub al-sitta*) in the Sunni world.

It is important to note that some scholars also compiled collections of weak and fabricated hadiths that were widely circulated and frequently cited by ordinary people. Collecting and identifying reports falsely attributed to the Prophet was another significant contribution to the study of hadith. Among the scholars who produced such compilations are Imam Suyuti, Ibn Qayyim (d. 1350), and Sakhawi (d. 1497).[39]

Hadith in the Shiite Tradition

As in Sunni Islam, hadith scholarship has been very important in the Shiite tradition as well.[40] Similar to the majority of Muslims, Shiite scholars maintained that the Qur'an should be interpreted in light of

---

39. Ghassan Abdul-Jabbar, "The Classical Tradition," in *The Wiley Blackwell Concise Companion to Hadith*, ed. Daniel W. Brown (Wiley Blackwell, 2020), 19.

40. There are nuanced differences in the approaches to hadith among various Shiite groups, such as the Ismailis and Zaydis. In this brief section, our focus is on Twelver Shiism.

the hadith.[41] However, their approach to hadith differed from the Sunni tradition in several ways. The most significant distinction concerns its approach to the chain of narration. For example, in the case of Twelver Shiism, unlike in the Sunni tradition, the chain of hadith does not continue primarily through the companions of the Prophet but rather through members of the Prophet's household, including Ali ibn Abi Talib, and then the Twelve Imams. The narrations in the hadith collections of Imami Shiism consist of three forms: a hadith attributed to the Prophet and transmitted through the chain of imams, a saying of an imam transmitted by later imams, and a saying of an imam transmitted by his followers with a chain (*isnad*).[42] In this context, for Shi'i scholars, hadith encompasses "the oral or behavioral teachings" of both the Prophet Muhammad and the Twelve Imams.[43] In other words, as described by a Shiite scholar, hadith is "all that is received from the Prophet or the Imams."[44] Shiite scholars generally distinguish between reports attributed to the Prophet and those originating from the imams. While reserving the term *hadith* exclusively for what is received from the Prophet, they use the term *khabar* (plural *akhbar*, meaning *news* or *reports*) to refer to narrations received from the Twelve Imams.[45] Eventually, four books of hadith (*al-kutub al-arba'a*) became prominent in the Shiite tradition and served as foundational texts for its jurisprudence and theology: *Al-Kafi* by Muhammad ibn Ya'qub al-Kulayni (d. 941 CE); *Man La Yahduruhu al-Faqih* by Ibn Babawayh al-Qummi, known as Al-Saduq (d. 991 CE); and *Tahdhib al-Ahkam* and *Al-Istibsar*, both by Abu Ja'far Muhammad ibn al-Hasan al-Tusi (d. 1067 CE).[46]

---

41. Ahmad Pakatchi, "Shi'ism," in *The Wiley Blackwell Concise Companion to Hadith*, ed. Daniel W. Brown (Wiley Blackwell, 2020), 281.

42. Brown, *Hadith*, 123–149.

43. Pakatchi, "Shi'ism," 281.

44. Zain al-Din al-Shahid al-Thani qtd. in Pakatchi, "Shi'ism," 281.

45. Pakatchi, "Shi'ism," 281.

46. Pakatchi, "Shi'ism," 287–290.

Hadith Commentaries

To understand the reports attributed to the Prophet, clarify their meanings, and explore their implications for the lives of Muslims, many scholars authored extensive commentaries on hadith collections. A typical hadith entry in a commentary includes several components. These may involve identifying other sources that contain the same hadith, discussing the identity and reliability of the narrators, evaluating the authenticity of the hadith, analyzing its linguistic and grammatical aspects, and exploring its implications for legal rulings and practical application.[47] For example, *Sahih al-Bukhari* alone has over a hundred commentaries. One of the most prominent is Ibn Hajar al-'Asqalani's (d. 1449) *Fath al-Bari*, which became a foundational text for interpreting the Prophet's hadiths. His student Sakhawi notes that Ibn Hajar studied under 628 teachers, 55 of whom were women.[48]

Examples from the Hadith Collections

Hadith collections contain descriptions of every aspect of the Prophet's life, including his spirituality, outward appearance, manners, morals, social relations, and family life. Significant portions of the hadiths focus on what the Prophet said about certain rituals and how he performed them. The following excerpts are examples:

> Whoever obeys me obeys God, and whoever disobeys me disobeys God.[49]

> There is no envy except in two cases: a person to whom God has given wealth and who spends it in the right way, and a person

---

47. Mustafa Macit Karagözoğlu, "Commentaries," in *The Wiley Blackwell Concise Companion to Hadith*, ed. Daniel W. Brown (Wiley Blackwell, 2020), 167–170.

48. M. Yaşar Kandemir, "İbn Hacer el-Askalani," in *İslam Ansiklopedisi* (Türkiye Diyanet Vakfı, 1999), 19:514.

49. *Sahih al-Muslim, kitab al-'imara, bab wujubi ta'a al-'umara*.

to whom God has given wisdom (i.e., religious knowledge) who makes decisions accordingly and teaches it to others.⁵⁰

God is beautiful and loves beauty.⁵¹

There are two blessings that many people squander: health and free time.⁵²

Live in this world as if you were a stranger or a traveler.⁵³

In the last third of the night, our Lord, the Blessed and Exalted, descends to the lowest heaven and says, "Is there anyone who prays to Me so that I may answer their prayer? Is there anyone who asks something of Me so that I may grant it to them? Is there anyone who seeks My forgiveness so that I may forgive them?"⁵⁴

God's Messenger (pbuh) used to pray, saying, "O God! I seek refuge in You from a heart that does not humble itself, from a prayer that is not heard, from a soul that is never satisfied, and from knowledge that brings no benefit. I seek refuge in You from these four."⁵⁵

Islam is based on five principles: testifying that there is no god but God and that Muhammad is the Messenger of God,

---

50. *Sahih al-Bukhari, kitab al-zakat, bab 'infaq al-mal fi haqqihi.*

51. *Sahih Muslim, kitab al-iman, bab tahrim al-kibr wa bayanihi.*

52. *Sahih al-Bukhari, kitab al-riqaq, bab ma ja'a fi al-riqaq wa 'an la 'aysha illa 'ayshu al-akhira.*

53. *Sahih al-Bukhari, kitab al-riqaq, bab qawli nabiyy salla Allahu 'alayhi wa sallam, "kun fi dunya kaannaka gharib aw 'abiru sabil."*

54. *Sahih al-Bukhari, kitab al-da'wat, bab al-du'a'i nisf al-layl.*

55. *Jami' al-Tirmidhi, kitab al-da'wat.*

performing the compulsory prayers, paying *zakat* (almsgiving), performing Hajj (the pilgrimage to Mecca), and fasting during Ramadan.[56]

Faith has over seventy branches, the most excellent of which is the declaration that there is no god but God, and the humblest of which is the removal of something harmful from the road. Modesty is also a branch of faith.[57]

I am a human being, so when I command you to do something related to religion, follow it. But when I give you an instruction based on my personal opinion, remember that I am just a human being.[58]

On Judgment Day, rights will be restored to the deserving, such that even the hornless sheep will receive what it is owed from the horned sheep.[59]

By Him who holds the soul of Muhammad in His hands! A believer is like a honeybee: it consumes good things, produces good things, lands on good places, and does not break or harm the place it lands on.[60]

The excellence in faith (*ihsan*) is to worship God as if you see Him. Even if you do not see Him, He sees you.[61]

---

56. *Jami' al-Tirmidhi, kitab al-iman, bab ma ja'a buniya al-'Islam 'ala khamsin.*
57. *Sahih Muslim, kitab al-iman, bab bayan 'adadi su'abi al-iman.*
58. *Musnad Ahmad*, 6872.
59. *Jami' al-Tirmidhi, kitab al-qiyama, bab ma ja'a fi sha'ni al-hisab wa al-qisas.*
60. *Musnad Ahmad*, 6872.
61. *Sahih al-Bukhari, kitab al-tafsir, bab qawlihi innallaha 'ilmu al-sa'ati.*

Whoever is not grateful to people is not grateful to God.[62]

The one who repents from sin is like one who has not sinned at all.[63]

On the implications of practicing good Islam: A man asked the Prophet (pbuh), "What deeds or qualities of Islam are considered good?" The Prophet (pbuh) replied, "To feed the poor and to greet both those you know and those you do not know."[64]

None of you will have faith until he wishes for his brother what he likes for himself.[65]

If a man provides for his family with the sincere intention of seeking God's reward, it is considered a form of charity in terms of the reward he will receive.[66]

You will be rewarded for whatever you spend for God's sake, even if it is just a morsel that you place in your wife's mouth.[67]

A man approached the Prophet (pbuh) seeking permission to participate in *jihad*. The Prophet (pbuh) asked him, "Are your

---

62. *Al-Tirmidhi, kitab al-birr, bab ma ja'a fi al-shukr liman ahsana ilayk.*

63. *Sunan ibn Majah, kitab al-zuhd, bab al-zuhd fi al-dunya.*

64. *Sahih al-Bukhari, kitab al-iman, bab it'amu al-ta'amai min al-'Islam.*

65. *Sahih al-Bukhari, kitab al-iman, bab it'amu al-ta'amai min al-'Islam.*

66. *Sahih al-Bukhari, kitab al-iman, bab ma ja'a anna a'mal bilniyyat walhisbati wa likulli amri'in ma nawa.*

67. *Sahih al-Bukhari, kitab al-iman, bab ma ja'a anna a'mal bilniyyat walhisbati wa likulli amri'in ma nawa.*

parents still alive?" When the man confirmed, the Prophet (pbuh) said, "Then devote your efforts to serving them."[68]

These examples show that the hadiths of the Prophet Muhammad address many aspects of Muslim life, guiding followers to conduct themselves in accordance with the teachings of the Qur'an and the Sunna of the Prophet.

What the Prophet Meant

Sorting hadiths based on a reliable chain of narration was not sufficient to fully understand the Prophet's words; the text of the hadith (*matn*) also needed careful study. It would be unrealistic to assume that the companions and the generations that followed were able to quote the Prophet word for word. In fact, many hadiths are likely the narrator's interpretation of the Prophet's words. To accurately understand the text of a hadith, scholars focused on several criteria: comprehending the language of the hadith, including both its literal and metaphorical meanings; interpreting the hadith in light of the Qur'an and the Sunna; considering the context in which the Prophet said or did something; and determining whether the hadith contradicts reason.

On one occasion, a companion of the Prophet came to Aisha and told her about a reported hadith: "God tortures a deceased believer because of the crying of his relatives."[69] She responded that the Qur'an is sufficient for clarification and that they should refer to it to resolve the matter. Aisha then pointed to a verse from the Qur'an: "Each soul is responsible for its own actions; no soul will bear the burden of another."[70] She emphasized the principle of individual responsibility and highlighted

---

68. *Sahih al-Bukhari, kitab al-jihad wa al-siyar, bab al-jihad bi'izni al-abawayn.*

69. *Jami' al-Tirmidhi, kitab al-jana'iz, bab ma ja'a fi al-rukhsati fi al-buka'i 'ala al-mayyit.*

70. Qur'an 6:164.

the misinterpretation of the hadith in question.⁷¹ In another instance, the following hadith was attributed to the Prophet and narrated by his companion Abu Hurayra: "Prayer is annulled by a dog, a donkey, and a woman [passing in front of the person praying]." When Aisha heard this report, she objected: "By God, I saw the Prophet (pbuh) praying while I lay in my bed between him and the direction of the qibla. Whenever I needed something, I would quietly slip away, as I disliked facing him."⁷² As someone who knew the Prophet better than anyone, Aisha pointed out that this hadith was inconsistent with the Prophet's practice.

In some instances, the Prophet used metaphors to convey a message. For example, he said, "Treat women nicely, for a woman is created from a rib, and the most curved portion of the rib is its upper portion. If you try to straighten it, it will break, but if you leave it as it is, it will remain crooked. So treat women nicely."⁷³ If we interpret this hadith literally, it might suggest that women were not created from dust like men were. However, focusing on the metaphorical interpretation provides a different understanding. The implication is not that women were literally created from a rib. As pointed out by a modern scholar, the Prophet "refers to women's sensitive and delicate nature and advises his followers to be careful not to oppress them, to respect their rights, to forgive their mistakes (if any), and to exercise patience in the face of their shortcomings."⁷⁴

Another example of the Prophet's use of metaphor is an incident when the companions heard a loud sound while they were with him. He then said, "This is the sound of a stone that has been rolling for seventy years and has just now reached the bottom of Hell."⁷⁵ A few moments later, someone arrived and reported that a well-known seventy-

---

71. *Islam Through Hadiths*, 1:108.

72. *Sahih al-Bukhari, kitab al-salat, bab man qala la yaqda'u al-salata shay'un.*

73. *Sahih al-Bukhari, kitab 'ahadith al-'anbiya, bab khalqi adam salawatu allahi 'alayhi wa dhurriyatihi.*

74. *Islam Through Hadiths*, 1:121.

75. *Sahih Muslim, kitab al-janna wa sifa na'imiha wa ahliha.*

year-old hypocrite had just died. If one were to take the Prophet's statement literally, its intended meaning might be difficult to grasp. However, he employs a metaphor to illustrate the fate of a hypocrite in the community, emphasizing the long, inevitable descent into punishment.[76] Similarly, in another hadith, the Prophet said, "Satan circulates in the human body as blood does."[77] The intended meaning is not that Satan physically flows through the body like blood but rather that his influence over human thoughts and emotions is subtle and continuous. Just as blood circulates rapidly and imperceptibly, Satan's whispers and influence can be swift and unnoticed.

The context in which the Prophet spoke is also crucial for understanding his intended meaning. It is reported that during one of his Friday sermons, the Prophet said, "Any one of you attending the Friday (prayers) should take a bath."[78] If we do not consider the context of this hadith, it might imply that it is obligatory for Muslims to shower before Friday prayers. However, when we study the context, the intended meaning becomes clear. A traveler once asked one of the companions whether it was required to take a bath before Friday prayer in light of this hadith. The explanation provided by Ibn Abbas, a companion of the Prophet, clarifies the Prophet's intent. In the past, people were poor, wore woolen clothes, and often carried heavy loads. Their mosque was small, with a low roof resembling a vine trellis. On a particularly hot day, the Prophet noticed that people were sweating heavily in their woolen garments, causing an unpleasant odor that made it uncomfortable for everyone. Observing this, the Prophet said, "O people, when Friday comes, you should take a bath, and each of you should anoint yourself with the best oil and perfume you have." Later, as the people became more prosperous, they wore different clothes, were no longer burdened with heavy labor, and their mosques became larger, eliminating the foul smell that had troubled them. Therefore, taking a bath on Fridays is not a religious obligation to honor

---

76. Nursi, *Lem'alar*, 165.

77. *Sahih al-Bukhari*, kitab al-i'tikaf, bab ziyara al-mar'a zawjaha fi i'tikafihi.

78. *Sahih al-Bukhari*, kitab al-jum'ah, bab al-duhn liljumu'a.

the day or the prayer itself but rather a practical measure to ensure that one does not disturb others in a communal setting. In other narrations, the Prophet also encouraged those attending Friday prayers to clean their teeth, wear their best clothes, and apply pleasant perfume.[79]

Despite the central role of hadith in Muslim life, some modern Muslim scholars have expressed skepticism about the hadith literature and its role in Islam. Several reasons contribute to this skepticism. First, hadiths attributed to the Prophet were primarily transmitted orally, and the major collections were compiled in the ninth century, more than two hundred years after the Prophet's death. Second, some hadiths in these collections are perceived as incompatible with contemporary values, particularly in areas such as human rights, gender equality, and science. As a response, some scholars advocate emphasizing the Qur'an over the hadith literature, arguing that any hadith contradicting Qur'anic principles should be disregarded. A few have even suggested that the hadith tradition should be completely abandoned, asserting that the Qur'an alone provides sufficient guidance for Muslims.[80]

Conclusion

The Prophet Muhammad was a living embodiment of the Qur'an, and his way—the Sunna—is regarded as the ideal implementation of God's words. His followers were deeply committed to preserving the spirit of the Prophet, understanding that following his example was a sign of their love for and obedience to God. The companions and the generations that followed were meticulous in observing the Prophet's actions and words. They dedicated themselves to safeguarding his spiritual legacy by embodying his teachings in their lives and transmitting them to future generations through the hadith collections. It is, therefore, fair to say that

---

79. *Sunan abi Dawud, kitab al-tahara, bab fi al-rukhsati fi tarki al-ghusl al-jumu'a* and *Islam Through Hadiths*, 1:117.

80. In this context, notable figures include the Egyptian-American scholar Rashad Khalifa (d. 1990), the Syrian philosopher Muhammad Shahrur (d. 2019), and the US-based Muslim scholars Fazlur Rahman and Amina Wadud.

no area of Islamic civilization remains untouched by the teachings of the Prophet Muhammad. Fundamental questions about life and faith find their answers in his example: Who is God, and how should one relate to Him? What are the responsibilities of being human? What are the dimensions of faith (*iman*)? How should one practice Islamic rituals such as prayer, fasting, charity, and pilgrimage? What are the attributes of an ethical person? How should one contribute to society? How are transactions conducted ethically? How does one prepare for life after death? Muslims seek guidance for these questions by following the Sunna of the Prophet, as recorded in the hadith collections. Moreover, Muslims have not only followed the example of the Prophet in every aspect of their lives but also remembered and celebrated his legacy across diverse cultures and contexts. This aspect of the Prophet's enduring spiritual influence will be explored further in the final chapter.

CHAPTER FIVE

Remembering the Prophet

An American Muslim friend of mine recently returned from Istanbul. During his time in the city, he visited the Eyub Sultan Mosque for the dawn prayer (*fajr*) on Sunday. After the prayers, hundreds of people stopped by the tomb in the mosque's courtyard to offer their private invocations (*du'a'*). My friend found it remarkable to see so many Muslim worshippers standing in front of the tomb before sunrise, offering supplications.

The mosque is located in the Eyup Sultan district of the city, and both the mosque and the district are named after Abu Ayyub al-Ansari, a companion of Muhammad who hosted him in his home for seven months after the Prophet had emigrated to Medina. Abu Ayyub died during an Islamic expedition to conquer Istanbul and was buried near the city walls in the late seventh century. His grave was rediscovered in a vision by the Ottoman scholar Akşemseddin (d. 1459) after the conquest of Istanbul. Akşemseddin was the teacher and spiritual mentor of Mehmed the Conqueror (d. 1481). Shortly after the conquest in 1453, Sultan Mehmed built a mosque complex (*külliye*) that included the tomb of Abu Ayyub, a school (*madrasa*), a mosque, a public kitchen, and a bathhouse. The Eyub Sultan complex became a major attraction throughout Ottoman history and remains so in modern Türkiye. The installation of Ottoman sultans often took place in front of Abu Ayyub's tomb.

Today, many newlywed couples include the site in their wedding programs, and those in need visit the tomb to pray to God for their requests to be fulfilled. The complex has become a pilgrimage site of sorts. Inside the Eyup Sultan Mosque, one of the calligraphies in the Ottoman Turkish reads:

Isn't this blessing of God enough for the people of this city?
The companion of the Noble Beloved [Muhammad], Abu
Ayyub al-Ansari.[1]

These lines suggest that the mere presence of the tomb of Abu Ayyub al-Ansari, the Prophet's companion, in the city is a sufficient blessing from God for the people of Istanbul.

Muslims' love for Abu Ayyub al-Ansari is rooted in their love for Muhammad, as he was the Prophet's companion and host in Medina. This chapter explores how Muslims have remembered the Prophet and expressed their love for him through culture and literature.

Sending Peace and Blessings Upon the Prophet (*Salawat*)

One of the most common ways of remembering the Prophet in the tradition is sending peace and blessings upon him (*salawat*), which is a fundamental aspect of Islamic piety. Whenever Muhammad's name is mentioned, Muslims say, "Peace and blessings of God be upon him" (*sallallahu 'alayhi wassallam*). This practice is also incorporated into the supplications recited during the five daily prayers (*salat*), which include this invocation: "O God! Send Your mercy on Muhammad and on the family of Muhammad, as You sent Your mercy on Abraham and on the family of Abraham, for You are the Most Praiseworthy, the Most Glorious."

Praising the Prophet and sending him peace and blessings have their foundations in the Qur'an and various sayings of Muhammad. For instance, the Qur'an states, "God and His angels send blessings on the Prophet: O you who believe! Send blessings on him, and salute him with all respect."[2] Sending peace and blessings upon the Prophet is thus

---

1. The original text of the calligraphic lines in Ottoman Turkish reads *Yetişmez mi bu şehrin halkına bu nimet-i Bârî, Habîb-i Ekrem'in yârî, Ebâ Eyyûbi'l-Ensârî*.

2. Qur'an 33:56.

Remembering the Prophet

seen as an expression of following the Qur'an's teaching and honoring the Prophet's spiritual legacy. As part of their invocations, Muslims ask God to elevate Muhammad's status. Numerous hadiths emphasize the importance of this practice, including one in which the Prophet said, "On the Day of Judgment, those closest to me will be those who send peace and blessings upon me."[3]

Sending peace and blessings upon the Prophet is an integral part of many occasions in Muslim societies. In Turkish Islamic culture, for example, *salawat* is often recited during weddings, when sending off pilgrims, or when someone is initiated into a Sufi order. A common form of sending peace and blessings upon the Prophet is known as *sala*, which is typically recited from the minarets of mosques. This melodic praise of the Prophet is invoked on Fridays, on special nights, during the two major religious holidays (Eid), and to announce the death of a community member. The text usually recited for the *sala* is as follows:

> Peace and blessings be upon you,
> O our master, the Messenger of God.
> Peace and blessings be upon you,
> O our master, the beloved of God.
> Peace and blessings be upon you,
> O master of the past and the future.
> And all praise belongs to God, Lord of the worlds.[4]

A culture surrounding the *salawat* is common in many other Muslim societies as well. In September 2024, a friend of mine from America traveled to Jakarta, Indonesia, for a conference with his family. During their visit, they included a stop at the Istiqlal Mosque, one of the largest mosques in the world. Their visit coincided with the evening (*maghrib*) prayer. While they were struck by the grandeur of the prayer hall—with multiple levels

---

3. *Jami' al-Tirmidhi, kitab al-witr, bab ma ja'a fi al-fadl 'ala nabiyy salla allahu 'alayhi wa sallam.*

4. Translation by author.

of balconies scaling its sides—they witnessed a remarkable experience unlike anything they had encountered at a typical mosque in America. As the prayer concluded, more than a hundred congregants slowly began a communal chant glorifying and praising God. The beautiful, rhythmic litany soon evolved, with teenagers playing *duff* drums joining the ensemble with practiced ease. Meanwhile, the Arabic phrases—along with their English translations—flashed across giant screens at the front of the sanctuary, serving as aids for the uninitiated. The recitation crescendoed, and a hush fell over the devotees as everyone rose to their feet, heads bowed in respect. Hymns of peace and blessings (*salawat*) now rang out in honor of the Prophet Muhammad. Watching the congregants chant solemnly as an expression of their love for the Messenger of God moved my friend and his family to tears.[5] In many Muslim societies, when the Prophet's name is mentioned alongside a *salawat*, it is common to stand or bow out of respect and reverence for Muhammad. Growing up in a Muslim community, I often observed this heartfelt gesture of love in remembrance of the Prophet.

Remembering the Prophet Through *Dalail*

Muslims have long remembered the Prophet through various supplications. One of the most comprehensive supplications for praising and venerating the Prophet is Imam al-Jazuli's (d. 1465) *Dalail al-Khayrat* (*Signs of Good Deeds*). This work has been widely read across Muslim societies. In the introduction, al-Jazuli states that those who recite this work will gain the Prophet's intercession (*shafa'a*) for salvation, have their sins forgiven, be edified with better character, be protected from sin, and find relief from worldly struggles. Many Muslims read the *Dalail* daily, and it was once "the most commonly owned" book after the Qur'an in some Muslim communities.[6] A section of the first chapter of *Dalail* reads:

> O God, bless our master Muhammad, and his wives and offspring, and all the Prophets and Messengers, the angels, those

---

5. I am grateful to the Munir family for sharing this experience with me.

6. Brown, *Muhammad*, 107.

brought near to God, and all the righteous servants of God as much as all the rain that has fallen from the sky since the time it was established. Bless our master Muhammad in quantity as great as all the plants the earth has brought forth since the time it was spread out. Bless our master Muhammad in quantity as great as the stars in the sky, for it is You who can count them. And bless our master Muhammad in quantity as great as the breaths that are breathed by souls since You created them. Bless our master Muhammad in quantity as great as what You have created and what You will create and what Your knowledge contains, and bless him immeasurably more than those quantities.

In the concluding part of *Dalail al-Khayrat*, the Prophet is praised with the following words:

O God, bless our master Muhammad and the family of our master Muhammad in quantity as great as the drops of rain. Bless our master Muhammad and the family of our master Muhammad in quantity as great as the leaves of the trees. Bless our master Muhammad and the family of our master Muhammad in quantity as great as the foam of the seas. Bless our master Muhammad and the family of our master Muhammad in quantity as great as the rivers. Bless our master Muhammad and the family of our master Muhammad in quantity as great as the sand of the deserts and wastelands. Bless our master Muhammad and the family of our master Muhammad in quantity as great as the weight of the mountains and rocks. Bless our master Muhammad and the family of our Muhammad in quantity as great as the inhabitants of the Garden and the inhabitants of the Fire. Bless our master Muhammad and the family of our master Muhammad in quantity as great as the righteous and the dissolute. And bless our master Muhammad and the family of our master Muhammad in quantity as great as the endless alternating cycles of day and night.

Al-Jazuli invokes blessings on Muhammad, his family, and the righteous, using poetic imagery to express abundance and vastness. The blessings are quantified in terms of rain, plants, stars, breaths, and all that God has created or will create, highlighting the boundless nature of God's mercy and the immeasurable honor due to the Prophet. The blessings are compared with drops of rain, leaves of trees, foam of seas, rivers, sand, mountains, and even the cycles of day and night.

This repetition and imagery reflect a profound attempt to convey infinite love to the Prophet, transcending human limitations of measurement. Through such vivid language, the *Dalail* not only inspires personal devotion but also fosters a sense of unity among Muslims in their shared love for Muhammad. The emphasis on limitless blessings underscores the Prophet's central role as a source of guidance and mercy for humanity.

Mawlid: Celebrating the Birth of the Prophet

Another important tradition in Islamic piety for remembering Muhammad is the *mawlid*, a celebration commemorating the Prophet's birth. While the specific forms of the celebration vary across cultures, they often include the recitation of a poetic genre known as *mawlid* (or *mawlidiyya* in parts of Africa). One of the most renowned examples of poetry associated with Muhammad is *Qasida al-Burda* (*The Poem of the Mantle*) by Ka'b ibn Zuhayr.

Initially a critic of the Prophet, Ka'b composed satirical poems against him. However, after visiting Muhammad, Ka'b converted to Islam and sought the Prophet's forgiveness. As a gesture of reconciliation, Ka'b recited a poem in praise of the Prophet, who was so pleased that he gifted Ka'b the cloak he was wearing.

This poem has since become a classic in Islamic literature, inspiring numerous commentaries and imitations. It has been widely recited throughout Islamic history and is known as *Qasida al-Burda* because of this story. In one part of the poem, Ka'b relates to the Prophet as follows:

They say the Messenger of God had threatened me,
but from him, I seek only pardon and mercy.

Go gently, and let the One who gave you
the gift of the Quran—filled with warnings and wisdom—be
your guide.

Do not hold me accountable for the words of my slanderers,
No matter how great their lies are, I am not as guilty as they
claim.

If an elephant stood in my place and heard what I hear
It would shake in terror and stay shaking until it received the
messenger's grace, God willing.[7]

These lines reflect Ka'b's humility, repentance, and appeal for forgiveness from the Messenger of God. In the last section, he uses the imagery of an elephant to illustrate the overwhelming awe and reverence he feels in the presence of the Prophet. He likens his own trembling to that of even the mightiest creature, expressing his vulnerability and desperate need for Muhammad's mercy.

Imam al-Busiri's *Qasida*

Another poem commonly recited during *mawlid* celebrations is Imam al-Busiri's famous *qasida*, also known as *Qasida al-Burda* (*The Poem of the Mantle*). Imam Busiri, a thirteenth-century Egyptian Sufi and poet, suffered from paralysis and persistently sought healing from God through worship and prayer. He also composed numerous poems in praise of Muhammad. According to tradition, the Prophet appeared

---

[7]. For Ka'b ibn Zuhary's poem and the translation, see Michael Anthony Sells, "Banat Su'ad: Translation and Interpretive Introduction," *Journal of Arabic Literature* 21, no. 2 (1990): 140–154.

to him in a dream one night and asked him to recite one of his poems. Unsure which poem to choose, as he had written many in praise of the Prophet, Busiri hesitated. The Prophet then recited the opening lines of one of the poems, prompting Busiri to continue reciting it while the Prophet listened. When Busiri finished, the Prophet removed his cloak and covered Busiri with it, then touched the paralyzed area of his body. On waking the next morning, Busiri found that he had been cured of his paralysis. This miraculous event became widely known, and the poem came to be known as *Qasida al-Burda* (*The Poem of the Mantle*). The poem is now commonly recited by Muslims as a form of remembrance of God and God's messenger and as a means of seeking healing for those suffering from paralysis.[8]

In his poem, Busiri reflects on various aspects of the Prophet's life and offers praise. In chapter 3, he praises the Prophet with the following words:

> He is like the sun: small to the eye when seen from afar,
> But dazzling to the sight when seen close up.
>
> How can his reality be grasped in this world
> By sleeping folk, distracted from him by dreams?
>
> It is as if precious hidden pearls, sparkling from their shells,
> came from the treasure-mine of his speech and smile.
>
> No perfume can match the ground that holds his bones.
> Blessed are those who breathe in its fragrance or kiss it!

In the last chapter, al-Busuri turns to God and the intercession of the Prophet, the Chosen One, on the day of judgment for the forgiveness of his sin:

---

8. Mahmut Kaya, "Kasidetü'l Bürde," in *İslam Ansiklopedisi* (Türkiye Diyanet Vakfı, 2001), 24:568–569.

O soul, despair not over a fault that is immense;
Enormities, with divine forgiveness, are like minor errors.

O Lord, by the Chosen One, allow us to attain our hopes
And forgive us for what has gone past, O Vastly Generous.[9]

These lines from *Qasida al-Burda* reveal Busiri's great admiration for the Prophet Muhammad and his role as an intercessor. The Prophet is compared to the sun, whose true brilliance is only fully appreciated up close, symbolizing Muhammad's unmatched greatness, which is beyond full comprehension in this world. Busiri laments humanity's distraction by worldly illusions, likening people to those dreaming, unable to grasp the reality of the Prophet's high status. The imagery of pearls emerging from the Prophet's speech and smile highlights the beauty and wisdom of his words and character, portraying him as a source of divine blessings. Busiri's love for the Prophet is vividly expressed in his praise of the earth that holds his blessed body, considering it sacred and fragrant. In the final chapter, Busiri shifts focus to repentance, seeking God's forgiveness through the intercession of Muhammad on the day of judgment. His prayer in the last lines encapsulates the essence of hope and mercy in Islamic spirituality, where even the gravest sins can be absolved through divine grace and the Prophet's intercession.

Süleyman Çelebi's *Mevlid*

In the Ottoman Empire and the Turkish-speaking world, the most renowned work of *mawlid* literature has been Süleyman Çelebi's (d. 1411) *Vesiletü'n Necat* (*The Path to Salvation*), commonly known as the *Mevlid*. It begins with praises to God and the creation of the universe, followed by the creation of Muhammad's soul and the extraordinary events surrounding his birth. In other sections of his *Mevlid*, Çelebi recounts Muhammad's prophethood and major miracles, including his ascension to heaven, his character, and his death. He concludes the

---

9. For the text and a translation of the *qasida*, see https://www.qasidaburda.com.

work with prayers and praises for Muhammad. For centuries, Çelebi's *Mevlid* has been recited to celebrate the birth of the Prophet, as well as at weddings, funerals, circumcision ceremonies, birth rituals, marriages, on sacred days and nights, and when sending people off for military service.[10] Regarding Muhammad's character, Çelebi writes,

> Withdrawing from the world, he did not favor,
> And those who loved the world only deceived themselves, he said.
>
> In all his lifetime, no lie ever crossed his lips,
> No shadow of falsehood ever cast upon him.
>
> He never harmed anyone with word or deed,
> Always obedient to the commands of the Lord.
>
> With unique attributes, he was a perfect king,
> These qualities drew him closer to the Lord.

In this section from *Mevlid*, the Prophet is praised as the epitome of moral excellence and divine obedience. Çelebi portrays him as a "perfect king," not in worldly power but in his unique virtues and closeness to the divine, emphasizing that his greatness lay in his spiritual and moral qualities. Regarding the death of the Prophet, Çelebi laments:

> This is the news of Mustafa's passing away,
> So when it reaches you, let grief and tears hold sway.
>
> Let your eyes flow with water because of this pain,
> Sacrifice your soul, and let your love for him be unchained.
>
> Whoever hears this news and does not lament or ache,
> Whose heart does not break with this distress:

---

10. A. Necla Pekolcay, "Mevlid," in *İslam Ansiklopedisi* (Türkiye Diyanet Vakfı, 2001), 29:486.

He would be considered worse than a tree or stone,
To call him a man, no one would ever agree.

Express your love for Mustafa if you truly love him,
For one who does not love Mustafa is a rebel grim![11]

Here, Çelebi calls on believers to openly grieve, shedding tears and offering their very souls as expressions of love for the Prophet. He makes the point that such grief is a natural and essential response for those who truly understand Muhammad's unparalleled status. For Çelebi, failing to feel sorrow because of the death of the Prophet reflects a lack of humanity, likening such a person to lifeless objects like trees or stones.

Seeing the Prophet in Your Dreams

Muslims have remembered the Prophet through dreams as well. Encountering the Prophet in a dream is a significant aspect of Sufism and Islamic piety. Many Sufi saints have reported seeing the Prophet in their dreams, citing a hadith in which the Prophet said, "He who sees me in a dream has indeed seen me, for Satan cannot assume my form."[12] Some Sufi saints have even attributed their teachings to the Prophet through these dream encounters. For instance, Ibn Arabi attributes his work *Fusus al-Hikam* (*The Bezels of Wisdom*) to the Prophet. In a dream, he saw the Prophet holding a book, and Muhammad told him, "This is the book of *Fusus al-Hikam*. Take it and share it with humanity so that they may benefit from it."[13]

---

11. For an introduction to and a translation of Celebi's *Mevlid*, see Syed Tenvir Wasti, "The Mevlid or Nativity Poem by Suleyman Celebi," *Tehseel* 11, no. 3 (2018): 1–76. I slightly revised the translation for accessibility.

12. *Sahih al-Bukhari, kitab al-ta'bir, bab man ra'a nabiyy salla allahu 'alayhi wa sallam fi al-manam.*

13. Ibn Arabi qtd. in Süleyman Uludağ, "Rüya: Tasavvuf," in *İslam Ansiklopedisi* (Türkiye Diyanet Vakfı, 2008), 35:309.

Reimagining the Prophet Through *Shamails*

It is also important to mention *shamail*, a genre in Islamic literature dedicated to the detailed descriptions of the Prophet Muhammad. Drawing from the Qur'an, hadith, and works about the Prophet's life and character, Muslim scholars compiled books that focused on his daily life, physical appearance, character, demeanor, spiritual practices, and habits. The purpose of these *shamail* works was to present an intimate portrait of the Messenger of God, inspiring love and emulation among Muslims. One of the most renowned *shamail* works was composed by Imam al-Tirmidhi, *Al-Shamail al-Muhammadiyya*. Although he included a section on the Prophet's virtues and character in his hadith collection, al-Tirmidhi also separately compiled a book focusing on the Prophet's physical features, habits, and demeanor. In this work, al-Tirmidhi provides a vivid description of the Prophet, covering aspects such as his hair, eating and drinking habits, clothing style, sitting posture, humor, walk, speech, worship, prayers, death, and the seal of prophethood on his shoulder. Below are a few examples from al-Tirmidhi's *Shamail*:

> Narrated by Abu Saiʿd al-Khudri: When God's Messenger (peace and blessings be upon him) put on a new garment, he would mention its name and then say: "O God, praise is to You, for You have clothed me with this. I ask You for its goodness and the goodness for which it was made, and I seek refuge with You from its evil and the evil for which it was made."
>
> Narrated by Al-Bara' ibn 'Azib: I have never seen anyone among the people more handsome in a red garment than God's Messenger (peace and blessings be upon him), with the hair of his head falling close to his shoulders.
>
> Narrated by Anas ibn Malik: When God's Messenger (peace and blessings be upon him) went to bed, he would say: "Praise be to God, who has fed us, provided us with drink, sufficed us, and granted us shelter, for how many are there who have neither a provider of sufficiency nor a provider of shelter!"

Narrated by Aisha: We, the wives of Muhammad, would sometimes go an entire month without cooking anything over a fire, having nothing to eat or drink except dates and water.

Narrated by Anas ibn Malik: There was no person dearer to them [the companions of the Prophet] than God's Messenger (peace and blessings be upon him). However, when they saw him, they refrained from standing up, because they knew he disliked people rising for him.

Al-Shifa of Qadi Iyad

Another major *shamail* work is *Al-Shifa* by the Moroccan scholar Qadi Iyad (d. 1149). In his introduction, Qadi Iyad explains that he was asked to write a work on the exalted status of the Prophet, the love and reverence due to him by Muslims, the status of those who show disrespect to him, and the rights the Prophet confers to believers. He clarifies that he wrote this book not for those who disbelieve in the Prophet but for those who have accepted his message, with the aim of increasing their faith in God, deepening their love for the Prophet, and motivating them to more closely follow his example.

The work is divided into four parts. The first section discusses the Prophet's physical and spiritual beauty, his elevated status before God, and his miracles, all of which demonstrate the respect and veneration owed to him. The second section emphasizes the reasons for believing in him, obeying him, loving him wholeheartedly, and sending blessings and peace upon him. Qadi Iyad describes the third section as the heart of the book, where he explains the attributes that may or may not be found in the Prophet, how God protected him from sins and evils, and the actions he performed as a human being. The fourth section addresses the legal rulings concerning those who speak ill of the Prophet.

In the second section, Qadi Iyad outlines some of the rights the Prophet holds over Muslims, including having faith in him; obeying him; following his example; and showing love and respect to him, his family, and his companions. Additionally, he emphasizes the importance of sending blessings upon the Prophet. To illustrate the companions' love for the Prophet, Qadi Iyad quotes Ali ibn Abi Talib, who was once asked about their devotion to him. Ali replied, "By God, he (peace be upon him) was dearer to us than our property, children, fathers, mothers, and even cold water to a thirsty person."[14]

Qadi Iyad also highlights the companion Bilal's attitude toward death as a testament to his love for the Prophet. He recounts that when Bilal was on his deathbed, his wife lamented, "Oh, what a grievous moment!" But Bilal responded, "Oh, what a moment of delight! Tomorrow I will meet the beloved ones: the Prophet and his companions."[15]

Muhammad in Calligraphy

The Prophet and his teachings have also played a significant role in the development of Islamic calligraphy. As reported in a hadith, "God is beautiful and loves beauty."[16] Muslim artists often expressed their love for the Prophet through their beautiful calligraphic works. While Islamic theology has generally discouraged visual depictions of the Prophet, there has been a strong focus on written descriptions that emphasize his appearance and virtues. One prominent example is *hilya*, particularly popular in the Ottoman Empire and modern Türkiye. *Hilya* is a genre of calligraphic art that depicts the Prophet's attributes in books and framed pieces. Examples of *hilya* are commonly found in Islamic calligraphy and often displayed on the walls of mosques, schools, and Muslim households.

Structurally, a *hilya* typically begins with the Qur'anic phrase "In the name of God, the Most Merciful, the Most Compassionate

---

14. Qadi Iyad, *Al-Shifa*, trans. Gehan Abdel-Raouf Hibah (Dar al-Kotob al-Ilmiyya, 2013), 453.

15. Qadi Iyad, *al-Shifa*, 454.

16. *Riyad al-Salihin, kitab al-muqaddamat, bab tahrim al-kibr wa al-i'jab.*

(*basmala*)." It features a large central disc that describes the physical appearance and character of the Prophet. Surrounding this central disc are four smaller discs containing the names of the four rightly guided caliphs: Abu Bakr, Umar, Uthman, and Ali. Below the central disc, there is usually a verse from the Qur'an related to the Prophet, such as "We have sent you [O Prophet] only as a mercy for the whole world"[17] or "And you are truly [a man] of outstanding character."[18] The final section of the *hilya* often includes the remainder of a hadith describing the Prophet. The most commonly used narration in *hilyas* comes from Ali ibn Abi Talib, the Prophet's cousin and son-in-law:

> He was not too tall nor too short. He was medium-sized. His hair was not short and curly, nor was it lank, but in between. His face was not narrow, nor was it fully round, but there was a roundness to it. His skin was white. His eyes were black. He had long eyelashes. He was big-boned and had wide shoulders. He had no body hair except in the middle of his chest. He had thick hands and feet. When he walked, he walked inclined, as if descending a slope. When he looked at someone, he looked at them in full face. Between his shoulders was the seal of prophecy, the sign that he was the last of the prophets. He was the most generous-hearted of men, the most truthful of them in speech, the most mild-tempered of them, and the noblest of them in lineage. Whoever saw him unexpectedly was in awe of him. And whoever associated with him familiarly, loved him. Anyone who would describe him would say, I never saw, before him or after him, the like of him. Peace be upon him.[19]

---

17. Qur'an 21:107.

18. Qur'an 68:4.

19. This description is based on the *Shamail* of Imam al-Tirmidhi.

Muhammad in Poetry

Considering the role of the Prophet in Islamic culture, he has naturally been a central theme in Islamic poetry and literature. We have already mentioned the poems of Ka'b Ibn Zuhayr and Imam Busiri in Arabic literature. Giants of Persian literature, such as Rumi (d. 1273), Saadi Shirazi (d. 1291), and Fariduddin Attar (d. 1221), also composed poems about the Prophet to express their deep love for him. For many of these poets, no story was more profound than that of Muhammad. As expressed by Hasan ibn Thabit, the Prophet's poet, in recounting Muhammad's story, their words were not sufficient to praise Muhammad; instead, their words gained beauty and worth because of mentioning him.[20]

In the introduction to his *Gulistan* (*The Rose Garden*), Saadi Shirazi offers praise to the Prophet and addresses him with the following words:

> What worry can the wall of the community have when it has one like you [Muhammad] as a supporter? What fear of the waves of the sea harbors he who has Noah as his captain?
>
> He [Muhammad] attained the heights with his perfection; he unveiled the dawn with his beauty. All of his qualities were beautiful: pray for him and his house.[21]

For Saadi, a community supported by the Prophet has nothing to fear, as it can overcome any struggle. He likens Muhammad's role to that of Noah, portraying him as the captain who safely guides his community to shore despite the tumultuous waves of the sea. Saadi also emphasizes that the Prophet was the epitome of the perfect human being, whose virtuous qualities illuminated the darkness of the world and hearts. He then urges his readers to send peace and blessings upon the Prophet and his family.

---

20. Nursi, *The Words*, 319.

21. Shaykh Mushrifuddin Sa'di of Shiraz, *The Gulistan of Sa'di*, trans. Wheeler M. Tackson (Ibex, 2017), 2.

Like Saadi, Rumi also expressed a profound love for the Messenger of God, viewing himself and his works as being in service to the Qur'an and the Prophet:

> I am a servant of the Qur'an as long as I live.
> I am but dust on the path of Muhammad, the Chosen One.
> If anyone interprets my words otherwise,
> I reject that person and his interpretation.[22]

Elsewhere, Rumi explains his reasoning for sending blessings upon the Prophet:

> I bring blessings upon you, (O Muhammad), so that the breeze of nearness (to God) may increase.
>
> Since, with the nearness of the Whole, all parts are allowed to approach.[23]

Rumi sees the Prophet as the embodiment of the entire community. His closeness to God benefits every member, including Rumi himself.

The Prophet is also a central theme in Ottoman literature, and many poets of the Ottoman era composed poems of praise (*qasida/naat*) dedicated to Muhammad. One of the most renowned examples is *The Qasida of Water* (*Su Kasidesi*) by Fuzuli (d. 1556). In this poem, every line ends with the word *su* (*water* in Turkish) as the rhyme. In certain sections, the flow of water symbolizes its longing to be united with the Prophet:

> It seems the water has fallen in love with the Beloved,
> For its course and flow lead toward the Prophet's abode.

---

22. Jalaluddin Rumi, *Divan*, trans. Abdulkadir Gölpınarlı (Kültür Bakanlığı, 2000), 2:1341.

23. Rumi, *Divan*, qtd. in Ibrahim Gamard, *Rumi and Islam* (Skylight, 2012), 136.

In another line, Fuzuli expresses his love for the Prophet as follows:

> O my friends, if I die without kissing the hand of my Beloved,
> Make a cup from the dust of my grave and present water with it to my Beloved.

In yet another couplet, Fuzuli uses the analogy of a rose for the Prophet:

> The gardener should quit watering the rose garden
> Even if he waters one thousand garden he would not have a rose like your face.

The rose symbolizes the Prophet in Ottoman literature, and there is none comparable to him. Fuzuli suggests that the gardener's labor is in vain; no matter how much effort he puts in, he will never grow a rose that matches the beauty of the Prophet's face.

Fuzuli concludes his lengthy poem with a prayer for union with the Prophet and the vision of his face on the Day of Resurrection:

> My hope is that on the Day of Resurrection, I will not be deprived
> Of the water from your fountain as I am so thirsty of seeing your face.

Here, the thirst symbolizes Fuzuli's deep longing to see the Prophet's face, and nothing can quench this thirst except the vision of Muhammad.

Many poems about the Prophet (*naat*) in Ottoman literature were also written by the sultans themselves. One such poet was Sultan Ahmed I (r. 1603–1617), who commissioned the construction of the Blue Mosque (Sultan Ahmed Camii) in Istanbul. Sultan Ahmed had a crest engraved with the footprint of Muhammad, which he would wear on Fridays and special nights. A poem was inscribed inside the crest, reflecting the sultan's great love for the Prophet Muhammad:

What if I always wear as a crown upon my head
The footprint of the king of prophets?

The owner of this footprint is the rose in the garden of prophethood.
Oh Ahmed, do not hesitate; bow your face to the footprint of that rose.

Like Fuzuli, in this line the sultan refers to the Prophet as a "rose." Many of these poems were later adapted into Islamic songs (*nasheed*), as Muhammad is a central theme in Islamic music.

Sacred Relics of the Prophet

Remembering Muhammad was not limited to poetry. Muslims have also sought to connect with the Messenger of God through his sacred relics. The companions of the Prophet had made efforts to collect and preserve relics of the Prophet, particularly when he had his haircut, as well as his other belongings.[24] Today, museums across the Muslim world house these relics, attracting millions of visitors each year.

The Topkapi Palace Museum, once the residence and administrative center of the Ottoman sultans, today houses many of the Prophet's relics, including his beard hair, mantle cloak, and personal belongings. For example, visiting the Prophet's mantle cloak during the month of Ramadan is a cherished tradition. As part of the ceremony, visitors are given specially designed handkerchiefs (*mendil*), which are touched to the cloak. The visitors then rub the handkerchiefs on their faces and kiss them, symbolically kissing the Prophet's cloak. These handkerchiefs are treasured for life, and it is customary for them to be included in the visitor's will, with instructions to be buried with the handkerchief covering their face. The following calligraphic lines are inscribed on the handkerchief:

---

24. *Hadislerle İslam*, 6:441.

Before the Prophet's mantle cloak,
Even the world's vast blue sky is unworthy as a doormat.
Turn to the Prophet with deep reverence,
And seek the intercession of the one who intercedes for all.

These lines inscribed on the handkerchief highlight the immense reverence Muslims hold for the Prophet Muhammad, portraying even the grand expanse of the sky as unworthy of serving as a doormat for his cloak, a metaphor emphasizing his unparalleled spiritual stature.

In addition, the Prophet is buried in Medina, and many Muslims include a visit to Medina as part of their *hajj*. Visiting the Prophet's tomb and spending time in his city is a spiritually uplifting experience for them.

Conclusion

In this chapter, we have explored the ways in which Muslims have remembered and honored the Prophet Muhammad through various cultural, spiritual, and literary traditions. From devotional poetry and supplications to sacred relics and artistic representations, these expressions highlight the deep love and reverence for the Prophet in Islamic piety. The widespread readings of works such as *Dalail al-Khayrat*, *Qasida al-Burda*, *al-Shifa*, and the *mawlid* genre illustrate the centrality of Muhammad in the spiritual and cultural lives of Muslim communities. Whether through prayers, dreams, or calligraphies, these acts of devotion serve as timeless reminders of the Prophet's lasting legacy as a source of guidance, mercy, and inspiration for Muslims.

Conclusion

In September 2024, I offered a seminar on the life of the Prophet Muhammad and his spiritual legacy at a local mosque in the state of Maryland in the United States. The participants came from diverse backgrounds and were highly educated, including college students, physicians, academics, engineers, and scientists. Notably, most of those enrolled in the seminar were women. During my introduction, I asked the participants, "Who is the Prophet to you?" The overwhelming majority responded that the Prophet was a role model for them. Both women and men confidently expressed that they viewed the Prophet as a guide for leading a life rooted in spirituality and morality.

One participant's response stood out as particularly remarkable. He shared that the Prophet was not only a role model for him but also the one who "raised" him. He explained that he had learned from the Prophet how to conduct his life: how to enter his home, use the bathroom, eat, sleep, perform rituals, interact with society, nurture relationships, be a father, and treat his parents. This way of relating to the Prophet beautifully captures his lasting impact on the lives of Muslims and the deep love they hold for him.

Throughout this book, I have sought to provide a portrait of the Prophet Muhammad, highlighting the reasons Muslims are deeply drawn to his teachings and legacy. The Prophet's life had humble beginnings. He was raised as an orphan, was unlettered (*ummi*), and worked as a shepherd within his community. His influence and impact were not rooted in worldly power or material wealth but rather in divine revelation. It was through this revelation that the Prophet was transformed and empowered to fulfill his mission.

While facing violent opposition and relentless persecution against himself and his followers, the Prophet remained steadfast and resilient in his cause. Through the mission of revelation, Muhammad eventually became the most influential and powerful figure in Arabia. Yet, despite his power and the loyalty of his followers, he never used religion for personal gain. He lived a life of humility and simplicity until his death. There were times when he and his family went without sufficient food, yet he did not seek a luxurious lifestyle or accumulate wealth. He left behind only a few modest belongings. The Prophet was not a kingly figure but a servant, a truth emphasized in the testimony of faith (*shahada*), the first pillar of Islam: "There is no god but God, and Muhammad is His servant and messenger."

Muhammad led a God-centered life. He was deeply mindful of the Creator in every aspect of his life. His was not a life of comfort or luxury. In addition to his daily prayers, he would rise during the night to spend significant time in prayer, which he regarded as the most precious part of his day. Beyond fasting during Ramadan, he would frequently fast in other months, using these practices as opportunities to deepen his connection with God. The Prophet found ways to remember God in almost every moment—when he slept, woke up, ate, traveled, received blessings, or endured illness. He remained constantly aware of the fleeting nature of this world and often reflected on death as a transition to the hereafter and a reunion with God. The Prophet is also renowned for his exemplary character. He was kind, generous, courageous, humble, just, faithful, trustworthy, patient, and compassionate. Muhammad forgave his enemies, not out of weakness but because his goal was to bring their hearts and minds closer to God. He did not seek revenge for the wrongs they had inflicted on him.

From the very beginning, Muslims have understood their love for the Prophet as an extension of their love for God. Following his example (Sunna) is regarded as an act of obedience to God, and emulating the Prophet's model is seen as a way to draw closer to God. To Muslims, the Prophet is seen as a healer of the heart and soul (*tabib*) and a beloved friend (*habib*), embodying the ideal of a life devoted to God. The Prophet's followers have not only embodied his teachings in their daily lives but also faithfully transmitted them to future generations. Beyond living according to his example, they have celebrated and remembered him through art, poetry, music, and collections of prayers. As Muhammad Iqbal puts it, "Love of the Prophet runs like blood in the veins of his community."[1] Despite their love and reverence for him, Muslims acknowledge the Prophet Muhammad as a human being. However, they regard him as the best of all humanity. This sentiment is articulated in these widely quoted lines among Muslims: "Muhammad is a human being, but not just any human being. He is like a ruby among stones."[2]

To know the Prophet Muhammad, one should observe the beautiful traits reflected in the lives of Muslims. Their spiritual practices, charitable works, character, manners, and contributions to society are all deeply rooted in the example set by the Prophet. Another way to gain insight into the Prophet's legacy is by examining the spiritual luminaries shaped by his teachings and spirituality. These include not only his companions but also renowned figures like Rabia al-Adawiyya, Imam al-Ghazali, Abdul Qadir Gilani, and Jalaluddin Rumi. Each of them became influential spiritual guides by following the Prophet's example.

To understand Muslims' love for the Prophet Muhammad, a comparison with the story of Laila and Qays, an account prominent in Arab, Persian, Turkish, and Urdu literature, may be helpful. Qays, the son of a noble family, grew up in the same village and fell deeply in love with Laila. However, their families opposed their union, and they were forced apart. Laila's family compelled her to marry another man. Heartbroken, Qays abandoned his home and retreated into the wilderness, consumed by his love for Laila. His devotion earned him the nickname Majnun (literally *madman*).

---

1. Sir Muhammad Iqbal, *Rumuz-i bekhudi*, cited in Annemarie Schimmel, *And Muhammad Is His Messenger: The Veneration of the Prophet in Islamic Piety* (The University of North Carolina Press, 1985), 256.

2. These lines about the Prophet are commonly written in the calligraphic frames. The Arabic transliteration of them is *Muhammad basharun la kalbashar, bal huwa kalyaqut bayn al-hajr*.

Rumi frequently alludes to the story of Laila and Majnun in his *Masnavi*. In one instance, Majnun visits Laila's neighborhood and tenderly pets and cares for a dog he finds there. When people mock him for being so invested in the dog, pointing out its flaws, Majnun responds that they fail to see it from his perspective. To him, he points out, even the ground touched by the paw of a dog from his beloved's neighborhood is nobler than the mightiest lions. In another instance, the caliph meets Laila and, puzzled by her appearance, questions why Majnun's love for her became so legendary. He remarks that there are many women in the town far more beautiful than Laila. Laila responds, "Be silent, for you are not Majnun."

Similarly, Muslims' relationship with the Prophet is a great story of love. Just as Majnun cherished anything connected to Laila, Muslims treasure everything associated with the Prophet—his words, actions, manners, companions, and relics. For them, these connections are precious reminders of their beloved. This deep reverence is exemplified in the life of Malik ibn Anas (d. 795), the founder of the Maliki school of jurisprudence and a renowned hadith scholar. Imam Malik displayed unparalleled respect for the hadiths of the Prophet. Before beginning a session, he would perform ablution, dress in clean garments, wear a new turban, and sit with solemnity and seriousness. Incense would be burned continuously during the lecture, creating a sacred atmosphere. Such was his dedication that, during one session, he endured sixteen scorpion stings without showing any sign of discomfort, out of respect for the sacred words of the Prophet.[3] This reverence was a testament to Imam Malik's great love for Muhammad.

Like the story of Laila and Majnun, the deep love Muslims have for the Prophet might seem astonishing to outsiders. However, such love can only be understood by viewing it through the eyes of Muslims. Otherwise, their view of Muhammad would be no different from that of those who criticized Majnun for caring for a dog in Laila's neighborhood

---

3. Schimmel, *And Muhammad Is His Messenger*, 29.

or the caliph who failed to perceive Laila's beauty and understand Majnun's profound love for her.[4]

I conclude this book with a heartfelt prayer from Imam al-Jazuli's *Dalail al-Khayrat*, which beautifully reflects Muslims' deep love and longing for the Prophet Muhammad: "O God, guide us to follow his example (*sunna*) and help us live as dedicated members of his community. Unite us in his company, under his banner, and count us among his closest companions. Lead us to his wellspring, allow us to share in his blessings, and let us experience the beauty of his love."[5]

---

4. Omid Safi uses a similar analogy based on the account from Saadi's *Gulustan* to illustrate the significance of the Prophet in Islamic piety, and I am thankful to him for this inspiration. See Omid Safi, *Memories of Muhammad: Why the Prophet Matters* (HarperOne, 2010), 263–265.

5. This prayer can be found in the seventh chapter of al-Jazuli's *Dalail al-Khayrat*.

BIBLIOGRAPHY

Abdul-Jabbar, Ghassan. "The Classical Tradition." In *The Wiley Blackwell Concise Companion to Hadith*, edited by Daniel W. Brown. Wiley Blackwell, 2020.
Ahmad Ibn Hanbal. *Kitab al-Zuhd*, edited by Muhammad Ahmad ʿIsa. Dar al-Ghad al-Jadid, 2005.
Ali ibn Abi Talib. *Nahjul Balagha*, edited by Yasin T. Al. Jiouri. Tahrike Tarsile, 2009.
———. "Qasida al-Jaljalutiya." In *Mealli Büyük Cevşen*. Hayrat Neşriyat, 2015.
Atar, Fahrettin. "Teşehhüd." In *İslam Ansiklopedisi*. Türkiye Diyanet Vakfı, 2011.
Bardakoğlu, Ali. "Had." In *İslam Ansiklopedisi*. Türkiye Diyanet Vakfı, 1996.
Brown, Jonathan A. C. *Hadith: Muhammad's Legacy in the Medieval and Modern World*. Oneworld, 2009.
———. *Muhammad: A Very Short Introduction*. Oxford University Press, 2011.
Donner, Fred M. *Muhammad and the Believers*. Harvard University Press, 2012.
Ersoy, Mehmet Akif. *Safahat*. Bağcılar Belediyesi, 2014.
Erul, Bünyamin. "Veda Hutbesi." In *İslam Ansiklopedisi*. Türkiye Diyanet Vakfı, 2012.
———. "Ümmü Eymen." In *İslam Ansiklopedisi*. Türkiye Diyanet Vakfı, 2012.
Fayda, Mustafa. "Muhammed." In *İslam Ansiklopedisi*. Türkiye Diyanet Vakfı, 2020.
———. "Ömer." In *İslam Ansiklopedisi*. Türkiye Diyanet Vakfı, 2007.
Gamard, Ibrahim. *Rumi and Islam*. Skylight, 2012.
Ghazali, al-. *Ihya' 'Ulum al-Din*. 5 vols. al-Quds, 2012.
Hadislerle İslam. 7 vols. Diyanet İşleri Başkanlığı, 2014.
Haley, Alex. *The Autobiography of Malcolm X*. Grove Press, 1965.

Hodgson, Marshall G. S. *The Venture of Islam: Conscience and History in a World Civilization*. Vol. 1, *The Classical Age of Islam*. University of Chicago Press, 1977.
Ibn al-Jawzi, Jamal al-Din Abi al-Faraj. *Sifat al-Safwa*, edited by Khalid Mustafa Tartusi. Dar al-Kitab al-Arabi, 2012.
Ibn Ishaq. *The Life of Muhammad*. Translated by A. Guillaume. Oxford University Press, 1967.
Ibn Kathir. *Al-Bidaya wa al-Nihaya*, edited by Abdullah ibn Abdulmuhsin al-Turki. Dar Hijr, 1998.
Ibn Saʿd. *Kitab al-Tabakat al-Kubra*, edited by ʿAli Muhammad ʿAmr. 11 vols. Maktabah al-Khanji, 2001.
Iyad, Qadi. *Al-Shifa*. Translated by Gehan Abdel-Raouf Hibah. Dar al-Kotob al-Ilmiyya, 2013.
Kandemir, M. Yaşar. "Al-Camiu's Sahih." In *İslam Ansiklopedisi*. Türkiye Diyanet Vakfı, 1993.
———. "İbn Hacer al-Askalani." In *İslam Ansiklopedisi*. Türkiye Diyanet Vakfı, 1999.
Karagözoglu, Mustafa Macit. "Commentaries." In *The Wiley Blackwell Concise Companion to Hadith*, edited by Daniel W. Brown. Wiley Blackwell, 2020.
Kaya, Mahmut. "Kasidetü'l Bürde." In *İslam Ansiklopedisi*. Türkiye Diyanet Vakfı, 2001.
Kurt, Abdurrahman. "Demografik Değiskenler Açısından İlk Müslümanlar." *Uludağ İlahiyat Fakültesi Dergisi* 18, no. 2 (2009): 27–41.
Lings, Martin. *Muhammad: His Life Based on the Earliest Sources*. Inner Traditions, 2006.
Nasr, Seyyed Hossein, Caner K. Dagli, Maria Massi Dakake, Joseph E. B. Lumbard, and Mohammed Rustom, eds. *The Study Quran: A New Translation and Commentary*. HarperOne, 2015.
Nursi, Bediuzzaman Said. *Emirdağ Lahikası II*. Söz Basım, 2012.
———. *İşaratül İ'caz*. Söz Basım, 2012.
———. *Lem'alar*. Söz Basım, 2012.
———. *Mesnev-i Nuriye*. Söz Basım, 2012.
———. *Sözler*. Söz Basım, 2012.
———. *Şualar*. Söz Basım, 2012.
———. *Tarihçe-i Hayat*. Söz Basım, 2012.
Pakatchi, Ahmad. "Shiʿism." In *The Wiley Blackwell Concise Companion to Hadith*, edited by Daniel W. Brown. Wiley Blackwell, 2020.
Pekolcay, A. Necla. "Mevlid." In *İslam Ansiklopedisi*. Türkiye Diyanet Vakfı, 2004.

Peters, F. E. *The Hajj: The Muslim Pilgrimage to Mecca and to Holy Places*. Princeton University, 1994.
Rabb, Intisar A. "Reasonable Doubt in Islamic Law." *Yale Journal of International Law* 40, no. 1 (2015): 41–94.
Rahman, Sofia Abdur. *Gendering the Hadith Tradition: Recentering the Authority of Aisha, Mother of the Believers*. Oxford University Press, 2024.
Rumi, Jalaluddin. *Divan*. Translated by Abdulkadir Gölpınarlı. Kültür Bakanlığı, 2000.
———. *The Masnavi of Rumi*. Translated by Alan Williams. I. B. Tauris, 2022.
———. *The Mathnavi of Jalalu'ddin Rumi*. Translated by Reynold A. Nicholson. Cambridge University Press, 1926.
———. "On the Day of My Death." In *Diwan-e Kabir*. Translated by Ibrahim Gamard. Dar al-Masnavi. Accessed January 5, 2025. https://www.dar-al-masnavi.org/gh-0911.html.
Saʻdi, Shaykh Mushrifuddin. *The Bustan of Saadi*. Translated by A. Hart Edwards. Bibliotech Press, 2018.
———. *The Gulistan of Saʻdi*. Translated by Wheeler M. Tackson. Ibex, 2017.
Sells, Michael Anthony. "Banat Suʻad: Translation and Interpretive Introduction." *Journal of Arabic Literature* 21, no. 2 (1990): 140–154.
Siddiqi, Muhammad Zubayr. *Hadith Literature: Its Origin, Development, and Special Features*. Islamic Text Society, 1993.
Suyuti, Imam Jalal al-Din. *The Virtue of Remaining Steadfast When Losing a Child (Fadl al-Jalad 'Inda Faqd al-Walad)*. Translated by Abu Muhammad Zaid ibn Mahmud Haspatel. Inprint, 2016.
Tabari, al-. *Tarikh al-Tabari: Tarikh al-Rusul wa al-Muluk*, edited by Muhammad Abu al-Fadl Ibrahim. 10 vols. Dar al-Maʼarif, 1967.
Wasti, Syed Tanvir. "The Mevlid or Nativity Poem by Suleyman Celebi." *Tehseel* 1, no. 3 (2018): 1–76.
Yesevi, Hoca Ahmed. *Divan-ı Hikmet*. Ahmet Yesevi Üniversitesi, 2016.

INDEX

'*am al-huzn*. See Year of Sadness
'*aziz,* 182
'*ibadah*. See worship.
'Isa. See Jesus

Abd al-Muttalib, Muhammad's grandfather, 11–13, 18, 104n96
Abdullah ibn Amr, 126, 179
Abdullah ibn Jud'an, 20
Abdullah ibn Masud, 110, 130
Abdullah ibn Salaam, 51
Abdullah ibn Ubayy, 56
Abdullah ibn Zayd, 79; vision of the call to prayer (*adhan*), 79–80
Abdullah, Muhammad's father, 12–14: marriage to Amina, 13–14; death, 14, 17
Abdullah, Muhammad's foster brother, 16
Abdullah, Muhammad's son, 21
Abraha, 11
Abu Ayyub al-Ansari, 45, 197–98
Abu Bakr, 27, 32, 37, 41, 43–45, 66, 134, 142–45, 159–66, 211
Abu Dawud al-Sijistani, 185
Abu Hassan al-A'raj, 164
Abu Hurayra, 49, 164, 179, 182, 192
Abu Jahl, 32, 35–36, 55
Abu Lahab, 27–28, 37

Abu Sufyan, 20, 54, 62
Abu Talib, Muhammad's uncle, 18; wife, 18, business travel to Syria, 19; faith, 26–27; support for Muhammad, 36–37; death, 37
Abu Ubayda ibn Jarrah, 161–62
Abyssinia, 11, 32–33, 35, 60, 153, 161
Adam, the Prophet, 63, 102, 106, 114, 154, 179
adhan, 79–81
ahad, 182
ahl al-kitab. See People of the Book
Ahmad ibn Hanbal, 183
Aisha, Muhammad's wife, 4, 21, 64, 67, 83, 85, 92, 98, 109, 127, 133, 142, 163–67, 171, 178, 191–92, 209
akhira. See hereafter.
akhlaq. See character
Akşemseddin, 197
Al-Aqsa Mosque, 41
al-hajar al-aswad, 22
al-Jawshan al-Kabir, 147–49
al-kutub al-arba'a, 186
Al-Nasa'i, 185
Al-Shamail al-Muhammadiyya, 208–09
Al-Shifa of Qadi Iyad, 209–10

Ali ibn Abi Talib, 21, 26, 43, 73, 134, 145–52, 166, 172, 186, 210–11; on death, 149
Allah. See God
Alliance of Virtues (*hilf al-fudul*), 20
Amina, Muhammad's mother, marriage to Abdullah, 13–14; birth to Muhammad, 14; death 17–18
Anas ibn Malik, 49, 65, 128, 208–09
animals, 21, 105, 132, 172, 174–75
Ankara, 169
ansar, 46–47, 139
Aqaba pledges, 41–42
Aristotle, 134
ashab al-kahf, 31–72
Asia Minor, 162
Attar, Fariduddin, 212
Aws, 42
ayat, in creation, 40, 47, 68, 87, 111

Balkh, 183
Banu Hashim, 11
Banu Saʻd, 15, 17
baraka, 110
basmala, 147, 211
Basra, 183
Battle of Badr, 39, 54–55, 57, 130, 153
Battle of Camel, 166
Battle of Trench, 56–57, 162
Battle of Uhud, 55–56
Bilal ibn Rabah, 27, 32, 67, 143, 162–63; on death, 210
Blue Mosque, 214
Bukhari, 183–84
Busiri, 203–05, 212

calligraphy, 145, 197, 210, 215–16
Cave of Hira, 23
Çelebi, Süleyman, *Mewlid*, 205–06; on death of Muhammad, 206–07; on Muhammad's character, 206
character, 7, of Muhammad, 4, 127–36
charity, 34, 63, 68, 72, 82, 88, 96; in life of Muhammad, 97–100
Christians, 11, 19, 20, 25, 29, 33, 54, 60, 73, 162
companions of Muhammad, 16–18, 33, 35, 44–46, 49–50, 55–59, 63–65, 69, 72–73, 75, 77–79, 98 99, 110, 126, 129–34, 137–67, 171–74, 177, 179–80, 182–83, 186, 191–94, 209–10, 215, 219–21
compassion, of God, 8, 95, 113, 116, 131; of Muhammad, 24, 33, 39, 69, 95, 97, 129, 131–32
contemplation, 111–18
courage, 151, 159, 167; of Muhammad, 69, 133–35

daʻif, 181
dabt, 181
Dalail al-Khayrat, 200–02, 216, 221
Damascus, 16, 163, 183–84
dar al-arkam, 73, 77
Day of Judgment, 48, 50, 53, 86, 101, 107, 111, 113, 132, 189, 199, 204–05
death, of Muhammad's children, 1–3; in the Qurʾan, 2, 26; inflictor of, 6; in teachings of Muhammad, 118–23; announcement of, 199
dhikr, 110

Index

dreams, 16; about Muhammad, 204, 207
du'a'. See invocations

Egypt, 60, 183–84
Ersoy, Mehmet Akif, 159
Eve, 63, 102
Eyub Sultan Mosque, 197

faith, 7
farewell sermon, 63–64
fasting, 7, 34, 48, 76, 143; in the life of Muhammad, 90–93; hadith on, 189
Fath al-Bari, 187
Fatima, Abu Talib's wife, 18
Fatima, Muhammad's daughter, 21, 26, 65; marriage, 147
fiqh, 100
forgiveness, 124–25, 133, 166, 192, 205; of God, 62, 77, 85, 170, 179, 188; of Muhammad, 8, 33, 132, 202–04
Friday prayers, 81–82
funeral, 7, 122, 129, 138, 143, 147, 154, 206
Fusus al-Hikam, 207
Fuzuli, 213

Gabriel (archangel), 7n11, 23–24, 29, 39–40, 63, 69, 71, 73, 91, 142
gharib, 182
Ghazali, 148–49, 154, 219; on death, 100, 123–24; on fasting, 95–96; on night prayer, 86; on charity, 100–01; on contemplation, 114–16; on *sunna,* 175
ghusl, 71, 82–83,

Gilani, Abdul Qadir, 219
God, names and attributes of, 6, 147–48; reliance on, 3, 30; obedience to, 4; worshiping, 6–8, 79; love for, 8, 170–71; closeness to, 41, 74; signs of, 68; mercy of, 70, 131–33; glorifying, 71, 77; submission to, 74; forgiveness of, 77, 166; generosity of, 99; contemplating, 111–18; remembering, 124–26

habib, 218
hadith al-qudsi, 178–79
hadith, definition, 1n1; on child loss, 1–2: and Sunna, 175–76; classifications, 179–82; collections, 183–85; in Shiite tradition, 185–86; commentaries, 187; examples, 187–91; interpretation, 191–94. Also see *Sunna*.
Hafsa, Muhammad's wife, 156
Hagar, Abraham's wife, 12n2, 102–03
hajj, 7, 63, 76, 91, 102–08. See also *umrah*
halal, 114, 176
Halima, Muhammad's foster mother, 15–17
hamd, 76
Hamza ibn Abd al-Muttalib, 35, 56
Hamzaname, 35
hanif, 23, 73
Hasan ibn Ali, 26
hasan, 181
Haspatel, Zaid, 3
heaven, 5n8, 142, 144
hell, 27, 86, 99, 132, 192

hereafter, 7, 26, 48, 53, 86, 88, 95, 101, 107, 118–24, 127, 138–39, 154–55, 218
Hijaz, 184
hijra, 45, 54, 78, 81
hilya, 210–11
Homs, 183
honey bee, 113–14
Hudaybiyya, 58–60, 154
humility, 6–8, 68–69, 79, 84, 105–06, 108; of Muhammad, 127–31
Husayn ibn Ali, 26

i'tikaf, 92, 169
Ibn Arabi, 149, 207
Ibn Hajar al-'Asqalani, 187
Ibn Jubayr, 106–07
Ibn Majah, 185
Ibn Qayyim, 185
Ibn Shihab al-Zuhri, 181–83
iftar, 90
ihram, 58, 105
Imam Malik, 182–83, 220
Imam Muslim, 184–85
iman. See faith
Infaq. See charity
invocations, 68, 70, 74, 81, 87, 108, 110, 138, 182, 197; in Muhammad's spirituality, 124–26
Iqbal, Muhammad, 219
Iraq, 184
Ishmael, the Prophet, 12–13, 22n25, 92, 103
isnad, 181, 186
Istanbul, 166, 197–98, 214
istighfar, 124
istirja', 2
ittisal al-isnad, 181

Ja'far ibn Abi Talib, 33–35
Jacob, the Prophet, 165
jahiliyya, 135
Jannat al-Baqi', 64
Jazuli, 200, 202
Jerusalem, 40–41, 73, 143
Jesus, 16, 19, 34–35, 40, 72–73, 129
Jews, 19, 20, 30, 33, 42, 51–52, 54, 57, 60–61, 79, 84, 104, 162
John (Yahya), the Prophet, 72
Joseph, the Prophet, 62, 165
Jubayr ibn Mut'im, 39
justice, 4, 7–8, 20, 26, 33, 48, 54, 69, 134–36, 148, 151–52, 156, 158–59, 167, 181

Ka'b ibn Zuhayr, 202, 212
Kaaba, 7, 11–12, 22–23, 36–37, 40, 45, 58–60, 62, 70, 73, 76, 79, 102–05, 141
karaha, 176
khabar, 186
Khadija bint Khuwaylid, wife of Muhammad, marriage, 21; children, 21; death, 22, 37; support for Muhammad, 24–26, 37, 97; life and spirituality, 141–42
Khazraj, 42
Khurasan, 184
Kufa, 183
Kulayni, Muhammad ibn Ya'qub, 186
külliye, 197
kutub al-sitta, 185

Layla and Majnun, 219–21
Laylat al-Qadr, 92

madrasa, 197
Malcolm X, 107

Index

Maqam Mahmud, 81
Maria al-Qibtiyya, 22
Mary, mother of Jesus, 19, 22, 34–35, 72, 129
Maryam. See Mary
Maryland, 217
mashhur, 182
Masjid al-Nabawi, 45, 78, 164, 170
masjid, 73, 78
mawlid, 202–07, 216
Mecca, 11, 14–19, 32–33, 38, 41, 44–45, conquest of, 61–63
Medina, 13–17, 45; revelations in, 47–49; religion in, 51–52
Mehmed the Conqueror, 197
mendil, 215
Merv, 183
mi'raj, 39–40, 71, 73, 143
mi'rajname, 41
minbar, 172
Monk Bahira, 19
Mosul, 162
muezzin, 32, 163
muhajirun, 46–47 139
Muhammad, the Prophet, on death, 65; death of, 65–66; spiritual personality, 5; light, 5; as the living Qur'an 4, 112; spiritual practices, 67–126; character of, 127–36
muqabala, 91
Mus'ab ibn Umayr, 42, 56
Mut'im ibn 'Adi, 39
mutawatir, 181–82
muttasil, 180
Muwatta' of Imam Malik, 182–83

naat, 214
Nahjul Balagha, 147
nasheed, 215

night prayer, 68; of Muhammad, 83–85; Ghazali on, 86
Nishabur, 183–84
Nur Mountain, 23
Nursi, Bediuzzaman Said, on Muhammad's spiritual personality, 5; on fasting, 93–95, on *salat*, 75–77; on contemplation, 116–18; on death, 122–23

patience, 1, 150, 165, 192; of Muhammad, 132–33, 136
People of the Book, 33, 60, 84
pilgrimage. See *hajj*
prayer. See *salat*

Qadi Iyad, 209–10
Qasida al-Burda, 202–05, 216
Qasida al-Jaljalutiya, 149
Qasim, Muhammad's son, 21
Qummi, ibn Babawayh, 186
Qur'an, 4, love for Muhammad, 4, 170; worship, 6; reciting, 7, 96, 108–11; God's mercy, 8, 131; Christians, 19, 33–35, 60–61; Jesus,19–20, 34–35; first revelation, 23–24; major themes, 26, 47–48; Mecca opposition, 29–32; seven sleepers, 31; Jews, 33; Mary 34–35; the night journey, 40; plot against Muhammad, 43; immigrants (*muhajirun*) and helpers (*ansar*), 47; hypocrites, 52–53; permission to fight, 53–54; Joseph, 62; Muhammad, 66, 138, 144, 198; contemplation, 68; ablution (*wudu*), 71; *salat*, 72,

75, 78; Friday prayer, 81–82; night prayer, 84; fasting, 90; *i'tikaf*, 92; Night of Power (*Laylat al-Qadr*), 92; charity, 97–98; death, 118; manners, 128; forgiveness, 133, courage, 134; justice, 135; companions of Muhammad, 139–40; remembering God, 148
Quraysh, 11, 23, 27, 39, 43, 52–56, 58, 60, 62–63, 156

Rabia al-Adawiyya, 219
Ramhormoz, 162
Rayy, 184
resurrection, 7–8, 26, 48, 65, 88, 111, 113, 119–20, 141, 214
revelation, 24–25, 27–32, 34, 40, 42, 60, 71, 73, 97, 104, 111, 141, 165, 176–77, 217
ruh, 31
Rumi, Jalaluddin, 50, 124, 157–58, 212–13, 219–20
Ruqayya, Muhammad's daughter, 21, 33, 153

Saadi Shirazi, 101, 212
sacred relics, 215–16
sadaqa. See charity
Safa and Marwah, 105
Sahih al-Bukhari, 184, 187
sahih, 181
Sahihayn, 185
Said ibn al-Musayyab, 182
Sakhawi, 185
salat al-duha, 89
salat al-eid, 90, 108
salat al-istisqa, 88–89
salat al-jum'a. See Friday prayers

salat al-kusuf and al-khusuf, 86–88
salat, 24, 42, 63, 68, of Muhammad, 69–75; communal, 77–79
salawat, 198–200
Salman al-Farisi, 57, 162
Samarkand, 183
Sanaa, 11
sanad, 180
Sarah, Abraham's wife, 102
Satan, 49, 63, 101, 129, 193, 207
Saudi Arabia, 169
Sawda bint Zam'a, Muhammad's wife, 22
seven sleepers, 31
shadh, 181
shafa'a, 200
shahada, 71, 76, 218
shamail, 208–10
sira, 9
Spain, 106
spirituality, Islamic, 6–8: of Muhammad, 67–126; in moderation, 126
Su Kasidesi, 213
Sufism, 70, 123, 145, 149n32, 150–51, 154, 199, 207
suhoor, 90–91
sujud al-shukr, 90
Sultan Ahmed I, 214
Sumayya bint Khabbat, 27, 32, 152–53
Sunna, 64, 66, 170–75, 218; understanding, 175–76, transmission, 176–83
Surat al-Ahzab, 57
Surat al-Fatiha, 76, 162
Surat al-Isra, 40
Surat al-Nas, 109
Surat al-Nisa, 110

Surat Falaq, 109
Suyuti, Jalal al-Din, 1, 185; on death, 2; loss of a child, 1–2
Syria, 14, 19, 54

tabib, 218
tafakkur. See contemplation
tahajjud. See night prayer
Taif, 38, 161
takbir, 76
Talha ibn Ubaydullah, 166
taqwa, 4, 106, in relation to Sunna, 172–75
tarawih, 91–92, 169
tasbih, 76
tawba, 124
the call to prayer. See *adhan*
Tirmidhi, 185, 208
Topkapi Palace, 215
Tuba tree, 5
Türkiye, 145, 148, 169, 197, 210
Tusi, Muhammad ibn al-Hasan, 186

Umar ibn al-Khattab, 35–36, 42, 45, 55, 58–59, 65, 73, 77, 127, 153, 155–59
Umayya ibn Khalaf, 32, 55
Umm Ayman, 17, 159–61

Umm Kulthum, Muhammad's daughter, 21, 153
umma, 22
ummi, 24, 217
umrah, 22n25, 58, 103, 105
Usama ibn Zayd, 160–61
Uthman ibn Affan, 33, 153–56, 211

Vesiletü'n Necat, 14, 205–07

wahy. See revelation
Waraqa ibn Nawfal, 25
worship, in Islam, 6–8. See also spirituality
wudu, 24, 49, 71, 73, 77, 83, 184

Yasir ibn Amir, 27, 32, 152
Year of Sadness, 37, 142
Yemen, 11–12
Yesevi, Ahmed, 158

Zainab, Muhammad's daughter, 21
Zakariyya, the prophet, 72
zakat. See charity
Zamzam, 12, 103–04
Zarkashi, 163
Zayd ibn Haritha, 27, 38, 160–61
Zoroastrians, 60, 90, 162
Zubayr ibn Awwam, 166

www.ingramcontent.com/pod-product-compliance
Ingram Content Group UK Ltd.
Pitfield, Milton Keynes, MK11 3LW, UK
UKHW040042030426
469647UK00005B/303

A loving introduction to the Prophet of Islam

Biographies of the Prophet Muhammad often focus on his historical context in seventh-century Arabia. Yet understanding the Prophet solely through the lens of ancient history fails to capture the significance and meaning of this individual, whose teachings have shaped the world and continue to guide nearly a quarter of the global population today.

With this book, Salih Sayilgan provides a loving portrait of the Prophet as he has lived in the hearts of Muslims across the centuries: as a religious light and spiritual guide. Drawing on a diverse body of Islamic literature on the Prophet, Sayilgan offers a vista onto the expansive and variegated legacy of this vitally significant religious figure. Examining how Muslims have remembered and reimagined the Prophet's spirit in different ways as expressions of their love for God and God's messenger, this book highlights the central place of the Prophet Muhammad in the religious lives of Muslim believers.

Praise for *Following the Prophet*

For many, the hardest thing to understand about Muhammad is that his greatest legacy is the immense love for him in the hearts of Muslims worldwide. This book guides readers into the world of that love, why and how it has grown over the centuries, and how it has been expressed.

Jonathan A. C. Brown, professor of Arabic and Islamic studies, Georgetown University

This accessible and thoughtful work offers a nuanced portrait of the Prophet Muhammad and other important figures, and a historical overview of early Islam, grounded in a wide range of Islamic sources. By presenting the Prophet's enduring legacy through the lens of Muslim devotional and historical memory, this book provides valuable insight for both Muslim readers seeking deeper spiritual understanding and non-Muslim readers interested in the foundations of early Islam.

Syed Atif Rizwan, assistant professor of Islamic and interreligious studies, Catholic Theological Union

Salih Sayilgan is an associate teaching professor in the Department of Theology and Religious Studies at Georgetown University. His previous books include *Exploring Islam: Theology and Spiritual Practice in America* (Fortress Press, 2021) and *God, Evil, and Suffering in Islam* (Cambridge University Press, 2023).

Islamic Studies/Religious Studies